The Least You Should Know about Eng...

TWELFTH Edition

WRITING SKILLS

Paige Wilson
Pasadena City College

Teresa Ferster Glazier
Late, Western Illinois University

CENGAGE
Learning

Australia • Brazil • Mexico • Singapore • United Kingdom • United States

CENGAGE
Learning®

The Least You Should Know about English: Writing Skills, Twelfth Edition
Paige Wilson and Teresa Ferster Glazier

Product Director: Todd Annie

Associate Content Developer: Elizabeth Rice

Product Assistant: Luria Rittenberg

Media Developer: Amy Gibbons

Marketing Manager: Lydia Lestar

Art and Cover Direction, Production Management, and Composition: PreMediaGlobal

Manufacturing Planner: Betsy Donaghey

Rights Acquisitions Specialist: Ann Hoffman

Cover Image: ©Andrew Buckin /Shutterstock

For product information and technology assistance, contact us at
Cengage Learning Customer & Sales Support, 1-800-354-9706

For permission to use material from this text or product,
submit all requests online at **www.cengage.com/permissions**
Further permissions questions can be emailed to
permissionrequest@cengage.com

Library of Congress Control Number: 2013953089

ISBN-13: 978-1-285-44353-9

ISBN-10: 1-285-44353-5

Cengage Learning
200 First Stamford Place, 4th Floor
Stamford, CT 06902
USA

Cengage Learning is a leading provider of customized learning solutions with office locations around the globe, including Singapore, the United Kingdom, Australia, Mexico, Brazil and Japan. Locate your local office at **www.cengage.com/global.**

Cengage Learning products are represented in Canada by Nelson Education, Ltd.

To learn more about Cengage Learning Solutions, visit **www.cengage.com**

Purchase any of our products at your local college store or at our preferred online store **www.cengagebrain.com.**

Printed in the United States of America
1 2 3 4 5 6 7 17 16 15 14 13

CONTENTS

Introducing *The Least You Should Know about English* in its new single-book format:

Forms A, B, and C of *The Least You Should Know about English* have been combined into one convenient form for the twelfth edition and beyond:

- The twelfth edition blends the best exercises and samples from the previous three forms and offers fresh perspectives and updated content throughout.

- The coverage remains the same as in the previous editions, with the addition of a new section in Part 4 on "Writing in Response to a Reading" that includes sample reading prompts, student samples using quotations, and a new chart with "Tips for In-Class Writing."

- Continuing its 35-year tradition, *The Least 12e's* upbeat explanations, abundant exercises, and complete set of answers allow for flexible coursework and self-directed learning.

- *The Least* helps student writers receive "just-in-time support" in any area, in any type of course (traditional, accelerated, stretch, or pathways), and through any delivery method (face-to-face, hybrid, or online).

The Least You Should Know about English has been helping students master the core content of basic writing skills for thirty-five years with its unique simplicity and self-teaching format that provides clear explanations, abundant exercises, and complete answers for instant insights about writing.

As in all previous editions, Parts 1 to 3 cover the essentials of "Word Use," "Sentence Structure," and "Punctuation." Part 4 on "Writing" clarifies the basic structures of the paragraph and the essay, along with the skills necessary to produce them (writing a thesis, finding a voice, organizing, summarizing, arguing, quoting and—*new to this edition—in-class writing and writing in response to a reading*). Part 4 contains writing exercises and helpful samples of real student work, as well as professional articles and excerpts from full-length texts.

The "least you should know" approach offers basic-skills support at any point in the learning process. It describes how writing actually works, rather than focusing on common errors. Explanations in *The Least* include timesaving memory devices that grow from familiar concepts, instead of linguistic distinctions that students may never use again. For example, in Part 3 we describe what we call "scoopable" elements, certain structures that can be "scooped" out of sentences and that need commas to enclose them. Students learn the *reasons* for putting commas around "scoopable" structures, not the technical terms to identify these structures as "nonrestrictive modifying clauses" or "appositives."

In line with core standards, the exercises in the twelfth edition continue to include thematically-related sentences and paragraphs from a variety of academic areas: science, art, history, film, literature, social studies, and the media. Students learn new, complex vocabulary as they read about both timely and timeless subjects—anything from the production of eco-friendly denim to the discovery of prehistoric artwork in the caves of Lascaux. Such thematic, cross-discipline exercises reinforce breadth of understanding and the need for coherent details in students' own writing.

The Least You Should Know about English functions equally well on the go as a self-tutoring text and in the classroom (in person or online). It provides students with everything they need to progress on their own. Students who have been previously overwhelmed by the complexities of English should, by practicing essential skills and through writing and rewriting their papers, gain the ability and confidence to fulfill all of their future writing needs.

A **Test Booklet** by Paige Wilson is available to instructors; it includes sixty tests that correspond to the book's content. Alternatively, these "tests" can act as additional exercises for which only instructors have the answers.

ACKNOWLEDGMENTS

For their extremely helpful commentary on the book, I would like to thank the following reviewers:

Melissa Barrett, *Portland Community College, Clark Community College*
Michelle Abbott, *Georgia Highlands College*
Virginia Gates, *Northwest Vista Community College*
Tammy White, *Forsyth Technical Community College*
Christina De La Rosa, *Northwest Vista College*
Judy Convington, *Trident Technical College*
Craig Bartholomaus, *Metropolitan Community College—Penn Valley*
Angela Taylor, *El Centro College*
Michelle Cristiani, *Portland Community College*
Aileen Gum, *City College*
Margie Dernaika, *Southwest TN Community College*

I would also like to extend my gratitude to the following students for their specific contributions to the twelfth edition: Catherine Alarcon, Frances Castanar, Eric Coffey, Christine Foy, Juan Grandez, Vanessa Horta, Jessica Ovando, and Maggie Wong.

As always, I am indebted to my publishing team for their expertise and hard work, especially the tireless efforts of my editors, Annie Todd and Elizabeth Rice. And for the ongoing support and encouragement of my family, friends, students, and colleagues, I am so grateful.

Paige Wilson
Pasadena City College

This book is dedicated to Teresa Ferster Glazier (1907–2004). In creating *The Least You Should Know about English*, she discovered a way to teach grammar and writing that students and teachers have actually enjoyed for over thirty years. Her original explanations and approaches have been constant sources of inspiration for this and all previous coauthored editions, as they will be for all future editions of her text.

What Is the Least You Should Know?

Most English textbooks try to teach you more than you need to know. This book will teach you the least you should know—and still help you learn to write clearly and acceptably. You won't have to learn grammatical terms like *gerund, auxiliary verb,* or *demonstrative pronoun.* You can get along without knowing such technical labels if you understand a few key concepts. You *should* know about the parts of speech and how to use and spell common words; you *should* be able to recognize subjects and verbs; you *should* know the basics of sentence structure and punctuation—but rules, as such, will be kept to a minimum.

The English you'll learn in this book is sometimes called Standard Written English, and it may differ slightly or greatly from the English you use when speaking. Standard Written English is the form of writing accepted in business and the professions. So no matter how you speak, you will communicate better in writing when you use Standard Written English. For instance you might *say,* "That's a whole nother problem," but you would probably want to *write,* "That's a completely different problem." Knowing the difference between spoken English and Standard Written English is essential in college, in business, and in life.

Until you learn the least you should know, you may have difficulty communicating in writing. Look for the misused word in the following sentence, for example:

I hope that the university will except my application for admission.

The writer probably relied on the sound, not the meaning, of the word *except* to choose it. The two words *except* and *accept* sound similar but have completely different meanings. (See page 08.) The writer should have used the one that means approve the application (*accept* it):

I hope that the university will *accept* my application for admission.

Then all of the words would have communicated clearly. Here's another example, this time with missing punctuation:

The manager fired Kevin and Chloe and I received a promotion.

This sentence needs a comma to separate its two independent clauses:

The manager fired Kevin and Chloe, and I received a promotion.

But perhaps the writer meant the following:

The manager fired Kevin, and Chloe and I received a promotion.

Punctuation changes the meaning of the sentence, especially for Chloe. With the help of this text, we hope that your writing will become so clear that no one will misunderstand it.

As you make your way through the book, it's important to remember information after you learn it because many concepts and structures build upon others. For example, once you can identify subjects and verbs, you'll be better able to recognize fragments, understand subject-verb agreement, and use correct punctuation. Explanations and examples are brief and clear, and it shouldn't be difficult to learn from them—*if you want to.* But you have to want to!

HOW TO LEARN THE LEAST YOU SHOULD KNOW

1. Read each explanatory section carefully (aloud, if possible).

2. Do the first exercise. Compare your answers with those at the back of the book. If they don't match, study the explanation again to find out why.

3. Do the second exercise and correct it. If you miss a single answer, go back once more to the explanation. You must have missed something. Be tough on yourself. Don't just think, "Maybe I'll get it right next time." Reread the examples, and *then* try the next exercise. It's important to correct each group of ten sentences before moving on so that you'll discover your mistakes early.

4. You may be tempted to quit after you do one or two exercises perfectly. Instead, make yourself finish another exercise. It's not enough to *understand* a concept or structure. You have to *practice* using it.

5. If you're positive that you've learned a concept or structure after doing several exercises, move on to the proofreading and sentence composing exercises, where you can apply that knowledge to your writing.

Learning the basics of spelling and word choice, sentence structure, and punctuation does take time. Generally, college students should study a couple of hours outside of class for each hour in class. You may need to study more. Undoubtedly, the more time you spend, the more your writing will improve.

P A R T   1

Word Use

Anyone can learn to use words more effectively. You can eliminate most of your spelling and word choice errors if you want to. It's just a matter of deciding you're going to do it.

THE IMPORTANCE OF A GOOD DICTIONARY

A current, full-featured dictionary is a basic but commonly underused resource for many writers. College-level print dictionaries provide the spelling, pronunciation, definitions, usage, and sources of words, as well as foreign phrases, famous names, and geographical locations. The latest dictionaries also offer online resources, including audio and video features that bring words, people, and places to life. Of course, most computers and word-processing programs have built-in dictionaries and spell-check capabilities. However, the automatic "corrections" they suggest may at times cause more damage to your meaning than your original mistakes would. The good news is that dictionaries of all kinds will become more useful once you learn the "least you should know" about spelling and word choice.

If you really intend to improve your spelling and choice of words, study each of the following sections until you make no mistakes in the exercises.

Your Own List of Misspelled Words

Words That Can Be Broken into Parts

Guidelines for Doubling a Final Letter

Words Often Confused (Set 1)

Words Often Confused (Set 2)

The Eight Parts of Speech

Adjectives and Adverbs

Contractions

Possessives

Your Own List of Misspelled Words

You can create your own personal dictionary on the inside cover of your English notebook or in some other obvious place by making a corrected list of all the misspelled words from your graded papers. Review and practice using the correct spellings until you're sure of them, and edit your papers to find and fix repeated errors.

Words That Can Be Broken into Parts

Breaking words into their parts will often help you spell them correctly. Each of the following words is made up of two shorter words. Note that the word then contains all the letters of the two shorter words.

chalk board	. . . chalkboard	room mate	. . . roommate
over due	. . . overdue	home work	. . . homework
super market	. . . supermarket	under line	. . . underline

Becoming aware of prefixes such as *dis, inter, mis,* and *un* is also helpful. When you add a prefix to a word, note that no letters are dropped, either from the prefix or from the word.

dis appear	disappear	mis represent	misrepresent
dis appoint	disappoint	mis spell	misspell
dis approve	disapprove	mis understood	misunderstood
dis satisfy	dissatisfy	un aware	unaware
inter act	interact	un involved	uninvolved
inter active	interactive	un necessary	unnecessary
inter related	interrelated	un sure	unsure

Have someone dictate the preceding list for you to write and then mark any words you miss. Memorize the correct spellings by noting how each word is made up of a prefix and a word.

Guidelines for Doubling a Final Letter

Most spelling rules have so many exceptions that they aren't much help. But here's one worth learning because it has very few exceptions.

Double a final letter (consonants only) when adding an ending that begins with a vowel (such as *ing, ed, er*) if all three of the following are true:

1. The word ends in a single consonant,

2. which is preceded by a single vowel (the vowels are *a, e, i, o, u*),

3. and the accent is on the last syllable (or the word only has one syllable).

We'll try the rule on a few words to which we'll add *ing, ed,* or *er.*

begin
    1. It ends in a single consonant—*n,*
    2. preceded by a single vowel—*i,*
    3. and the accent is on the last syllable—be *gín.*
        Therefore, we double the final consonant and write *beginning, beginner.*

stop
    1. It ends in a single consonant—*p,*
    2. preceded by a single vowel—*o,*
    3. and the accent is on the last syllable (there is only one).
        Therefore, we double the final consonant and write *stopping, stopped, stopper.*

filter
    1. It ends in a single consonant—*r,*
    2. preceded by a single vowel—*e,*
    3. But the accent isn't on the last syllable. It's on the first—*fíl* ter.
        Therefore, we *don't* double the final consonant. We write *filtering, filtered.*

keep
    1. It ends in a single consonant—*p,*
    2. but the *p* isn't preceded by a single vowel. There are two *e*'s.
        Therefore, we *don't* double the final consonant. We write *keeping, keeper.*

NOTE 1—Be aware that *qu* is treated as a consonant because *q* is almost never written without *u*. Think of it as *kw*. In words like *equip* and *quit,* the *qu* acts as a consonant. Therefore, *equip* and *quit* both end in a single consonant preceded by a single vowel, and the final consonant is doubled in *equipped* and *quitting.*

> **NOTE 2**—The final consonants *w, x,* and *y* do not follow this rule and are not doubled when adding *ing, ed,* or *er* to a word (as in *bowing, fixing,* and *enjoying*).

E X E R C I S E S

Add *ing* to these words. Correct each group of ten before continuing so you'll catch any errors early.

Exercise 1

1. mask
2. defer
3. push
4. wax
5. fit

6. offer
7. row
8. click
9. feed
10. review

Exercise 2

1. tow
2. rip
3. peel
4. refer
5. invest

6. order
7. profit
8. scream
9. slip
10. predict

Exercise 3

1. trip
2. munch
3. roll
4. mop
5. flavor

6. cash
7. beep
8. talk
9. travel
10. plan

Exercise 4

1. pat	**6.** brush
2. saw	**7.** gather
3. feed	**8.** knot
4. play	**9.** offer
5. occur	**10.** box

Exercise 5

1. help	**6.** wish
2. flex	**7.** try
3. assist	**8.** construct
4. need	**9.** polish
5. select	**10.** lead

Words Often Confused (Set 1)

Learning the difference between words often confused will help you overcome many of your word-use problems. We've divided the most commonly confused words into two sets. Study the pairs of words in Set 1 carefully, with their helpful memory tips and examples, before trying the exercises. Then move on to Set 2. If you practice each set thoroughly, your spelling should improve.

a, an

Use *an* before a word that begins with a vowel sound (*a, e, i,* and *o,* plus *u* when it sounds like *uh*) or silent *h.* Note that it's not the letter but the *sound* of the letter that matters.

an apple, *an* essay, *an* inch, *an* onion

an umpire, *an* ugly design (The *u*'s sound like *uh.*)

an hour, *an* honest person (The *h*'s are silent.)

Use *a* before a word that begins with a consonant sound (all the sounds except the vowels, plus *u* or *eu* when they sound like *you*).

a chart, *a* pie, *a* history book (The *h* is not silent in *history.*)

a union, *a* uniform, *a* unit (The *u*'s sound like *you.*)

a European vacation, *a* euphemism (*Eu* sounds like *you.*)

accept, except

Accept means "to receive or agree to take." Think of the two *c*'s in *accept* as two hands curling up to receive something.

I *accept* this award on my mother's behalf.

Except means "excluding" or "but." Think of the *x* in *except* as two arms crossed to block something or someone.

The airline upgraded everyone *except* Stanley.

advise, advice

Advise is a verb. (*Wise* people *advise.* Note the *s* sounds like *z.*)

I *advise* you to apply for a seasonal job.

Advice is a noun. (You can give or take *advice* like a bowl of *rice.*)

I took my math tutor's *advice.*

affect, effect	*Affect* is almost always a *verb* that means "to alter or influence someone or something." Try substituting another *verb* that starts with *a*—like *alter* or *amaze* or *astound*—to see if it works. If it does, then use this verb that starts with *a: affect.*

All quizzes will *affect* the final grade. (All quizzes will *alter* the final grade.)

That story *affected* everyone who heard it. (That story *amazed* everyone who heard it.)

Effect is most commonly used as a *noun* and means "a result." Focus on the *e* sound in *effect* and *result,* and try substituting *result* for *effect* as a test.

The strong coffee had a powerful *effect.* (The strong coffee had a powerful *result.*)

We studied the *effects* of sleep deprivation in my psychology class. (We studied the *results.* . . .)

all ready, already   If you can leave out the *all* and the sentence still makes sense, then *all ready* is the form to use.

That box is *all ready* to go. ("That box is *ready* to go" makes sense.)

But if you can't leave out the *all,* use *already.*

That box is *already* full. ("That box is *ready* full" does not make sense, so use *already.*)

are, our   *Are* is a present form of the verb "to be."

We *are* going to Colorado Springs.

Our is a pronoun that shows we possess something.

We painted *our* fence to match the house.

brake, break   *Brake* used as a verb means "to slow or stop motion." It's also the device that slows or stops motion in a *car.* Remember that both *car* and *brake* both have an *a* in the middle.

I had to *brake* quickly to avoid an accident.

Luckily I just had the *brakes* on my car fixed.

Break used as a verb means "to shatter" or "to split." It's also the name of an interruption, as in "a coffee break."

She never thought she would *break* a world record.

Enjoy your spring *break.*

choose, chose   The difference here is one of time. Use *choose* for present and future; use *chose* for past.

I will *choose* a new major this semester.

They *chose* the wrong time of year to travel to India.

clothes, cloths   *Clothes* are garments people wear; *cloths* are pieces of material you might clean or polish something with.

I love the *clothes* that characters wear in old movies.

Workers at car washes use special *cloths* to dry the cars.

coarse, course   *Coarse* describes a rough texture.

I used *coarse* sandpaper to smooth the surface of the board.

Course is used for all other meanings.

Of *course* we visited the golf *course* at Pebble Beach.

complement, compliment   *Complement,* spelled with an *e,* means to complete something or bring it to perfection.

Use a color wheel to find a *complement* for purple.

Juliet's personality *complements* Romeo's: she is practical, and he is a dreamer.

Compliment, spelled with an *i,* has to do with praise. Remember the *i* in "*I* like compliments," and you'll remember to use the *i* spelling when you mean praise.

In my evaluation, I got a nice *compliment* from my new boss.

We *complimented* them on their new home.

conscious, conscience   *Conscious* means "awake" or "aware."

They weren't *conscious* of any problem at the time.

Conscience means that inner voice of right and wrong. The extra *n* in *conscience* should remind you of "No," which is what your conscience often says to you.

My *conscience* told me not to keep the money I found.

dessert,
desert

Dessert is the sweet one, the one people like two helpings of. So give it two helpings of *s*. Remember also that "stressed" spelled backwards is *desserts*.

When I'm stressed, I can eat two *desserts* in a row.

The other one, *desert,* is used for all other meanings and has two pronunciations.

I promise that I won't *desert* you at the party.

The snake slithered slowly across the *desert*.

do, due

Do is a verb, an action. You *do* something.

I *do* most of my homework on the weekends.

But a payment a paper is *due;* it is scheduled for a certain time.

Our first essay is *due* tomorrow.

Due also comes before *to* in a phrase that means *because of*.

The outdoor concert was canceled *due to* rain.

feel, fill

Feel describes *feel*ings.

Whenever I stay up late, I *feel* sleepy in class.

Fill is the action of pouring into or packing something fully.

I want to *fill* my essay with memorable details.

fourth, forth

The word *fourth* has *four* in it. But note that *forty* does not. Remember the word *forty-fourth* to help you spell both of these words related to numbers.

This is our *fourth* quiz in forty-eight hours.

My grandparents celebrated their *forty-fourth* anniversary.

If you don't mean a number, use *forth*.

The ship's passengers walked back and *forth* on deck.

have, of

Have is a verb. Sometimes, in a contraction, it sounds like *of*. When you say *could've,* the *have* may sound like *of,* but it is not written that way. Always write *could have, would have, should have, might have*.

We should *have* planned our vacation sooner.

Then we could *have* used our coupon for a free ticket.

Use *of* only in a prepositional phrase. (See page 64.)

She sent me a box *of* chocolates for my birthday.

hear, here   The last three letters of *hear* spell "ear." You *hear* with your ear.

When I listen to a seashell, I *hear* ocean sounds.

The other spelling *here* tells "where." Note that the three words indicating a place or pointing out something all have *here* in them: *here, there, where.*

I'll be *here* for three more weeks.

it's, its   *It's* is a contraction and means "it is" or "it has."

It's hot. (*It is* hot.)

It's been hot all week. (*It has* been hot all week.)

Its is a possessive. Pronouns such as *its, yours, hers, ours, theirs,* and *whose* are already possessive forms and never need an apostrophe. (See page 47.)

The jury had made *its* decision.

The dog pulled at *its* leash.

knew, new   *Knew* has to do with *knowledge;* both start with a silent *k.*

New means "not old."

Her friends *knew* that she wanted a *new* bike.

know, no   *Know* has to do with *knowledge;* both start with a silent *k.*

By Friday, I must *know* all the state capitals.

No means "not any" or the opposite of "yes."

My boss has *no* patience. *No,* I am not exaggerating.

E X E R C I S E S

Circle the correct words in parentheses. Don't guess! If you aren't sure, turn back to the explanatory pages. Correct each set of ten sentences before continuing so you'll catch your mistakes early.

Exercise 1

1. People have (a, an) exciting (knew, new) way to buy books.

2. (It's, Its) all (do, due) to a device called the Espresso Book Machine—or EBM.

3. At bookstores and libraries, users can (choose, chose) titles from (a, an) online list and send the data directly to the EBM to be printed on the spot.

4. The EBM prints (a, an) 300-page book in only three minutes then binds (it's, its) pages in a traditional paperback cover.

5. Many booksellers and coffee shops (all ready, already) offer the services of this new kind of "Espresso" machine.

6. Some libraries use these instant book printers to (complement, compliment) the books in their regular holdings.

7. People can also (choose, chose) to print books that they have written themselves.

8. (It's, Its) too soon to (know, no) whether readers and writers will (accept, except) the idea of instant books.

9. Once they (hear, here) about the EBM, however, most people (do, due) want to try one.

10. The cost of printing (a, an) instant book is reasonable too; (it's, its) about one penny a page.

Source: ondemandbooks.com

Exercise 2

1. I took my family's (advise, advice) and enrolled at (a, an) community college.

2. I wanted to apply to (a, an) university as soon as I graduated from high school.

3. My friend sent in several applications, but the schools didn't (accept, except) him.

4. After he received the news, he decided to take a (brake, break) from school.

5. Now that I'm taking community college classes, I can relax and (choose, chose) the right university for me.

6. I've (all ready, already) taken one (coarse, course) in math and one in history.

7. The classes (are, our) challenging but manageable as long as I keep up with all of the assignments that are (do, due).

8. The instructors make sure that students (know, no) what to (do, due) to complete the assignments.

9. Even though I could (have, of) started at a four-year school, I'm glad that I (choose, chose) a community college.

10. I definitely (feel, fill) that (it's, its) the right place for me.

Exercise 3

1. (It's, Its) never too late to learn something (knew, new).

2. After living for nearly one hundred years without knowing how to read or write, George Dawson could (have, of) just (accepted, excepted) his life as it was.

3. But he never did (feel, fill) good about hiding his illiteracy from his children or signing his name with (a, an) X.

4. In 1996, George Dawson (choose, chose) to start school for the first time at the age of ninety-eight.

5. Dawson, who was (all ready, already) in his teens when the *Titanic* sank, worked all of his life to support his family and even outlived his (fourth, forth) wife.

6. He had enough memories to (feel, fill) a book, (accept, except) he wouldn't (have, of) been able to read it.

7. When a man in Seattle came to (hear, here) of Dawson's long life and strong desire for (a, an) education, he gave Dawson some (advise, advice).

8. Richard Glaubman, a teacher himself, suggested that Dawson share his experiences in a book; they (are, our) now coauthors of Dawson's autobiography.

9. In the (coarse, course) of his life as an African-American man and the grandson of slaves, Dawson witnessed and felt the (affects, effects) of racism and oppression.

10. But Dawson always believed that the joyful moments in life more than (complemented, complimented) the painful ones, and he titled his book *Life Is So Good*.

Source: Jet, April 17, 2000

Exercise 4

1. If you wear any (clothes, cloths) made of polyester, you may be wearing what used to be (a, an) old movie print.

2. (Do, Due) to the huge numbers of reels of film needed to meet the demands of today's movie audiences, recycling is (a, an) necessary part of the motion picture industry.

3. Companies such as Warner Bros. and New Line Cinema (accept, except) the responsibility for film recycling.

4. Of (coarse, course), the best prints of movies are saved for the future, but there (are, our) usually thousands of leftover copies (all ready, already) to be turned into something else.

5. The recycling process begins by chopping the film into (course, coarse) pieces, then transforming the rubble into a (knew, new) substance, such as polyester fabric.

6. Movie distributors are (conscious, conscience) that collectors and other interested parties would love to get their hands on these extra movie prints.

7. Therefore, security is (a, an) essential part of the movie-recycling process.

8. Someone trying to (brake, break) into a warehouse in search of last month's hottest release would (feel, fill) very disappointed.

9. The five to six reels of each film would (have, of) (all ready, already) been separated and mixed together with other films' reels.

10. (It's, Its) (know, no) surprise that movie companies want to protect their interests.

Source: Los Angeles Times, February 17, 2003

Exercise 5

1. Dentists (are, our) hardworking professionals, but most of us don't want to visit them.

2. Almost all of us hate to have (are, our) teeth drilled.

3. Most of us do, however, (accept, except) the need for dental work as a part of modern life.

4. (It's, Its) surprising to learn that dentists used drills on their patients 9,000 years ago.

5. (Knew, New) scientific discoveries have brought (fourth, forth) the remains of nomads who lived in the Stone Age.

6. Amazingly, many of their teeth revealed the (affects, effects) of drilling to eliminate decay.

7. Scientists don't (know, no) exactly what substance was used to (feel, fill) the cavities.

8. (It's, Its) also unclear whether patients were given anything so that they didn't (feel, fill) pain.

9. Based on the drilling patterns, scientists believe that some Stone Age people took advantage of the holes in their teeth for a decorative (affect, effect).

10. They may have used precious stones to (feel, fill) these holes as (a, an) ancient form of "mouth bling."

Source: National Geographic News, April 4, 2006

PROOFREADING EXERCISE

Find and correct the ten errors contained in the following paragraph. All of the errors involve Words Often Confused (Set 1).

In the middle of a debate in my speech class last week, I suddenly became very self-conscience. My heart started beating faster, and I didn't no what to due. I looked around to see if my show of nerves was having a affect on the audience. Of coarse, they could here my voice trembling. The topic that we were debating involved whether it would be best to eliminate letter grades in college, and everyone else was doing so well. But for some reason, my face turned red, and I would of left the room if the door had been closer. After the debate, my classmates tried to give me complements, but I new that they were just trying to make me feel better.

SENTENCE WRITING

The surest way to learn these Words Often Confused is to use them immediately in your own writing. Choose the five pairs of words that you most often confuse from Set 1. Then use each of them correctly in a new sentence. No answers are provided, but you can see if you are using the words correctly by comparing your sentences with the examples in the explanations.

Words Often Confused (Set 2)

Study this second set of words as carefully as you did the first. Read the short explanations, helpful hints, and sample sentences before attempting the exercises. By learning all of the word groups in both sets, you can eliminate many basic spelling problems.

lead, led   *Lead* is the metal that rhymes with *head*.

Old paint is dangerous because it often contains *lead*.

The past form of the verb "to lead" is *led*.

What factors *led* to your decision?

I *led* our school's debating team to victory last year.

If you don't mean past time, use *lead*, which rhymes with *seed*.

I will *lead* the debating team again this year.

loose, lose   *Loose* means "not tight." Note how *l o o s e* that word is. It has plenty of room for two *o*'s. Remember that *loose* and *tooth* both have two *o*'s in the middle.

My sister has a *loose* tooth.

Lose is the opposite of win. Pronounce the *s* like a *z*.

If we *lose* the next game, we will be out for the season.

passed, past   *Passed* is a form of the verb "to pass."

Nanette easily *passed* her math test.

The runner *passed* the baton to her teammate.

I *passed* your house on my way to the store.

Use *past* when you mean "*by*" or to refer to the time that came before the present.

I drove *past* your house. (Meaning "I drove *by* your house." The verb in the sentence is *drove*.)

It's best to learn from *past* experiences.

In the *past*, he worked for a small company.

personal, personnel   Pronounce these two correctly, and you won't confuse them—*pérsonal, personnél*.

She shared her *personal* views as a parent.

Personnel means "a group of employees."

I had an appointment in the *personnel* office.

piece, peace   Remember "a *piece* of *pie*." The word meaning "a *piece*" always begins with *pie*.

> Some students asked for an extra *piece* of scratch paper.

The other word, *peace,* means "the opposite of war."

> The two sides finally signed a *peace* treaty.

principal,   *Principal* means "main." Both words have *a* in them: **principle**   princip*a*l, m*a*in.

> The *principal* concern is safety. (main concern)

> We paid both *principal* and interest. (main amount of money)

Also, think of a school's "princi*pal*" as your "*pal*."

> An elementary school *principal* must be kind. (main administrator)

A *principle* is a "rule." Both words end in *le:* princip*le*, ru*le*.

> I am proud of my *principles*. (rules of conduct)

> We value the *principle* of truth in advertising. (rule)

quiet, quite   Pronounce these two correctly, and you won't confuse them. *Quiet* means "free from noise" and rhymes with *diet*.

> Golfers often ask spectators to be *quiet*.

Quite means "really" or "very" and ends with the same three letters as *white*.

> The bleach made my towels *quite* white.

right, write   *Right* means "correct," "proper," or "the opposite of left."

> You will find your keys if you look in the *right* place, on the *right* side of the coffee table.

It also means "in the exact location, position, or moment."

> Your keys are *right* where you left them.

> Let's go *right* now.

Write means "to compose sentences, poems, essays. . . ."

> I *write* in my journal every day.

than, then

Than is used to compare. Remember that both *than* and *compare* have an *a* in them.

I am taller *than* my sister.

Then tells when. *Then* and *when* rhyme, and both have an *e* in them.

I always write a rough draft of a paper first; *then* I revise it.

their, there, they're

Their is a possessive, meaning "belonging to them."

They read *their* essays out loud.

There points out something. Remember that the three words indicating a place or pointing out something all have *here* in them: *here, there, where.*

I know that I haven't been *there* before.

In Hawaii, *there* is always a rainbow in the sky.

They're is a contraction and means "they are."

They're living in Canada now. (*They are* living in Canada now.)

threw, through

Threw is the past form of "to throw."

The students *threw* snowballs at each other.

I *threw* away my application for a scholarship.

If you don't mean "to throw something," use *through.*

We could see our beautiful view *through* the new curtains.

They worked *through* their differences.

two, too, to

Two is a number.

We have written *two* papers so far in my English class.

Too means "very" or "also," and so it also has an extra *o.*

The movie was *too* long and *too* violent. (very)

They are enrolled in that biology class, *too.* (also)

Use *to* for all other meanings.

They like *to* ski. They're going *to* the mountains.

weather,
whether

Weather refers to conditions of the atmosphere.

Snowy *weather* is too cold for me.

Whether means "if."

I don't know *whether* it is snowing there or not.

were, wear,
where

These words are pronounced differently but are often confused in writing.

Were is a past form of the verb "to be."

We *were* interns at the time.

Wear usually means "to have on," as in wearing clothes.

I always *wear* a scarf in winter.

Where refers to a place. Remember that the three words indicating a place or pointing out something all have *here* in them: *here, there, where.*

Where are the teachers' mailboxes?

who's, whose

Who's is a contraction and means "who is" or "who has."

Who's responsible for the checks? (*Who* is responsible?)

Who's been signing them? (*Who has* been signing them?)

Whose is a possessive. Words such as *whose, its, yours, hers, ours,* and *theirs* are already possessive forms and never need an apostrophe. See page 47.

Whose keys are these? We don't know *whose* keys they are.

woman,
women

The difference here is one of number: wo*man* refers to one adult female; wo*men* refers to two or more adult females.

I know a *woman* who has bowled a perfect game.

I bowl with a group of *women* from my work.

you're, your

You're is a contraction and means "you are."

You're as smart as I am. (*You are* as smart as I am.)

Your is a possessive meaning "belonging to you."

I borrowed *your* lab book.

EXERCISES

Circle the correct words in parentheses. As you finish each exercise, check your answers so that you will catch any mistakes early.

Exercise 1

1. (Their, There, They're) is a new way to prepare children for earthquakes.
2. Researchers use current technology to put kids (threw, through) a simulated earthquake using virtual reality headphones and goggles.
3. Children in Greece have been the first (two, too, to) receive the training.
4. (Their, There, They're) very likely to experience a real earthquake, according to scientists.
5. The (personal, personnel) who teach students with special needs have seen very positive results from earthquake training.
6. In the (passed, past), children with Down syndrome, for example, would (loose, lose) control and panic during a frightening event such as an earthquake.
7. In a twist of fate, (their, there, they're) was an earthquake in Greece just a few months after some children were trained.
8. After being (lead, led) (through, threw) an artificial quake using virtual reality, the children with Down syndrome (were, wear, where) able to remain calm and follow directions.
9. In fact, all of the children who had experienced a virtual earthquake coped with the event better (than, then) those who hadn't.
10. It's unclear (weather, whether) virtual earthquake training will work as well with adults.

Source: Science News, August 5, 2006

Exercise 2

1. Knut is the name of a polar bear (who's, whose) early life made headlines in 2007.
2. Knut became (quiet, quite) a celebrity in Germany after being born in captivity and rejected by his mother at the Berlin Zoo.

3. The tiny abandoned polar bear was no bigger (than, then) a fat kitten when (personal, personnel) at the zoo had to make a difficult decision.

4. They had to decide (weather, whether) to let the little bear cub die naturally or to go against nature and raise him themselves.

5. At the time, some people voiced (their, there, they're) strong belief in the (principal, principle) that humans should not artificially raise wild animals.

6. As a small cub, Knut's fluffy white fur and adorable personality (lead, led) newspapers, magazines, and television stations (two, too, to) spread stories and photos of him around the world.

7. Children and adults (were, wear, where) equally impressed with Knut, and they wrote songs and books about him.

8. Companies even designed candy and other products (two, too, to) look like him.

9. Sadly, Knut (passed, past) away unexpectedly in March of 2011.

10. Knut lived a shorter life (than, then) most polar bears and was only four years old when he died.

Source: http://www.dailymail.co.uk/news/article-1367921

Exercise 3

1. You've probably been (threw, through) this experience.

2. (You're, Your) in a theater, auditorium, or intimate restaurant, and someone's cell phone rings.

3. The person (who's, whose) phone it is becomes (two, to, too) embarrassed (two, to, too) answer it.

4. In the (passed, past), (their, there, they're) was no way to keep this unfortunate event from happening.

5. Now scientists have invented a type of magnetic wood paneling that will maintain the (piece, peace) and (quiet, quite) of public places even if people still refuse to turn off (their, there, they're) cell phones.

6. This new wood will block radio signals and therefore keep such calls from going (threw, through) the walls of a theater, auditorium, restaurant, or anywhere else (their, there, they're) not wanted.

7. Of course, (their, there, they're) are people who do not want to (loose, lose) (their, there, they're) (right, write) to make (personal, personnel) calls wherever they want.

8. One of the best uses of magnetic wood will be to protect areas (were, wear, where) signals interfere with each other.

9. (Than, Then) wooden panels will be used (two, too, to) divide wireless signals rather (than, then) block calls altogether.

10. (Weather, Whether) (you're, your) for it or against it, magnetic wood will probably be used worldwide (quiet, quite) soon.

Source: New Scientist, June 27, 2002

Exercise 4

1. The three days following September 11, 2001, (were, wear, where) unique.

2. They offered an unprecedented opportunity to study an aspect of the (whether, weather) that could not be studied under normal conditions.

3. The situation that (lead, led) to the study was the temporary ban on nearly all airline flights over America.

4. In the (passed, past), scientists had wondered (whether, weather) the clouds produced by airplane engines affected temperatures on land.

5. These man-made clouds, called contrails, are the streaks left behind after an airplane has (passed, past) across the sky.

6. Never in the recent (passed, past) had (their, there, they're) been days when the skies were clear of contrails.

7. The absence of air traffic also produced an eerie kind of (quiet, quite).

8. Not wanting to (loose, lose) the chance to discover the effects of contrails, (two, too, to) scientists went (right, write) to work.

9. David Travis and Andrew Carleton discovered, (threw, through) comparisons of temperatures from the three days without air traffic and the same days for the (passed, past) thirty years, that the contrails do cause temperatures to cool slightly.

10. This (piece, peace) of scientific data may lead to a greater understanding of our impact on the planet's (whether, weather) overall.

Source: Discover, August 2002

Exercise 5

1. One beautiful morning, you may receive a phone call that changes (you're, your) life.

2. The caller will tell you that (you're, your) half a million dollars richer and that you don't have to do anything other (than, then) be yourself to deserve the money.

3. You might wonder (weather, whether) it is a real or a crank call.

4. Believe it or not, this wonderful (piece, peace) of news is delivered to between twenty and thirty special men and (woman, women) in America every year.

5. (Their, There, They're) unofficially called the "Genius Awards," but (their, there, they're) real title is the MacArthur Fellowships.

6. The MacArthur Foundation awards its fellowships each year based on the (principal, principle) that forward-thinking people deserve an opportunity to pursue their ideas freely and without obligation to anyone.

7. No application is necessary (two, too, to) receive the gift of $100,000 a year plus health insurance for five years, and no particular field of work receives more consideration (than, then) another.

8. The (principal, principle) characteristic that MacArthur Fellows share is (their, there, they're) creative potential—in any area.

9. Each year, the MacArthur Foundation sends about one hundred "scouts" across the country looking for people with untapped potential (two, too, to) nominate; (than, then) another anonymous group selects the year's recipients.

10. The nominees don't even know that (their, there, they're) going (threw, through) the process until the phone rings on that fateful morning one day.

Source: http://www.macfound.org/fellows-faq/

PROOFREADING EXERCISE

Find and correct the ten errors in this paragraph. All errors involve Words Often Confused (Set 2).

Yesterday, we watched and discussed a short animated video in my philosophy class. The film shows office workers in a high-rise building looking down from there windows and watching pedestrians walk passed a small construction site on the street below, wear a jack hammer has broken a peace of the sidewalk. As pedestrians walk over the lose brick, several of them trip and fall but are not injured. The office personnel who are watching from above find each accident funnier then the one before until an old man with a cane approaches the dangerous site. His weak condition makes the office workers remember their principals of write and wrong, and they all try too warn the old man before he falls too. The film ends in a way that is quiet a surprise.

Source: http://responsibility-project.libertymutual.com/films/good-vibrations

SENTENCE WRITING

Write several sentences using any words you missed in the exercises for Words Often Confused (Set 2). Use one of the topics below or a new topic of your own.

- Something you would like to accomplish this year
- Qualities of a good friend
- All-time favorite TV shows movies
- Places you would like to know more about
- Reasons why you're in school

The Eight Parts of Speech

Choosing the right word is an important aspect of writing. As we've explained, some words sound alike but are spelled differently and have different meanings (*past* and *passed,* for instance), and some words are spelled the same but sound different and mean different things (*lead,* for the action of "leading," and *lead,* for the stuff inside pencils). Besides learning to use the right words, it is important to understand the roles that words play in sentences.

Just as one actor can play many different parts in movies (a hero, a villain, a humorous sidekick), single words can play different parts in sentences (a noun, a verb, an adjective). These are called the *eight parts of speech,* briefly defined with examples below.

1. **Nouns** name *people, places, things,* or *ideas* and are used as subjects and objects in sentences. **Proper nouns** that name *specific people, places, things,* or *ideas*—such as *Marie Curie, New York City, Kleenex,* and *Freemasonry*—are capitalized and can include more than one word. (See pages 57, 64, and 137 for more about nouns as subjects and objects. See page 197 for more about capitalizing specific nouns.)

    Ms. Kim and the other **librarians** are proud of the **success** of the new **library**.

2. **Pronouns** are special words—such as *I, she, him, it, they, who, that,* and *us*—that replace nouns to avoid repeating them. (See page 155 for more about pronouns.)

    In fact, **they** (the librarians) are very proud of **it** (the new library's success).

3. **Adjectives** add description to nouns and pronouns—telling *which one, how many, what kind, color,* or *shape* they are. (See page 34 for more about adjectives.)

    The **head** librarian designed the **new, state-of-the-art** facilities.

    The words *a, an,* and *the* are special forms of adjectives called **articles.** They always introduce a noun or a pronoun and are used so often that there is no need to label them.

4. **Verbs** show action or link a subject with a description. One verb can also help another verb in a verb phrase. (See pages 57, 93, and 137 for more about verbs.)

    She **was teaching** in France before she **retired** and **became** a librarian.

5. **Adverbs** add information—such as *when, where, why,* or *how*—to verbs, adjectives, other adverbs, and whole clauses. (See page 35 for more about adverbs.)

    The library steps are marble; people **often** slip **there** on the **very** slick ice.

6. **Prepositions** show position in *space* and *time* and are followed by noun objects to form prepositional phrases. (See page 64 for more about prepositions.)

    The computers lounges **in** the library are full **by** the middle **of** the morning.

7. **Conjunctions** are connecting words—such as *and, but,* and *or*—and words that begin dependent clauses—such as *because, since, when, while,* and *although.* (See pages 70 and 85 for more about conjunctions.)

> The library **and** its landscaping impress people **when** they first see the campus.

8. **Interjections** interrupt a sentence to convey a greeting or to show surprise or other emotions and are rarely used in Standard Written English.

> When they walk up or drive by, they say, "**Oh**, what a great building!"

To find out what parts of speech an individual word can play, look it up in a good, college-level dictionary. (See page 3.) You'll find a list of definitions beginning with an abbreviated part of speech (*n, adj, prep,* and so on) that identifies its possible uses. However, seeing how a word is used in a particular sentence is the best way to identify its part of speech. Look at these examples:

> Our **train** arrived at exactly three o'clock.
>
> (*Train* is a noun in this sentence, naming the vehicle we call a "train.")
>
> Sammy and Helen **train** new employees at Sea World.
>
> (*Train* is a verb in this example, showing the action of "training.")
>
> Students can take a shuttle from the **train** station.
>
> (*Train* is an adjective here, adding description to the noun *station.*)

All of the words in a sentence work together to create meaning, but each one serves its own purpose by playing a part of speech. Think about how each of the words in the following sentence plays the particular part of speech labeled:

> n   prep   adj   n   adv   v   adj   n   prep   n   conj   v
> Students at community colleges often attend several classes in a day and are
>
> adv   adj   conj   pro   adv   v   adv
> very tired when they finally go home.

Below, you'll find an explanation for each label:

> Students   n (*names the people* who are the subject of the sentence)
>
> at   prep (*begins a prepositional phrase* showing position in space)
>
> community   adj (*adds description* to the noun *colleges,* telling what kind)

colleges	n (*names the place* that is the object of the preposition *at*)
often	adv (*adds to the verb,* telling when students *attend* classes)
attend	v (*shows an action,* telling what the students do)
several	adj (*adds description* to the noun *classes,* telling how many)
classes	n (*names the things* that the students *attend*)
in	prep (*begins a prepositional phrase* showing position in time)
a	no label (an article that *points to the noun day*)
day	n (*names the thing* that is the object of the preposition *in*)
and	conj (*joins* the two verbs *attend* and *are*)
are	v (*links* the subject *students* with the descriptive word *tired*)
very	adv (*adds to the adjective* that follows, telling how *tired* the students are)
tired	adj (*describes the noun* subject *students*)
when	conj (*begins a dependent clause*)
they	pro (*replaces* the noun *students* to avoid repetition)
finally	adv (*adds to the verb,* telling when they *go* home)
go	v (*shows an action,* telling what they do)
home.	adv (*adds to the verb,* telling where they *go*)

Familiarizing yourself with the parts of speech will help you use words more correctly now and understand phrases and clauses better later. Each of the eight parts of speech has characteristics that distinguish it from the other seven, but it takes practice to learn them.

E X E R C I S E S

Label the parts of speech above all of the words in the following sentences using the abbreviations **n**, **pro**, **adj**, **v**, **adv**, **prep**, **conj**, and **interj**. Remember that proper nouns can include more than one word and that you may ignore the words *a, an,* and *the.* Refer back to the definitions and examples of the parts of speech whenever necessary. When in doubt, leave a word unmarked until you check the answers after each set of ten sentences.

Exercise 1

1. Bette Nesmith Graham invented correction fluid in the 1950s.
2. She originally called her invention Mistake Out.
3. Later, she changed its name to Liquid Paper.
4. Originally, Graham worked as a typist, and she often made mistakes.
5. She brought white paint to work and covered her typos with it.
6. Soon everyone wanted a bottle of Graham's correction paint.
7. She mixed the product in her kitchen and bottled it like fingernail polish.
8. Single-handedly, Graham developed a product that made millions of dollars.
9. Her son, Michael Nesmith, also benefited from her success.
10. He was a member of The Monkees, a popular boy band in the 1960s.

Source: Invention and Technology, Fall 2009

Exercise 2

1. Clyde Tombaugh discovered the ninth "planet," Pluto, in 1930.
2. Tombaugh died in 1997 at the age of 90.
3. Scientists loaded Tombaugh's ashes onto New Horizons, a space probe that was launched in January of 2006.
4. New Horizons will arrive near Pluto in 2015.
5. After the launch of New Horizons, astronomers deleted Pluto from the list of real planets.

6. They determined that real planets must control their own orbits.

7. Pluto is an icy ball under the influence of Neptune's orbit.

8. Astronomers put Pluto into a new category.

9. Therefore, the official number of planets has changed to eight.

10. Wow! That is an amazing development.

Source: Newsweek, September 4, 2006

Exercise 3

1. In the summer of 2005, London Zoo opened a temporary exhibit.

2. The title of the exhibit was "The Human Zoo."

3. Zoo officials selected eight human volunteers.

4. Then they put the humans on display for several days.

5. Dozens of people had applied online for the project.

6. The exhibit showcased three males and five females.

7. They dressed in fake fig leaves that covered their shorts and bikini tops.

8. With its rocky ledges and cave-like structures, the enclosure had previously housed bears.

9. The eight humans talked, played games, and received a lot of attention.

10. Outside the exhibit, the zoo posted signs about human diet, habitat, and behavior.

Source: BBC News, August 25, 2005

Exercise 4

1. Wow, pigeons have a built-in compass in their brains!

2. This compass points them in the right direction as they fly.

3. Recently, pigeon experts in England conducted a study of these birds.

4. The study tracked the flights of certain pigeons for two years.

5. The results were very surprising.

6. Modern pigeons usually ignored their inner compasses.

7. They navigated by other methods instead.

8. The pigeons simply looked down and followed human highways.

9. They remembered roads from previous flights and took the same roads home again.

10. The pigeons even traced the roads' turns, curves, and roundabouts as they flew.

Source: The Daily Telegraph, February 6, 2004

Exercise 5

1. Some people collect rare coins and paper money.

2. The Del Monte twenty-dollar bill is very famous.

3. The mint made a mistake when it printed this bill.

4. A sticker from a banana accidentally attached itself to the paper during the printing process.

5. The round green and red sticker became a part of the bill.

6. Such mistakes usually lead to a bill's destruction.

7. This flawed note, however, left the mint with the normal twenties.

8. Experts immediately authenticated its rare status.

9. The bill first sold on eBay for $10,000.

10. Eventually, a couple from Texas paid $25,000 for this one-of-a-kind note.

Source: www.delmontenote.com

PARAGRAPH EXERCISE

Here is a brief excerpt from the book *The Pact: Three Young Men Make a Promise and Fulfill a Dream* by Drs. Sampson Davis, George Jenkins, and Rameck Hunt. Their dream was for all three of them to become doctors, and they did. Label the parts of speech above as many of the words as you can before checking your answers.

When I look back over my life and the lives of my friends, I also see that involvement in school and community activities helped us [when we felt] the negative pull of our peers. I joined the Shakespeare Club in elementary school and the Police Athletic League in junior high school, and I played baseball in high school. Sam took karate lessons from grade school through his early years in high school and also played on our high-school baseball team. And Rameck took drama lessons in junior high school, and in high school he joined the drama club. . . .

Source: The Pact: Three Young Men Make a Promise and Fulfill a Dream (Riverhead Books, 2002)

SENTENCE WRITING

Write ten short sentences (under ten words each) about the good qualities of a person you know well, perhaps a sibling or close friend. Be sure to avoid using "to _____" forms of verbs. Label the parts of speech above the words in your sentences.

Adjectives and Adverbs

English has only two kinds of modifiers: adjectives and adverbs. "To modify" means to change or improve something, usually by adding to it. Two of the eight parts of speech, adjectives and adverbs, are used to *add* information to other words. Try to remember that both *ad*jectives and *ad*verbs *add* information.

ADJECTIVES

- Adjectives *add to nouns and pronouns* by answering these questions: *Which one? What kind? How much or how many? What size, what color, or what shape?*

                        adj   n   adj   n   adj adj adj
    She bought a *new* textbook with *multicolored* tabs. It has *one large blue*

      n   adj   adj   adj   n   adj adj adj pro
    tab, *two medium yellow* tabs, and *three small red* ones.

- Adjectives usually come *before the nouns they modify.*

            adj   n   adj   n   adj adj   adj   n
    The *new* library stands on the *north* side of *our big beautiful* campus.

- However, adjectives can also come *after the nouns they modify.*

                n   adj   adj   adj   n   adj   n
    The land, *flat* and *accessible,* was the *perfect* location for the *new* building.

- Adjectives may also come *after linking verbs* (*is, am, are, was, were, feel, seem, appear, taste* . . .) to add description to the subject. For further discussion of these special verbs, see page 137.

                n   lv   adj   adj
    The trees are *lush* and *plentiful.*

                n   lv   adj   adj   n   lv   adj   adj
    The juice tasted *fresh* and *delicious.* (or) The juice was *fresh* and *delicious.*

- Adjectives can be *forms of nouns and pronouns* that are used to add information to other nouns.

            adj   n   adj   n   adj   adj   n
    The *tree's* owner always trims *its* branches during *his summer* vacation.

                adj   n   adj   n
    I love *chocolate* cake for *my* birthday.

Adverbs

- Adverbs *add to verbs, adjectives, other adverbs, and whole clauses* by answering these questions: *How? When? Where? Why? In what way?*

         adv   v   adv   v   adv adv
  I *quickly* typed my paper and *reluctantly* turned it *in late*.

            v   adv   v
  She did *not* accept my paper at first.

          adv   adj
  I was *very* nervous about it.

              adv   adj   n
  She had an *extremely* disappointed look on her face.

              adv adj   adv   adj
  The deadline was *very* clear and *quite* reasonable.

           adv   adv adv
  Students *often* work *really hard* at the end of the term.

- Unlike adjectives, some adverbs can move around in sentences without changing the meaning.

    adv
  Now I have enough money for a vacation.

      adv
  I *now* have enough money for a vacation.

               adv
  I have enough money *now* for a vacation.

                         adv
  I have enough money for a vacation *now*.

Notice that many—but not all—adverbs end in *ly*. Be aware, however, that adjectives can also end in *ly*. Remember that a word's part of speech is determined by how the word is used in a particular sentence. For instance, in the old saying "The early bird catches the worm," *early* adds to the noun, telling which bird. *Early* is acting as an adjective. However, in the sentence "The teacher arrived early," *early* adds to the verb, telling when the teacher arrived. *Early* is an adverb.

     Now that you've read about adjectives and adverbs, try to identify the question that each modifier (adj or adv) answers in the example below. Refer back to the questions listed under Adjectives and Adverbs.

    adj   n   adj   n   adv   adv   v
My family and I went to the farmer's market yesterday. There we watched the

adj   adj   n   adv   v   adv adj

decoration of a huge wedding cake. The baker skillfully squeezed out colorful

n   adj   n   adv adj   adj   n   adj   adj

flowers, leaf patterns, and pale pink curving letters made of smooth, creamy

n

frosting.

NOTE—Although we discuss only single-word adjectives and adverbs here, phrases and clauses can also function as adjectives and adverbs following similar patterns.

CHOOSING BETWEEN ADJECTIVES AND ADVERBS

Knowing how to choose between adjectives and adverbs is important, especially in certain kinds of sentences. See if you can make the correct choices in these three sentences:

We did (good, well) on that test.

I feel (bad, badly) about quitting my job.

Your friend speaks (really clear/really clearly).

Did you choose *well, bad,* and *really clearly?* If you missed *bad,* you're not alone. You might have reasoned that *badly* adds to the verb *feel,* but *feel* is acting in a

v

special way here—not naming the action of feeling with your fingertips (as in "I *feel*

adv   n   adj

the fabric *carefully*"), but describing the feeling of it (as in "The *fabric* feels *smooth*"). To understand this concept, try substituting "I feel (happy, happily)" instead of "I feel (bad, badly)" and note how easy it is to choose.

Another way that adjectives and adverbs work is to compare two or more things by describing them in relation to one another. The *er* ending is added to both adjectives and adverbs when comparing two items, and the *est* ending is added when comparing three or more items.

adj   n   adj   adj   n   adj   adj   n

The *first* peach was *sweet.* The *second* peach was *sweeter.* The *third* peach was

adj   pro

the *sweetest* one of all.

v   adv   v   adv   v   adv

You work *hard;* he works *harder;* I work *hardest.*

In some cases, such comparisons require the addition of a word (*more* or *most*, *less* or *least*) instead of a change in the ending from *er* to *est*. Longer adjectives and adverbs usually require these extra adverbs to help with comparisons.

adj   adv   adj   adv   adj

Food is *expensive*; gas is *more expensive*; rent is the *most expensive*.

adv   adv   adv   adv   adv

He dances *gracefully*; you dance *less gracefully*; I dance *least gracefully*.

E X E R C I S E S

Remember that adjectives add to nouns and pronouns, while adverbs add to verbs, adjectives, and other adverbs. If you learn the difference between adjectives and adverbs, your word choice will improve. Check your answers frequently.

Exercise 1

Identify whether each *italicized* word is used as an adjective or an adverb in the sentence.

1. The "New Books" displays at bookstores *always* attract me. (adjective, adverb)

2. These displays usually stand right next to the *front* entrance. (adjective, adverb)

3. They hold everything from *tiny* paperbacks to huge reference works. (adjective, adverb)

4. The books are brand new and cover *various* topics. (adjective, adverb)

5. *Yesterday,* I discovered a whole book about flowers. (adjective, adverb)

6. The book's title was *very* straightforward: <u>Flowers</u>. (adjective, adverb)

7. I loved its *intriguing* subtitle: <u>How They Changed the World</u>. (adjective, adverb)

8. The *bright* pink tulip on its cover also appealed to me. (adjective, adverb)

9. I had *never* considered the effects of flowers on the world. (adjective, adverb)

10. Therefore, I bought the book and took it *home* to read. (adjective, adverb)

Exercise 2

Identify whether the word *only* is used as an adjective or an adverb in the following sentences. In each sentence, try to link the word *only* with another word to figure out if *only* is an adjective (adding to a noun or pronoun) or an adverb (adding to a verb, adjective, or other adverb). Have fun with this exercise!

1. I reached into my wallet and pulled out my *only* coupon.

2. I had *only* one coupon.

3. *Only* I had a coupon.

4. That company *only* sells the software; it doesn't create the software.

5. That company sells *only* software, not hardware.

6. Other companies deal in hardware *only*.

7. In my Spanish class, the teacher speaks in Spanish *only*.

8. *Only* the students use English to ask questions or to clarify something.

9. My best friend is an *only* child, and so am I.

10. *Only* she understands how I feel.

Exercise 3

Choose the correct adjective or adverb form required to complete each sentence.

1. We have many (close, closely) relatives who live in the area.

2. We are (close, closely) related to many of the people in this area.

3. During the holidays, we feel (close, closely) to everyone in town.

4. My sister suffered (bad, badly) after she fell and broke her leg.

5. She felt (bad, badly) about tripping on a silly little rug.

6. Her leg itched really (bad, badly) under her cast.

7. The classroom hamster runs (very happy, very happily) on his exercise wheel.

8. The children are always (very happy, very happily) when he exercises.

9. My group received a (good, well) grade on our project.

10. The four of us worked (good, well) together.

Exercise 4

Choose the correct adjective or adverb form required to complete each sentence.

1. Of all my friends' cars, Jake's is (small, smaller, the smallest).

2. Janna has (a small, a smaller, the smallest) car, too.

3. Her car is (small, smaller, smallest) than mine.

4. Ken bought his car last week, so it's (a new, a newer, the newest) one.

5. Mine has (new, newer, newest) tires than Ken's since my tires were put on yesterday.

6. Jake's car is (new, newer, newest) than Janna's.

7. Ken looked for a car with (good, better, best) gas mileage than his old one.

8. Of course, Jake's tiny car gets (good, better, the best) gas mileage of all.

9. I do get (good, better, best) gas mileage now that I have new tires.

10. These days, gas mileage is (important, more important, most important) than it used to be.

Exercise 5

Label all of the adjectives (adj) and adverbs (adv) in the following sentences. Mark the ones you are sure of; then check your answers and find the ones you missed.

1. I took a helpful class online in the spring.

2. An Internet specialist taught me research skills.

3. I discovered very useful tools for Web research.

4. The instructor clearly explained various kinds of online resources.

5. She gave me several optional topics for each assignment.

6. I especially enjoyed the articles from my two projects about world music.

7. Now I fully understand the benefits of online classes.

8. They are fun and rewarding because students work at their own pace.

9. I am definitely less confused about online sources.

10. I can do research online and enjoy the process completely.

PROOFREADING EXERCISE

Correct the five errors in the use of adjectives and adverbs in the following paragraph. Then try to label all of the adjectives (adj) and adverbs (adv) in the paragraph for practice.

I didn't do very good during my first semester at community college. I feel badly whenever I think of it. I skipped classes and turned in sloppy work. My counselor warned me about my negative attitude, but I was real stubborn. I dropped out for a year and a half. Now that I have come back to college, I am even stubborner than before. I go to every class and do my best. Now, a college degree is only my goal.

SENTENCE WRITING

Write a short paragraph (five to seven sentences) describing your favorite singer and song at the moment. Then go back through the paragraph and label your single-word adjectives and adverbs.

Contractions

When two words are shortened into one, the result is called a *contraction*. A contraction pulls two words together in the same way that a muscle contraction pulls your forearm and upper arm together. Use an apostrophe to show where the letter or letters have been squeezed out in most contractions.

is not ·····➤ *isn't*   you have ·····➤ *you've*

Here's a list of the most common contractions:

I am	I'm
I have	I've
I shall, I will	I'll
I would	I'd
you are	you're
you have	you've
you will	you'll
she is, she has	she's
he is, he has	he's
it is, it has	it's
we are	we're
we have	we've
we will, we shall	we'll
they are	they're
they have	they've
are not	aren't
cannot	can't
do not	don't
does not	doesn't
have not	haven't
let us	let's
who is, who has	who's

where is	where's
were not	weren't
would not	wouldn't
could not	couldn't
should not	shouldn't
would have	would've
could have	could've
should have	should've
that is	that's
there is	there's
what is	what's

Notice that one contraction does not follow this rule: *will not* becomes *won't*.

In all other contractions that you're likely to use, the apostrophe goes exactly where the letter or letters are left out. Note especially that *it's, they're, who's,* and *you're* are contractions. Use them when you mean *two* words. (See page 49 for more about the possessive forms—*its, their, whose,* and *your*—which *don't* need apostrophes.)

E X E R C I S E S

Add the missing apostrophes to the contractions in the following sentences. A few of the sentences do not include any contractions. Be sure to correct each exercise before going on to the next so you'll catch your mistakes early.

Exercise 1

1. We modern folks arent the only ones to love movies and animation.

2. Ancient Europeans created their own animated images in caves 30,000 years ago.

3. Their moving pictures werent projected but painted on walls and twirled on strings.

4. The walls of prehistoric caves in France display scenes that appear to move due to tricks of perspective and repetition.

5. In one image, theres a bison painted in various positions with eight legs instead of four to suggest running.

6. In parts of France and Spain, scientists have also discovered ancient animated toys.

7. Theyve found flat, two-sided objects carved with pictures of the same animal on both sides.

8. On one side, the animal is lying down, and on the other, its standing on four legs.

9. When the disk is spun on string, the viewer sees a moving image of the animal standing up by itself.

10. Its fascinating to think of people creating animated images so long ago.

Source: Science News, June 30, 2012

Exercise 2

1. Whats a strong natural substance that might save thousands of lives in the future?

2. Youre right if youre thinking of bamboo.

3. Engineers from around the world have recently tested its strength and flexibility.

4. Experts found that its equally impressive when its used in its natural state and when its mixed with more traditional building materials, such as concrete.

5. Structures made from bamboo-based products are clearly safer when theres an earthquake.

6. They dont crack or crumble, even when theyre shaken violently by powerful earthquake simulators.

7. Theres a long list of factors that make bamboo a promising building material of the future.

8. It doesnt cost much and wont catch on fire.

9. Its lightweight but isnt brittle.

10. And although theyll be easy and quick to build, bamboo-reinforced buildings wont need repair for decades.

Source: Discover, August 2004

Exercise 3

1. Theres a new kind of addiction to be worried about.

2. Experts call it "infomania," and its having an impact on people's lives.

3. If someones addicted to e-mail, cell phone calls, and text messages, that person suffers from infomania.

4. That persons not alone.

5. A recent study shows that around sixty percent of us have at least a mild case of infomania.

6. If theres a computer around, well check our e-mail, even if were in the middle of a meeting or some other important activity.

7. Well check our messages when we should be resting at home or on vacation.

8. The results of the study showed that theres a price to be paid.

9. People lose approximately 10 points of their IQ scores if theyre distracted by e-mails and phone calls.

10. Thats double the amount of a decline in intelligence than if they were smoking marijuana.

Source: BBC News, April 22, 2005

Exercise 4

1. "Music wasnt made to make us wise, but better natured." Josh Billings

2. "Give me a laundry list, and Ill set it to music." Rossini

3. "I know only two tunes. One of them is 'Yankee Doodle'—and the other one isnt." Ulysses S. Grant

4. "Its not me. Its the songs. Im just the postman. I deliver the songs." Bob Dylan

5. "If you think youve hit a false note, sing loud. When in doubt, sing loud." Robert Merrill

6. "I dont know anything about music. In my line, you dont have to." Elvis Presley

7. "If the king loves music, theres little wrong in the land." Mencius

8. "When you got to ask what jazz is, youll never get to know." Louis Armstrong

9. "I havent understood a bar of music in my life, but I have felt it." Igor Stravinsky

10. "There are more love songs than anything else. If songs could make you do something, wed all love one another." Frank Zappa

Source: Music: A Book of Quotations (Dover, 2001)

Exercise 5

1. This week, Im helping my sister with her research paper, and shes chosen chocolate as her topic.

2. Weve been surprised by some of the things weve discovered.

3. First, the cocoa beans arent very appetizing in their natural form.

4. They grow inside an odd-shaped, alien-looking pod, and theyre surrounded by white mushy pulp.

5. After cocoa beans have been removed from the pods, theyre dried, blended almost like coffee beans, and processed into the many types of chocolate foods available.

6. In fact, the Aztecs enjoyed chocolate as a heavily spiced hot drink that was more like coffee than the sweet, creamy chocolate thats popular today.

7. Weve also learned that white chocolate cant be called chocolate at all since it doesnt contain any cocoa solids, only cocoa butter.

8. With an interest in organic foods, wed assumed that organic chocolate would be better than conventional chocolate.

9. But thats not true either because its got to be grown on pesticide-free trees, and theyre the strongest but not the tastiest sources of chocolate.

10. Unfortunately, the best cocoa trees are also the most vulnerable to disease, so it isnt easy to grow them organically.

Source: The Chocolate Companion (Simon & Schuster, 1995)

PARAGRAPH EXERCISE

In the following paragraph, cross out the ten pairs of italicized words and rewrite them as correct contractions (for example, ~~you are~~ = *you're*).

I have had the same group of friends since I was in junior high school. Now that *we are* all in college, my friends *do not* spend as much time on schoolwork as I do. Whenever *I am* studying for an exam or working on a project, they call and ask if *I would* like to see a movie or go to a game. *It is* the worst in the summer. *I have* been enrolling in summer school classes for the past two years so that *I will* be ready to transfer soon. However, none of my friends has taken a class during the summer. At the rate *they are* going, my friends *will not* ever transfer.

SENTENCE WRITING

Write ten new sentences to practice using contractions. In these sentences, try to describe your dream vacation or the types of recycling you participate in at home, work, or school.

Possessives

Words that clarify ownership are called *possessives*. The trick in writing possessives is to ask the question "Who (or what) does the item belong to?" Modern usage has made *who* acceptable when it begins a question. More correctly, of course, the phrasing should be "*Whom* does the item belong to?" or even "*To whom* does the item belong?"

In any case, if the answer to this question does not end in *s* (as in *player, person, people, children, month*), simply add an *apostrophe* and *s* to show the possessive. Look at the first five examples in the chart below.

However, if the answer to the question already ends in *s* (as in *players and Brahms*), add only an apostrophe after the *s* to show the possessive. See these two examples in the chart and say them aloud to hear that their sound does not need to change when made possessive.

Finally, some *s*-ending words need another sound to make the possessive clear. If you need another *s* sound when you *say* the possessive (for example, *the office of my boss* becomes *my boss's office*), add the apostrophe and another *s* to show the added sound.

a player (uniform)	Who does the uniform belong to?	a player	Add *'s*	a player's uniform
a person (clothes)	Who do the clothes belong to?	a person	Add *'s*	a person's clothes
people (clothes)	Who do the clothes belong to?	people	Add *'s*	people's clothes
children (games)	Who do the games belong to?	children	Add *'s*	children's games
a month (pay)	What does the pay belong to?	a month	Add *'s*	a month's pay
players (uniforms)	Who do the uniforms belong to?	players	Add *'*	players' uniforms
Brahms (Lullaby)	Who does the Lullaby belong to?	Brahms	Add *'*	Brahms' Lullaby
my boss (office)	Who does the office belong to?	my boss	Add *'s*	my boss's office

The trick of asking "Who does the item belong to?" will always work, but you must ask the question every time. Remember that the key word is *belong*. If you ask the question another way, you may get an answer that won't help you. Also, notice that the trick does not depend on whether the answer is *singular* or *plural,* but on whether it ends in *s* or not.

> ## To Make a Possessive
>
> 1. Ask "Who (or what) does the item belong to?"
> 2. If the answer doesn't end in *s,* add an *apostrophe* and *s.*
> 3. If the answer already ends in *s,* add just an *apostrophe* or an *apostrophe* and *s* if you need an extra sound to show the possessive (as in *boss's office*).

EXERCISES

Follow the directions carefully for each of the following exercises. Because possessives can be tricky, we include explanations in some exercises to help you understand them better.

Exercise 1

Cover the right column and see if you can write the following possessives correctly. Ask the question "Who (or what) does the item belong to?" each time. Don't look at the answer before you try!

1. the jury (reaction)   _____ the jury's reaction

2. an umpire (decision)   _____ an umpire's decision

3. Jess (remarks)   _____ Jess's (or Jess') remarks

4. Alice (company)   _____ Alice's company

5. Dr. Porter (car)   _____ Dr. Porter's car

6. the Johnsons (cat)   _____ the Johnsons' cat

7. a parent (advice)   _____ a parent's advice

8. parents (advice)   _____ parents' advice

9. a woman (watch)   _____ a woman's watch

10. two women (watches)   _____ two women's watches

(Sometimes you may have a choice when the word ends in *s. Jess's remarks* may be written *Jess' remarks.* Whether you want your reader to say it with or without an extra *s* sound, be consistent when given such choices.)

CAUTION—Don't assume that every word that ends in *s* is a possessive. The *s* may indicate more than one of something, a plural noun. Make sure the word actually possesses something before you add an apostrophe.

A few commonly used words have their own possessive forms and don't need apostrophes added to them. Memorize this list:

our, ours	its
your, yours	their, theirs
his, her, hers	whose

Note particularly *its, their, whose,* and *your.* They are already possessive and don't take an apostrophe. (These words sound just like *it's, they're, who's,* and *you're,* which are *contractions* that use an apostrophe in place of their missing letters.)

Exercise 2

Cover the right column and see if you can write the required form. The answer might be a *contraction* or a *possessive.* If you miss any, go back and review the explanations.

1. (She) the best teacher I have.	She's
2. (They) remodeling next door.	They're
3. Does (you) computer work?	your
4. (Who) traveling with us?	Who's
5. My parrot enjoys (it) freedom.	its
6. (They) presentation delighted everyone.	Their
7. (Who) shoes are those?	Whose
8. My apartment is noisy; (it) by the airport.	it's
9. (He) going to give his speech today.	He's
10. (There) a pie in the refrigerator.	There's

Exercise 3

Here's another chance to check your progress with possessives. Cover the right column again as you did in Exercises 1 and 2, and add apostrophes correctly to any possessives. Each answer is followed by an explanation.

1. The students went to their counselors offices.

counselors' (You didn't add an apostrophe to *students,* did you? The students don't possess anything.)

2. The teams bus broke down with all the players on board.

The team's (Who does the bus belong to? The players don't possess anything.)

3. I was invited to my friends graduation.

friend's (if it belongs to one friend), friends' (to two or more friends)

4. That writers ideas are very clever.

writer's (The ideas don't possess anything in the sentence.)

5. Gus opinion is similar to mine.

Gus's (The *s* after the apostrophe adds the extra letter Gus' needs to *sound* possessive.)

6. Last semesters grades were the best yet.

semester's (The grades belong to last semester.)

7. The Millers house is just outside of the city.

The Millers' (Who does the house belong to? No need to add an extra *s* to Millers'.)

8. I'm reading many books in my childrens literature class.

children's (The literature belongs to children, but the books don't possess anything.)

9. The students handed the teacher their essays.

No apostrophe. *Their* is already possessive.

10. The sign on the door said, "Employees Entrance."

Employees' (The entrance is for employees only.)

Exercises 4 and 5

Now you're ready to add apostrophes to the possessives that follow. But be careful. *First,* make sure the word really possesses something; not every word ending in *s* is a possessive. *Second,* remember that certain words already have possessive forms and don't use apostrophes. *Third,* even though a word ends in *s,* you can't tell where the apostrophe goes until you ask the question, "Who (or what) does the item belong to?" The apostrophe or apostrophe and *s* should follow the answer to that question. Check your answers after the first set.

Exercise 4

1. Claude Monets paintings of water lilies are world famous.
2. Monet also created a series of paintings that captured the beauty of Londons bridges at the turn of the twentieth century.
3. Monet was inspired by the fogs influence on light, color, and texture.
4. He wrote about the foggy weathers positive effect on his mood and creativity.
5. Now historians and scientists know more about the unusually thick fog that hung over London at that time.
6. It was really smog—fog mixed with soot, smoke, and other pollutants.
7. Peoples health suffered so much that hundreds died each week at its worst.
8. Monet himself had lung disease.
9. The artists views of London in the fog went on tour as an exhibition in 2005.
10. The exhibit was called "Monets London."

Source: Discover, September 2005

Exercise 5

1. David Mannings reputation as a movie reviewer was destroyed in the spring of 2001.
2. This critics words of praise had been printed on several of Columbia Pictures movie posters at the time and had helped to convince the public to see the films.
3. Mannings glowing quotations appeared on ads for *A Knights Tale, The Patriot,* and *Hollow Man.*
4. However, there was a problem with this particular writers opinions.
5. David Mannings praise was empty because David Manning didn't exist.
6. One of the movie studios employees had invented Manning and made up the quotations printed on the posters.

7. A news writer discovered that Mannings identity was a fake.

8. The publics reaction surprised both news people and entertainment industry executives.

9. Many moviegoers said that they expected movie poster quotations to be false and therefore weren't surprised when the studio admitted the truth.

10. The entertainment industry took the deception very seriously, however, and all of the films posters with phony quotes on them were reprinted.

Source: BBC News, August 3, 2005

PROOFREADING EXERCISE

Find the six errors in the following paragraph. All of the errors involve possessives.

I'm not satisfied with my cars ride; it's too rough. For instance, when a roads surface has grooves in it, the wheels get pulled in every direction. My tires treads seem too deep for ordinary city driving. Bumps and potholes usually send my passenger's heads straight into the roof. When I bought my car, I asked about it's stiff suspension and heavy-duty tires. The salesperson told me that the suspension's elements would eventually soften for a smoother ride, but they haven't. I should have known not to trust anyones words more than my own instincts.

SENTENCE WRITING

Write ten sentences using the possessive forms of the names of your family members or the names of your friends. You could write about a recent event that brought your family or friends together. Just tell the story of what happened that day.

REVIEW OF CONTRACTIONS AND POSSESSIVES

Here are two review exercises. First, add the necessary apostrophes to the following sentences. Try not to make the mistake of placing an apostrophe where it isn't needed. Don't excuse an error by saying, "Oh, that was just a careless mistake." A mistake is a mistake. Be tough on yourself.

1. According to artist Eric Sloane, it isnt easy to draw or paint clouds.
2. A clouds shape is difficult to capture because its always moving.
3. Clouds arent static bumps that float in the sky.
4. Theyre like living things—constantly building up or disintegrating.
5. Sloanes suggestions for capturing clouds beauty make good sense.
6. Artists shouldnt forget that clouds are "wet air in action."
7. Theyre not solid; theyre transparent.
8. Color choices will affect an artists ability to recreate clouds on paper or canvas.
9. An artist who wants to paint a cloudy sky mustnt rely on blue and white alone.
10. Its better to use gray, yellow, and pink to capture a cloudscapes full effect.

Source: Skies and the Artist (Dover, 2006)

Second, add the necessary apostrophes to the following paragraph.

I consider my friend Alexis to be one of the smartest people I know. Alexis is a twenty-five-year-old film student at a nearby university. Shes presently in her senior year, but thats just the beginning for Alexis. She plans to take full advantage of her universitys resources to learn what she needs before starting her own filmmaking career. She has access to her fellow students talent, her different teachers equipment and experience, and the film schools many contacts. Alexis doesnt agree with a lot of the advice she gets from people in the film industry. They try to discourage her sometimes, but she wont let anything distract her from her goal of making great movies. Ive always been impressed by Alexis self-confidence, and its inspired me to believe in myself more than I ever have before.

PROGRESS TEST

This test covers everything you've studied so far. One sentence in each pair is correct. The other is incorrect. Read both sentences carefully before you decide. Then write the letter of the incorrect sentence in the blank. Try to isolate and correct the error if you can.

1. _____ **A.** Their presentations didn't go very well.

    _____ **B.** They should of practiced more.

2. _____ **A.** Kyle bought a knew phone with his first paycheck.

    _____ **B.** It's got all of the best features.

3. _____ **A.** My teacher complemented me on my writing style.

    _____ **B.** He also said that I have excellent study skills.

4. _____ **A.** My friend misunderstood the compliment I gave him.

    _____ **B.** I feel badly whenever I hurt someone's feelings.

5. _____ **A.** The tutors didn't know wear the extra handouts were.

    _____ **B.** We had to look in all of the cabinets.

6. _____ **A.** I recently learned how to drive a motorcycle.

    _____ **B.** Its fun to shift gears.

7. _____ **A.** Our new computer has all ready frozen several times.

    _____ **B.** We're not happy with its performance so far.

8. _____ **A.** My philosophy class has two teachers.

    _____ **B.** I'm learning more from one of them then the other.

9. _____ **A.** Eating a snack before an exam can have positive affects.

    _____ **B.** Food affects the brain's ability to concentrate.

10. _____ **A.** I always except my best friend's advice.

    _____ **B.** She seems to know what's best for me.

Sentence Structure

Sentence structure refers to the way sentences are built using words, phrases, and clauses. Words are single units, and words link up in sentences to form clauses and phrases. Clauses are word groups *with* subjects and verbs, and phrases are word groups *without* subjects and verbs. Clauses are the most important because they make statements—they tell who did what (or what something is) in a sentence. Look at the following sentence as an example:

Over the summer, we visited the Grand Canyon with our geology club.

It contains twelve words, each playing its own part in the meaning of the sentence. But which of the words together tell who did what? *We visited the Grand Canyon* is correct. That word group is a clause. Notice that *over the summer* and *with our geology club* also link up as word groups but don't include somebody (subject) doing something (verb). Instead, they are phrases to clarify *when* and *how* we visited the Grand Canyon.

Importantly, you could leave out one or both of the phrases and still have a sentence—*We visited the Grand Canyon.* However, you cannot leave the clause out. Then you would just have *Over the summer with our geology club.* Remember, every sentence needs at least one clause that can stand by itself.

Learning about the structure of sentences helps you control your own. Once you know more about sentence structure, you can understand writing errors and learn how to avoid them.

Among the most common errors in writing are fragments, run-ons, and awkward phrasing.

Here are some fragments:

Wandering around the museum all afternoon.

Because I tried to handle too many responsibilities at once.

By tutoring the students in groups.

These groups of words don't make complete statements—not one has a clause that can stand by itself. Who was *wandering around the museum?* What happened *because you tried to handle too many responsibilities at once?* What did someone gain *by tutoring the students in groups?* These incomplete sentence structures fail to communicate a complete thought.

In contrast, here are some run-ons:

The forecast calls for heavy rain the parade might be canceled.

Taking the train will cut my travel time in half carpooling is also an option.

My employer offered incentives and they really worked to motivate us.

Unlike fragments, run-on sentences do make complete statements, but the trouble is they make two complete statements; the first *runs on* into the second. Without the help of proper punctuation, the reader has to go back and find the break between the two ideas.

Fragments don't make any complete statements, and run-ons make too many complete statements without punctuating between them. Another problem occurs when the phrasing in a sentence just doesn't make sense.

Here are a few sentences with awkward phrasing:

The problem from my grades started to end.

It was a great time at my sister's graduation.

She won me at chess every time we played.

Try to find the word groups that show who did what—that is, the clauses (*The problem started, It was,* and *She won*). Now try to put the clauses and phrases together to form a precise meaning. It's difficult, isn't it? You'll see that many of the words don't work together, such as *problem from my grades, started to end, it was a great time at,* and *won me at chess.* These sentences don't communicate clearly due to awkward phrasing.

Fragments, run-ons, and awkward phrasing confuse the reader. If you can learn to avoid these and other sentence structure errors, your writing will be stronger and easier to understand. Unfortunately, there is no quick, effortless way to strengthen your sentence structure. First, you need to understand how clear sentences are built. Then you can eliminate common errors in your own writing.

This section will describe areas of sentence structure one at a time and then explain how to avoid errors associated with the different areas. For instance, we start by helping you find subjects and verbs and understand dependent clauses; then we show you how to correct fragments. You can go through the whole section yourself to learn all of the concepts and structures. Or your teacher may assign only parts based on errors the class is making.

Finding Subjects and Verbs

The most important words in sentences are those that make up its independent clause—the subject and the verb. When you write a sentence, you write about a noun or pronoun (a person, place, thing, or idea). That's the *subject*. Then you write what the subject *does* or *is*. That's the *verb*.

Lightning strikes.

The word *Lightning* is the thing you are writing about. It's the subject, and we'll underline all subjects once. *Strikes* tells what the subject does. It shows the action in the sentence. It's the verb, and we'll underline all of them twice. Most sentences do not include only two words (the subject and the verb). However, these two words still make up the core of the sentence even if other words and phrases are included with them.

Lightning strikes back and forth from the clouds to the ground very quickly.

It often strikes people on golf courses or in boats.

When many words appear in sentences, the subject and verb can be harder to find. Because the verb often shows action, it's easier to spot than the subject. Therefore, always look for it first. For example, take this sentence:

The neighborhood cat folded its paws under its chest.

Which word shows the action? The action word is folded. It's the verb, so we'll underline it twice. Now ask yourself who or what folded? The answer is cat. That's the subject, so we'll underline it once.

Study the following sentences until you understand how to pick out subjects and verbs:

The college celebrates its fiftieth anniversary tomorrow. (Which word shows the action? The action word is celebrates. It's the verb, so we'll underline it twice. Who or what celebrates? The college does. It's the subject. We'll underline it once.)

The team members shared several boxes of chocolates. (Which word shows the action? Shared shows the action. Who or what shared? Members shared.)

Internet users crowd the popular services. (Which word shows the action? The verb is crowd. Who or what crowd? Users crowd.)

Often, the verb doesn't show action but links the subject with a description of what the subject *is, was,* or *will be.* Learn to spot such linking verbs—*is, am, are, was, were, has been, seem, feel, appear, become, look.* . . . (For more information on linking verbs, see the discussion of sentence patterns on page 137.)

Marshall is a neon artist. (First spot the verb <u>is</u>. Then ask who or what is? Marshall <u>is</u>.)

The sandwiches in the cafeteria look stale. (First spot the verb <u>look</u>. Then ask who or what look? <u>Sandwiches</u> <u>look</u>.)

Sometimes the subject comes after the verb, especially when a word like *there* or *here* begins the sentence without being a real subject.

In the audience were two reviewers from the *Times*. (Who or what were in the audience? Two <u>reviewers</u> from the *Times* <u>were</u> in the audience.)

There was a fortune-teller at the carnival. (Who or what was there? A <u>fortune-teller</u> <u>was</u> there at the carnival.)

There were nametags for all the participants. (Who or what were there? <u>Nametags</u> <u>were</u> there for all the participants.)

Here are two examples. (Who or what are here? The <u>examples</u> <u>are</u> here.)

NOTE—Remember that *there* and *here* (as used in the last three sentences) are not subjects. They simply point to something.

When a sentence is a command, it may appear to be missing a subject. However, an unwritten *you* is understood by the reader.

Fill in all spaces on the form. (*You* <u>fill</u> in all spaces on the form.)

Attach two copies of the application to your e-mail. (*You* <u>attach</u> two copies . . . .)

Make an appointment for Tuesday. (*You* <u>make</u> an appointment for Tuesday.)

A sentence may have more than one subject.

<u>Toys</u> and <u>memorabilia</u> from the 1950s to the 1990s <u>are</u> valuable collectibles.

Celebrity <u>dolls</u>, board <u>games</u>, and even cereal <u>boxes</u> from those decades <u>sell</u> for high prices online.

A sentence may also have more than one verb.

> Water boils at a certain temperature and freezes at another.

> The ice tray fell out of my hand, skidded across the floor, and landed under the table.

E X E R C I S E S

Identify the subjects and verbs in the following sentences. Remember that it's best to start by double underlining the verbs; then you can find and single underline their subjects. When you finish each exercise, compare your markings carefully with the answers. Refer back to the explanations and examples whenever necessary.

Exercise 1

1. Many people know the name of Uggie, the dog actor.
2. Uggie became famous in the Oscar-winning silent movie *The Artist.*
3. His big break came after ten years of work in other films and projects.
4. With his role in *The Artist,* Uggie showcased the skills and expressions of Jack Russell terriers and made them very popular.
5. Originally, Uggie's trainer rescued him from an animal shelter.
6. In June 2012, Uggie retired from his long acting career due to a physical setback.
7. Before his retirement, this famous little dog left his mark on Hollywood—literally.
8. On June 25, 2012, Uggie put his paw prints in cement at Grauman's Chinese Theater.
9. Crowds of fans gathered on Hollywood Blvd. in honor of Uggie's work in films.
10. They were the first canine footprints in the history of this famous landmark.

Source: San Francisco Chronicle, June 28, 2012

Exercise 2

1. In 1940, four teenagers took a walk and discovered something marvelous.
2. They entered an underground cavern in Lascaux, France, and found vivid images of animals on its walls.
3. There were horses, deer, bulls, cats, and oxen.
4. The prehistoric artists also left tracings of their handprints on the walls.
5. Scientists dated the paintings and engravings at approximately 17,000 years old.
6. After its discovery, the Lascaux cave became a popular tourist attraction.
7. Twelve hundred people visited the site daily.
8. These visitors had a negative impact on the cave's prehistoric artwork.
9. They breathed carbon dioxide into the cave and increased its humidity.
10. French officials closed the Lascaux cave to the public in 1963.

Source: The Cave of Lascaux official Web site (http://www.culture.gouv.fr:80/culture/arcnat/ lascaux/en/)

Exercise 3

1. Harold Lloyd became a star of comic films during the silent era of Hollywood.
2. Lloyd worked in Hollywood at the same time as Charlie Chaplin and Buster Keaton.
3. The name of Harold Lloyd's character in many of his films was also Harold.
4. One accessory distinguished Harold from other silent-film characters—a pair of perfectly round eyeglasses.
5. The glasses had no lenses but fit his face and gave him a distinct personality.
6. A suit and a straw hat completed Harold's simple yet memorable costume.

7. Unlike Chaplin and Keaton's clownish characters, Harold looked like a normal young man out for adventure—anything from good fun to a great fight.

8. As Harold, Lloyd performed incredible stunts in spite of an injury from an accident with a prop bomb early in his career.

9. He lost part of his hand and covered it in his films with a special glove.

10. In his most famous film, *Safety Last!*, Harold climbed outside a tall building and dangled dangerously from the hands of its clock.

Source: *Harold Lloyd: Magic in a Pair of Horn-Rimmed Glasses* (Bear Manor Media, 2009)

Exercise 4

1. There are a number of world-famous trees in California.

2. Among them are the oldest trees on the planet.

3. These trees live somewhere in Inyo National Forest.

4. One of these ancient trees is a bristlecone pine.

5. Scientists call it the Methuselah Tree.

6. They place its age at five thousand years.

7. The soil and temperatures around it seem too poor for a tree's health.

8. But the Methuselah Tree and its neighbors obviously thrive in such conditions.

9. Due to its importance, the Methuselah Tree's exact location is a secret.

10. Such important natural specimens need protection.

Source: Current Science, May 3, 2002

Exercise 5

1. Ancient Egyptians worshipped cats of all sizes.

2. Archaeologists find many mummies of cats in Egyptian tombs.

3. Carvings in the tombs reveal a strong belief in the god-like powers of large cats.

4. Scientists always look for new evidence of ancient beliefs.

5. Archaeologists recently discovered the mummy of a lion in a tomb in Saqqara, Egypt.

6. It is the first discovery of a lion skeleton in an Egyptian tomb.

7. There were no bandages around the lion.

8. But there were other signs of mummification.

9. The lion rested in the tomb of King Tutankhamen's nurse.

10. Archaeologists now have real evidence of lion worship in Egypt.

Source: Science News, January 31, 2004

PARAGRAPH EXERCISE

Identify the subjects and verbs in the following excerpt about an important time in film history from *The Knowledge Book: Everything You Need to Know to Get by in the 21st Century* by National Geographic. Remember to double underline the verbs first; then find and single underline their subjects. Check your answers often, and refer to the explanations and examples whenever necessary. Note that standard practice is to italicize or underline film titles; however, the writers of this excerpt have used quotation marks to identify film titles. See page 192 for more about the standard punctuation of titles.

The 1960s and 1970s: Renewal through Independence

The golden age of cinema was over. A new generation of filmmakers . . . emerged on the scene during this period of crisis.

Worldwide Awakening

Everywhere there was a renewal of film and cinema. In Latin America, the Brazilian Glauber Rocha provided the impetus for *Cinema Novo* with his cinema as political allegories. In the U.S., a group of young directors, actresses, and actors responded to the creative standstill of the large studios—the first [were] Dennis Hopper and Peter Fonda with their naively pessimistic interpretation of the American Dream in "Easy Rider" (1969). George Lucas ("THX 1138," 1970) and Steven

Spielberg ("Duel," 1971) made their debut. Martin Scorsese ("Mean Streets," 1973; "Taxi Driver," 1976; "Raging Bull," 1980) and Francis Ford Coppola ("The Conversation," 1974; "The Godfather," 1972; "Apocalypse Now," 1979) directed their best films. The decade of "New Hollywood" was a stroke of luck for cinema and the film industry.

SENTENCE WRITING

Write ten sentences about any subject—your favorite movies or movie snacks, for instance. Keep these ten sentences as short and simple as possible to make it easier to find their subjects and verbs. After you have written your sentences, go back and underline the verbs twice and their subjects once.

Locating Prepositional Phrases

Prepositional phrases are among the easiest structures in English to learn. Remember that a phrase is just a group of related words (at least two) without a subject and a verb. And don't let a term like *prepositional* scare you. If you look in the middle of that long word, you'll find a familiar one—*position*. In English, we tell the *positions* of people and things in sentences using prepositional phrases. Think of prepositional phrases as a type of GPS (Global Positioning System) in the sentences that you write and read.

Look at the following sentence with its prepositional phrases in parentheses:

Our trip (to the desert) will begin (at 6:00) (in the morning) (on Friday).

One phrase tells *where* the trip will take us (*to the desert*), and three phrases tell *when* the trip will begin (*at 6:00, in the morning,* and *on Friday*). Most prepositional phrases show the position of someone or something in *space* or in *time.*

Here is a list of some prepositions that can show positions in *space*:

to	across	next to	against
at	through	inside	under
in	beyond	between	beneath
on	among	above	around
by	near	behind	past
over	with	from	below

Here are some prepositions that can show positions in *time* (note some repeats):

at	for	past	within
by	after	until	since
in	before	during	throughout

These lists include only individual words, *not phrases*. Remember, a preposition must be followed by a noun or pronoun object—a person, place, thing, or idea—to create *a prepositional phrase*. Notice that as the preposition changes in the prepositional phrases below, the balloon's position in relation to the object, *the clouds,* changes completely.

The hot-air balloon floated *above the clouds.*
below the clouds.
within the clouds.
between the clouds.
past the clouds.
near the clouds.

Now notice how these other prepositions similarly affect the time of its landing:

> The balloon landed *before 3:30.*
> *at precisely 3:30.*
> *after 3:30.*
> *before the thunderstorm.*
> *during the thunderstorm.*
> *after the thunderstorm.*

NOTE—A few words—*of, as,* and *like*—are prepositions that do not fit neatly into either the space or time category, yet they are very common prepositions (book *of essays,* note *of apology,* type *of bicycle;* act *as a substitute,* use *as an example,* testified *as an expert;* sounds *like a computer,* acts *like a sedative,* moves *like an athlete*).

By locating prepositional phrases, you will be able to find subjects and verbs more easily. For example, you might have difficulty finding the subject and verb in a long sentence like this:

> During the rainy season, one of the windows in the attic leaked at all four of its corners.

But if you put parentheses around all the prepositional phrases like this

> (During the rainy season), one (of the windows) (in the attic) leaked (at all four) (of its corners).

then you have only two words left—the subject and the verb. Even in short sentences like the following, you might pick the wrong word as the subject if you don't put parentheses around the prepositional phrases first.

> A box (of books) arrived (with a return address) (from Italy).

> The mood (around campus) is cheerful today.

NOTE—Don't mistake *to* plus a verb for a prepositional phrase. Special forms of verbals always start with *to,* but they are not prepositional phrases (see page 125). For example, in the sentence "I like to take the train to school," *to take* is a verbal, not a prepositional phrase. However, *to school* is a prepositional phrase because it begins with a preposition (to), ends with a noun (school), and shows position in space.

E X E R C I S E S

Put parentheses around the prepositional phrases in the following sentences. Be sure to start with the preposition itself (*in, on, to, at, of . . .*) and include the word or words that go with it (*in the morning, on our sidewalk, to Hawaii . . .*). Then double underline the sentences' verbs and single underline their subjects. Remember that the subject and verb of a sentence will never be inside a prepositional phrase, so if you locate the prepositional phrases *first,* the subjects and verbs will be much easier to find. Check your answers for each exercise before continuing to the next.

Exercise 1

1. Viganella is a tiny village at the bottom of the Alps in Italy.

2. Due to its physical position between the mountains, the town of Viganella suffered from an unusual problem.

3. The sun's rays never reached the village from the middle of November to the first week in February.

4. The mountains kept the little town in shadow without any direct sunlight for several months each year.

5. Then Giacomo Bonzani found a high-tech solution to Viganella's dreary situation.

6. In 2006, engineers installed a huge mirror thousands of feet above Viganella on the side of one of the mountains around it.

7. A computer at the mirror's location keeps track of the sun's movements.

8. The computer's software rotates the mirror into the perfect position to reflect sunlight into the village square.

9. The mirror began its work in December of 2006.

10. Now the sun "shines" on the town of Viganella during all months of the year.

Source: International Herald Tribune, February 5, 2007

Exercise 2

1. One fact about William Shakespeare and his work always surprises people.

2. There are no copies of his original manuscripts.

3. No museum or library has even one page from a Shakespeare play in Shakespeare's own handwriting.

4. Museums and libraries have copies of the First Folio instead.

5. After Shakespeare's death in 1616, actors from his company gathered the texts of his plays and published them as one book, the First Folio, in 1623.

6. They printed approximately 750 copies at the time.

7. Currently, there are 230 known copies of the First Folio in the world.

8. Many owners of the Folio remain anonymous by choice.

9. One woman inherited her copy of the Folio from a distant relative.

10. Another copy of the First Folio recently sold for five million dollars.

Source: Smithsonian, September 2006

Exercise 3

1. Most of us remember playing with Frisbees in our front yards in the early evenings and at parks or beaches on weekend afternoons.

2. Fred Morrison invented the original flat Frisbee for the Wham-O toy company in the 1950s.

3. Ed Headrick, designer of the professional Frisbee, passed away at his home in California in August of 2002.

4. Working at Wham-O in the 1960s, Headrick improved the performance of the existing Frisbee with the addition of ridges in the surface of the disc.

5. Headrick's improvements led to increased sales of his "professional model" Frisbee and to the popularity of Frisbee tournaments.

6. After Headrick's redesign, Wham-O sold 100 million of the flying discs.

7. Headrick also invented the game of disc golf.

8. Like regular golf but with discs, the game takes place on special disc golf courses like the first one at Oak Grove Park in California.

9. Before his death, Headrick asked for his ashes to be formed into memorial flying discs for select family and friends.

10. Donations from sales of the remaining memorial discs went toward the establishment of a museum on the history of the Frisbee and disc golf.

Source: Los Angeles Times, August 14, 2002

Exercise 4

1. Roald Dahl is the author of *Charlie and the Chocolate Factory.*

2. In his youth, Dahl had two memorable experiences with sweets.

3. One of them involved the owner of a candy store.

4. Dahl and his young friends had a bad relationship with this particular woman.

5. On one visit to her store, Dahl put a dead mouse into one of the candy jars behind her back.

6. The woman later went to his school and demanded his punishment.

7. He and his friends received several lashes from a cane in her presence.

8. During his later childhood years, Dahl became a taste-tester for the Cadbury chocolate company.

9. Cadbury sent him and other schoolchildren boxes of sweets to evaluate.

10. Dahl tried each candy and made a list of his reactions and recommendations.

Source: Sweets: A History of Candy (Bloomsbury, 2002)

Exercise 5

1. At 2 a.m. on the second Sunday in March, something happens to nearly everyone in America: Daylight Saving Time.

2. But few people are awake at two in the morning.

3. So we set the hands or digits of our clocks ahead one hour on Saturday night in preparation for it.

4. And before bed on the first Saturday in November, we turn them back again.

5. For days after both events, I have trouble with my sleep patterns and my mood.

6. In spring, the feeling is one of loss.

7. That Saturday-night sleep into Sunday is one hour shorter than usual.

8. But in fall, I gain a false sense of security about time.

9. That endless Sunday morning quickly melts into the start of a hectic week like the other fifty-one in the year.

10. All of this upheaval is due to the Uniform Time Act of 1966.

PARAGRAPH EXERCISE

Put parentheses around the prepositional phrases in the following paragraph from the book *One Red Paperclip* by Kyle MacDonald. MacDonald is the young man who turned one red paperclip into a house of his own by trading it each time for something "bigger and better." In this paragraph, MacDonald describes the first moments of his world-famous adventure. Remember that a prepositional phrase must include a preposition followed by a noun or pronoun. After you have marked the prepositional phrases, go back and double underline the verbs and single underline their subjects for extra practice.

I put the red paperclip on the desk and took a picture of it. I walked to the door and pulled the handle. The door swung open. I lifted my right foot into the air. As my right foot came forward to the threshold of the doorframe, the phone rang. My foot hung in the air, just short of the outside hallway. The phone rang again. I spun around slowly, almost in slow motion. I slowly slunk away from the door and lifted the phone from the receiver.

SENTENCE WRITING

Write ten similar sentences describing a memorable moment of your own. When you finish your sentences, put parentheses around any prepositional phrases; then underline your verbs twice and their subjects once. For example, if you had been a contestant on a game show, you might write, "I stood (in front) (of the enormous wheel) and reached out to grab one (of the pegs) (with my hand)." Remember that "to grab" is a special form of verb, not a prepositional phrase. For more about verbs that start with *to*, see page 125.

Understanding Dependent Clauses

All clauses are groups of related words that contain a subject and a verb. However, there are two kinds of clauses: *independent* and *dependent*. Independent clauses have a subject and a verb and make complete statements by themselves. Dependent clauses also have a subject and a verb, but these clauses don't make complete statements because of the words that begin them. Here are some of the words (conjunctions or pronouns) that can begin dependent clauses:

after	since	where
although	so that	whereas
as	than	wherever
as if	that	whether
because	though	which
before	unless	whichever
even if	until	while
even though	what	who
ever since	whatever	whom
how	when	whose
if	whenever	why

When a clause begins with one of these dependent words, it is usually a dependent clause. To see the difference between an independent and a dependent clause, look at this example of an independent clause:

> We studied history together.

It has a subject (<u>We</u>) and a verb (<u>studied</u>), and it makes a complete statement. But as soon as we put one of the dependent words in front of it, the clause becomes *dependent* because it no longer makes a complete statement:

> *After* we studied history together . . .
>
> *Although* we studied history together . . .
>
> *As* we studied history together . . .
>
> *Before* we studied history together . . .
>
> *Since* we studied history together . . .
>
> *That* we studied history together . . .

When we studied history together . . .

While we studied history together . . .

Each of these dependent clauses leaves the reader expecting something more. Each would depend on another clause—an independent clause—to make it a sentence. For the rest of this discussion, we'll place a dotted line beneath dependent clauses.

After we studied history together, we went to the evening seminar.

We went to the evening seminar *after* we studied history together.

The speaker didn't know *that* we studied history together.

While we studied history together, the library became crowded.

As you can see in these examples, *when a dependent clause comes before an independent clause, it is followed by a comma.* Often the comma prevents misreading, as in the following sentence:

When we returned, our library books were on the floor.

Without a comma after *returned,* the reader would read *When we returned our library books* before realizing that this was not what the writer meant. The comma prevents misreading. Sometimes if the dependent clause is short and there is no danger of misreading, the comma can be left off, but it's safer simply to follow the rule that a dependent clause coming before an independent clause is followed by a comma. You'll learn more about the punctuation of dependent clauses on page 177, but for now just remember to use a comma when a dependent clause comes before an independent clause.

Note that a few of the dependent words (*that, who, which, what*) can do "double duty" as both the dependent word and the subject of the dependent clause:

Thelma wrote a poetry book *that* sold a thousand copies.

The manager saw *what* happened.

Sometimes the dependent clause is in the middle of the independent clause:

The book *that* sold a thousand copies was Thelma's.

The events *that* followed the parade delighted everyone.

The dependent clause can even be the subject of the entire sentence:

What you do also affects me.

How your project looks counts for ten percent of the grade.

Also note that sometimes the *that* of a dependent clause is omitted:

I know that you feel strongly about this issue.

I know you feel strongly about this issue.

Everyone received the classes *that* they wanted.

Everyone received the classes they wanted.

Of course, the word *that* doesn't always introduce a dependent clause. It may be a pronoun and serve as the subject or object of the sentence:

That was a really long movie.

We knew *that* already.

That can also be an adjective, a descriptive word telling *which one:*

That movie always makes me laugh.

We took them to *that* park last week.

EXERCISES

Exercise 1

Each of the following sentences contains *one* independent and *one* dependent clause. Draw a dotted line beneath the dependent clause in each sentence. Start at the dependent word and include all the words that go with it. Remember that dependent clauses can show up in the beginning, middle, or end of a sentence.

Example: We study together whenever we meet in the library.

1. Edgar and Nina Otto, who live in Florida, were the winning bidders in an unusual auction in 2008.

2. Whoever placed the highest bid won the opportunity of a lifetime: a chance to clone their dog.

3. The company that held the auction and provided the service was BioArts International.

4. The Ottos wanted to clone Sir Lancelot, a yellow Labrador that died in 2008.

5. The price that they paid exceeded $150,000.

6. Once the auction ended, the scientists at BioArts went to work.

7. They used the DNA that the Ottos saved from Sir Lancelot to produce a genetic match.

8. The complex process, which took place in South Korea, yielded an adorable puppy.

9. The puppy looked so much like Sir Lancelot that the company named him Encore Lancelot, Lancey for short.

10. At the first meeting with their new dog in January of 2009, the Ottos were overjoyed that Lancey walked with crossed feet, just like Sir Lancelot.

Source: www.Today.com, January 28, 2009

Exercises 2–5

Follow the same directions as in Exercise 1; however, this time draw your dotted lines far below the dependent clauses. Then go back to both the independent and dependent clauses and draw a double underline beneath the verbs and a single underline beneath their subjects.

Example: We study together whenever we meet in the library.

Exercise 2

1. When I was on vacation in New York City, I loved the look of the Empire State Building at night.

2. I thought that the colored lights at the top of this landmark were just decorative.

3. I did not know that their patterns also have meaning.

4. While I waited at the airport, I visited the building's Web site and read about the patterns.

5. Some of the light combinations reveal connections that are obvious.

6. For instance, if the occasion is St. Patrick's Day, the top of the building glows with green lights.

7. When the holiday involves a celebration of America, the three levels of lights shine red, white, and blue.

8. There are other combinations that are less well known.

9. Red–black–green is a pattern that signals Martin Luther King Jr. Day.

10. Whenever I visit the city again, I'll know that the lights on the Empire State Building have meaning.

Source: http://www.esbnyc.com/esb_led_lights.asp

Exercise 3

1. When people visit Google's homepage on one evening in March each year, they are often surprised.

2. They notice immediately that the whole page is black instead of white.

3. After they look into it further, they discover the reason for the temporary color change.

4. The black page signifies that Google is a participant in Earth Hour.

5. In 2008, Google joined countless cities, companies, and individuals who turn their lights off for one hour in an international effort to encourage energy conservation.

6. People around the globe cut their electricity and live in the dark as soon as the clocks strike 8 p.m. in their locations.

7. When the hour is up at 9 p.m., they turn the electricity back on.

8. Earth Hour is an idea that began in Australia.

9. In 2007, the first Earth Hour that the Australians celebrated occurred between 7:30 and 8:30 p.m. on March 31.

10. Even though some people dismiss Earth Hour as a minor event, others believe in its power as a symbol of environmental awareness.

Source: http://www.earthhour.org

Exercise 4

1. On June 8, 1924, George Mallory and Andrew Irvine disappeared as they climbed to the top of Mount Everest.

2. Earlier, when a reporter asked Mallory why he climbed Everest, his response became legendary.

3. "Because it is there," Mallory replied.

4. No living person knows whether the two British men reached the summit of Everest before they died.

5. Nine years after Mallory and Irvine disappeared, English climbers found Irvine's ice ax.

6. In 1975, a Chinese climber spotted a body that was frozen in deep snow on the side of the mountain.

7. He kept the news secret for several years but finally told a fellow climber on the day before he died himself in an avalanche on Everest.

8. In May 1999, a team of mountaineers searched the area that the Chinese man described and found George Mallory's frozen body, still intact after seventy-five years.

9. After they took DNA samples for identification, the mountaineers buried the famous climber on the mountainside where he fell.

10. The question remains whether Mallory was on his way up or down when he met his fate.

Source: Newsweek, May 17, 1999

Exercise 5

1. I just read an article with a list of "What Doctors Wish You Knew."

2. One fact is that red and blue fruits are the healthiest.

3. Patients who have doctor's appointments after lunchtime spend less time in the waiting room.

4. Drivers who apply more sunscreen to their left sides get less skin cancer.

5. People who take ten deep breaths in the morning and evening feel less stress.

6. A clock that is visible from the bed makes insomnia worse.

7. People often suffer from weekend headaches because they get up too late.

8. They withdraw from caffeine by skipping the coffee that they usually drink on workdays.

9. Doctors suggest that people maintain weekday hours on weekends.

10. I am glad that I found this list.

Source: Good Housekeeping, November 2005

PARAGRAPH EXERCISE

Draw a dotted line beneath the dependent clauses in the following paragraphs about the value of friendship from Alain de Botton's book *The Consolations of Philosophy.* We've added the word *that* in brackets to two of the clauses in which it was left out (as described on page 72). See if you can find all thirteen dependent clauses in this challenging exercise.

We don't exist unless there is someone who can see us existing, what we say has no meaning until someone can understand, while to be surrounded by friends is constantly to have our identity confirmed; their knowledge and care for us have the power to pull us from our numbness. In small comments, many of them teasing, they reveal [that] they know our foibles and accept them and so, in turn, accept that we have a place in the world. We can ask them "Isn't he frightening?" or "Do you ever feel that . . . ?" and be understood, rather than encounter the puzzled "No, not particularly"—which can make us feel, even when in company, as lonely as polar explorers.

True friends do not evaluate us according to worldly criteria, it is the core self [that] they are interested in; like ideal parents, their love for us remains unaffected by our appearance or position in the social hierarchy, and so we have no qualms in dressing in old clothes and revealing that we have made little money this year. The desire for riches should perhaps not always be understood as a simple hunger for a luxurious life, a more important motive might be the wish to be appreciated and treated nicely. We may seek a fortune for no greater reason than to secure the respect and attention of people who would otherwise look straight through us. Epicurus, discerning our underlying need, recognized that a handful of true friends could deliver the love and respect that even a fortune may not.

SENTENCE WRITING

Write ten sentence that express your *own* ideas about friendship. Try to write sentences that contain both independent and dependent clauses. Then underline the verbs twice, their subjects once, and draw a broken line beneath the dependent clauses. Take care not to use the same phrasing as in the excerpt by Alain de Botton (on the previous page) unless you punctuate it correctly to give him credit. For more about quoting from and responding to readings, see page 230 on "Choosing and Using Quotations" and page 234 on "Writing in Response to a Reading."

Correcting Fragments

To be a *sentence,* a group of words must include at least one independent clause (a subject + verb combination that forms a complete thought). A sentence *fragment* is a word group that is punctuated as a sentence—with a capital letter at the beginning and a period at the end—but some part of its phrasing or meaning is missing. In short, fragments are incomplete word groups posing as sentences. Here are a few examples:

Always reads a magazine at the break. (no subject—*Who* reads a magazine?)

The exhibit of graphic novels in the library. (no verb—What did the exhibit *do?*)

Once the plane finally landed. (no complete thought—*What happened* then?)

To correct these fragments, simply add the missing information:

My philosophy teacher always reads a magazine at the break. (subject added)

The exhibit of graphic novels in the library opened on Sunday. (verb added)

Once the plane finally landed, I felt so relieved. (complete thought added)

Other fragments need to be combined with the sentences around them:

The actors stood outside the director's office. Waiting for an audition. (fragment)

Waiting for an audition, the actors stood outside the director's office. (corrected)

The actors stood outside the director's office and waited for an audition. (corrected)

Finally, *dependent clauses* are fragments whenever they are punctuated as sentences because their meaning is incomplete. To correct a dependent clause fragment, combine it with an independent clause or remove the word that makes it dependent. See page 70 for more about dependent clauses:

Our presentations went well. *Because* we practiced every week. (fragment)

Our presentations went well *because* we practiced every week. (corrected)

Our presentations went well. We practiced every week. (corrected)

> **NOTE—**If you have trouble finding fragments, try making the word group into a question by adding *"Did you know that..."* in front of it and adding a question mark at the end. For example, to check whether "Water is a liquid" is a sentence, ask *"Did you know that* Water is a liquid?" Clearly, the question makes sense. "Water is a liquid" also includes a subject (water) and verb (is); therefore, this word group is a sentence.
>
> Now try using *"Did you know that..."* in front of "Unless it freezes or vaporizes." The result does not make sense—*"Did you know that* Unless it freezes or vaporizes?" This word group is a fragment. It does have a subject and two verbs (it freezes and vaporizes), but they are part of a dependent clause that does not form a complete thought.
>
> The *Did you know that...* method will help you identify fragments in the exercises and in your own writing. This method works with most standard sentences, but not with sentences that are already questions or commands.
>
> To check sentences that are commands (see page 58), use *"Did you know that you should..."* in front of the word group. For example, to confirm that "Insert flap A into slot B" is a sentence, ask *"Did you know that you should* Insert flap A into slot B"?

You might ask, "Are fragments ever permissible?" Professional writers sometimes use fragments in ads, articles, books, and other published writing. When professional writers use fragments, however, they do it intentionally, not in error. They understand how an occasional fragment might fulfill a stylistic purpose. Until you master writing complete sentences for academic or business purposes, you should avoid writing fragments.

EXERCISES

Some of the following word groups are sentences, and some are fragments. The sentences include subjects and verbs and make complete statements, but the fragments do not. Use the *"Did you know that..."* method to help you identify the fragments, as explained on page 79. Write "sentence" next to the word groups that qualify, and change the fragments into sentences by adding missing information or by combining them with a sentence before or after them. Check your answers frequently, and refer back to the examples whenever necessary.

Exercise 1

1. Soon we will wear clothes that clean themselves.
2. Improvements in fabric coatings making it possible.
3. Clothes treated with certain chemicals.
4. These chemicals kill bacteria and keep dirt from soaking into fabrics.
5. Already tested by the military for soldiers' uniforms.
6. U.S. soldiers wore self-cleaning T-shirts and underwear in one study.
7. The chemicals worked but eventually wore off.
8. Helped cure soldiers' skin problems, too.
9. Fabric that stays clean and dry is a great idea.
10. Also could be used for hospital bedding, kitchen linens, and sport-related clothing.

Source: Sunday Telegraph, December 30, 2006

Exercise 2

1. Duct tape has many uses.
2. Good at holding objects together firmly.
3. Campers using it to patch holes in backpacks and tents.
4. People are very creative with duct tape.
5. Books written about the unique uses for it.
6. A yearly contest by the makers of Duck Brand duct tape.
7. For the contest, high school couples make prom clothes entirely out of duct tape.
8. Strips of duct tape to form tuxedos, cummerbunds, gowns, hats, and corsages.
9. A $5,000 prize to the couple with the best use of duct tape and another $5,000 to their high school.
10. Hundreds of couples from across the country participate in this contest every year.

Source: http://www.ducktapeclub.com

Exercise 3

In this exercise, each pair contains one sentence and one fragment. Correct the fragment by combining it with the complete sentence before or after it.

1. A worker at the Smithsonian discovered an important historical object. On a shelf in one of the museum's storage rooms.

2. Made of cardboard and covered with short, smooth fur. It was a tall black top hat.

3. The hat didn't look like anything special. More like an old costume or prop.

4. It was special, however. Having been worn by Abraham Lincoln on the night of his assassination.

5. Once found and identified, Lincoln's hat traveled with the 150th anniversary exhibition. Called "America's Smithsonian."

6. For such a priceless object to be able to travel around the country safely. Experts needed to build a unique display case for Lincoln's top hat.

7. The design allowed visitors to view the famous stovepipe hat. Without damaging it with their breath or hands.

8. The hat traveled in a sealed box. Designed against even earthquakes.

9. Keeping the hat earthquake-proof was an important concern. Being on display in California for part of the time.

10. President Lincoln's hat is one of the most impressive. Among the millions of objects in the archives of the Smithsonian.

Source: Saving Stuff (Fireside, 2005)

Exercise 4

Each pair contains one sentence and one dependent clause fragment. Correct each dependent clause fragment by combining it with the complete sentence before or after it or by eliminating its dependent word.

1. When Nathan King turned twelve. He had a heart-stopping experience.

2. Nathan was tossing a football against his bedroom wall. Which made the ball ricochet and land on his bed.

3. In a diving motion, Nathan fell on his bed to catch the ball. As it landed.

4. After he caught the ball. Nathan felt a strange sensation in his chest.

5. To his surprise, he looked down and saw the eraser end of a no. 2 pencil. That had pierced his chest and entered his heart.

6. Nathan immediately shouted for his mother. Who luckily was in the house at the time.

7. Because Nathan's mom is a nurse. She knew not to remove the pencil.

8. If she had pulled the pencil out of her son's chest. He would have died.

9. After Nathan was taken to a hospital equipped for open-heart surgery. He had the pencil carefully removed.

10. Fate may be partly responsible for Nathan's happy birthday story. Since it turned out to be his heart surgeon's birthday too.

Source: Time, March 20, 2000

Exercise 5

All of the following word groups are fragments, incomplete word groups punctuated as sentences. Make the necessary changes to turn each fragment into a sentence that makes sense to you. Your corrections will most likely differ from the sample answers at the back of the book. But by comparing your answers to ours, you'll see that there are many ways to correct a fragment.

1. One of the people sitting next to me on the train.

2. Taking good pictures with my cell phone camera.

3. Before the paint was dry in the classrooms.

4. The judge's question and the answer it received.

5. Because there were fewer students in the program this year.

6. Since his speech lasted for over an hour.

7. Whenever the teacher reminds us about the midterm exam.

8. If we move to Kentucky and stay for two years.

9. As soon as the order form reaches the warehouse.

10. Buildings with odd shapes always of interest to me.

PROOFREADING EXERCISE

Find and correct the seven fragments in the following paragraphs:

On June 15, 2012, Nik Wallenda made history. By being the first person to walk on a tightrope from the U.S. to Canada directly above the raging falls of Niagara Gorge. His trip on the high wire that misty evening took 30 minutes. A nail-biting half hour that one major network, ABC, televised live. To be on the safe side, the network made sure that Wallenda attached himself to a safety cable in case he fell off the wire on live TV. Nik Wallenda comes from a long line of daredevil performers. From the famous family known as the Flying Wallendas. Nik represents the seventh generation of people willing to risk their lives in the name of entertainment. Before attempting his spectacular walk across Niagara Falls, Wallenda fought hard to get permission from both U.S. and Canadian officials. So that he was not arrested—as previous stunt performers have been—when he reached the other side. Instead of handcuffs waiting for him on the Canadian bank of the falls. Nik Wallenda heard the cheers of 100,000 supporters welcoming him back to earth.

A year later, Wallenda also succeeded in crossing a gorge near the Grand Canyon. This time without a safety cable. His tightrope being 1,500 feet above the canyon floor. Winds were so strong that he had to stop twice in the middle of the crossing and crouch down to maintain his position on the wire.

Sources: New York Times, June 15, 2012, and *CBSnews.com,* June 23, 2013

SENTENCE WRITING

Write ten fragments like the ones in Exercise 5 and revise them so that they are complete sentences. For even more good practice, exchange papers with another student and turn your classmate's ten fragments into sentences.

Correcting Run-on Sentences

A word group with a subject and a verb is a clause. As we have seen, the clause may be independent (making a complete statement and able to stand alone as a sentence), or it may be dependent (beginning with a dependent word and unable to stand alone as a sentence). When two *independent* clauses are written together without proper punctuation between them, the result is called a *run-on sentence*. Here are some examples.

> World music offers a lot of variety I listen to it in my car.

> I love the sound of drums therefore, bhangra is one of my favorite styles.

Run-on sentences can be corrected in one of six ways:

1. Separate the independent clauses into two sentences with a period.

> World music offers a lot of variety. I listen to it in my car.

> I love the sound of drums. Therefore, bhangra is one of my favorite styles.

2. Connect the two independent clauses with a semicolon alone.

> World music offers a lot of variety; I listen to it in my car.

> I love the sound of drums; therefore, bhangra is one of my favorite styles.

3. Connect the two independent clauses with a semicolon and a transition.

Look over the following list of connecting words (transitions):

also	however	otherwise
consequently	likewise	then
finally	moreover	therefore
furthermore	nevertheless	thus

When one of these words is used to join two independent clauses, a semicolon comes before the connecting word, and a comma usually comes after it.

> Mobile devices are essential in our society; however, they are very expensive.

> Earthquakes scare me; nevertheless, I live in Los Angeles.

> Yasmin traveled to London; then she took the "Chunnel" to Paris.

> The college recently built a large new library; thus we have more study areas.

NOTE—The use of the comma after the connecting word depends on how long the connecting word is. If it is only a short word, like *then* or *thus,* the comma is not necessary.

4. **Connect the two independent clauses with a comma and one of the following seven words (the first letters of which create the word *fanboys*, an easy way to remember them): *for, and, nor, but, or, yet,* or *so*.**

   Swans are beautiful birds, *and* they mate for life.

   Students may sign up for classes in person, *or* they may register online.

   Each of the *fanboys* has its own meaning when used as a connecting word. For example, *so* means "as a result," and *for* means "because":

   World music offers a lot of variety, *so* I never get bored with it.

   Bhangra is one of my favorite styles, *for* I love the sound of drums.

   I applied for financial aid, *but* (or *yet*) I make too much money to receive it.

   My brother doesn't know how to drive, *nor* does he plan to learn.

   Before you put a comma before a *fanboys,* be sure there are two independent clauses. Note that the first sentence that follows has two independent clauses. However, the second sentence contains just one clause with two verbs and therefore needs no comma.

   Registration begins next week, and it continues throughout the summer.

   Registration begins next week and continues throughout the summer.

5. **Add a dependent word—such as *when, since, after, while,* or *because*—to the clause used at the beginning of the sentence, and follow the dependent clause with a comma.**

   Because I enjoy the mellow sounds of acoustic guitar music, I listen to it in my car.

6. **Add a dependent word—such as *when, since, after, while,* or *because*—to the clause used at the end of the sentence (no comma necessary).**

   I listen to acoustic guitar music in my car *because* I enjoy its mellow sounds.

Learn these ways to join two clauses, and you'll avoid run-on sentences.

SIX WAYS TO CORRECT RUN-ON SENTENCES

Run-on: The movie had a dull plot many people left early.

1. The movie had a dull plot. Many people left early. (period)
2. The movie had a dull plot; many people left early. (semicolon)
3. The movie had a dull plot; therefore, many people left early.
   (semicolon + transition)
4. The movie had a dull plot, so many people left early.
   (comma + *fanboys*)
5. Because the movie had a dull plot, many people left early.
   (dependent clause at the beginning + comma)
6. Many people left early because the movie had a dull plot.
   (dependent clause at end—no comma)

EXERCISES

Exercises 1 and 2

CORRECTING RUN-ONS WITH PUNCTUATION

Some of the following sentences are run-ons. If the sentence contains two
independent clauses without proper punctuation, use one of the first four ways
to correct the run-on (using punctuation only). All existing punctuation in the
sentences is correct. When correcting run-ons with punctuation, remember to
capitalize after a period but not after a semicolon. Also remember to insert a
comma only when one of the *fanboys* (*for, and, nor, but, or, yet,* or *so*) has already
been used to join the two independent clauses.

Exercise 1

1. Mary Mallon is a famous name in American history but she is not
   famous for something good.

2. Most people know Mary Mallon by another name and that is "Typhoid
   Mary."

3. Mallon lived during the late nineteenth and early twentieth centuries.

4. At that time, there was little knowledge about disease carriers.

5. Mary Mallon was the first famous case of a healthy carrier of disease but she never believed the accusations against her.

6. Mallon, an Irish immigrant, was a cook she was also an infectious carrier of typhoid.

7. By the time the authorities discovered Mallon's problem, she had made many people ill a few of her "victims" actually died from the disease.

8. A health specialist approached Mallon and asked her for a blood sample she was outraged and attacked him with a long cooking fork.

9. Eventually, the authorities dragged Mallon into a hospital for testing but she fought them hysterically the entire time.

10. The lab tests proved Mallon's infectious status and health officials forced Mary Mallon to live on an island by herself for twenty-six years.

Source: Los Angeles Times, September 2, 2002

Exercise 2

1. I just read an article about prehistoric rodents and I was surprised by their size.

2. Scientists recently discovered the remains of a rat-like creature called *Phoberomys* it was as big as a buffalo.

3. *Phoberomys* sat back on its large rear feet and fed itself with its smaller front feet in just the way rats and mice do now.

4. This supersized rodent lived in South America but luckily that was nearly ten million years ago.

5. At that time, South America was a separate continent it had no cows or horses to graze on its open land.

6. South America and North America were separated by the sea so there were also no large cats around to hunt and kill other large animals.

7. Scientists believe that *Phoberomys* thrived and grew large because of the lack of predators and competitors for food.

8. The *Phoberomys'* carefree lifestyle eventually disappeared for the watery separation between North and South America slowly became a land route.

9. The big carnivores of North America could travel down the new land route and the big rodents were defenseless against them.

10. The rodents who survived were the smaller ones who could escape underground and that is the reason we have no buffalo-sized rats today.

Source: Science News, September 20, 2003

Exercises 3 and 4

CORRECTING RUN-ONS WITH DEPENDENT CLAUSES

Most of the following sentences are run-ons. Correct any run-on sentences by making one or more of the clauses *dependent.* You may rephrase the sentences, but be sure to use dependent words (such as *since, when, as, after, while, because,* or the other words listed on page 70) to begin dependent clauses. Since various words can be used to form dependent clauses, your answers might differ from those suggested in the answers.

Exercise 3

1. Pablo Wendel is a German student of art he feels a special connection with a particular group of ancient sculptures.

2. Pablo acted on this feeling in September of 2006 it won him his "fifteen minutes of fame."

3. He had always admired the terra cotta warriors that were discovered in the 2,200-year-old tomb of a Chinese emperor.

4. Pablo decided to see the famous army of clay soldiers first-hand and to document his trip with photographs.

5. He made a special clay-covered costume it was complete with armor and a helmet.

6. Pablo took this outfit and a pedestal with him to the museum it is located in Xian, China.

7. He planned to take a picture of himself in costume outside the museum, but his dream to stand among the soldiers was too strong.

8. He entered the excavation site, jumped into the excavation pit, and joined the terra cotta army.

9. Pablo, in disguise, stood among his fellow "soldiers" and didn't move eventually someone saw him.

10. The museum guards took Pablo's clay costume they let him go with just a warning.

Source: http://news.bbc.co.uk/2/hi/asia-pacific/5355546.stm

Exercise 4

1. I've been reading about sleep in my psychology class I now know a lot more about it.

2. Sleep has four stages we usually go through all these stages many times during the night.

3. The first stage of sleep begins our muscles relax and mental activity slows down.

4. During stage one, we are still slightly awake.

5. Stage two takes us deeper than stage one we are no longer aware of our surroundings.

6. We spend about half our sleeping time in the second stage.

7. Next is stage three in it we become more and more relaxed and are very hard to awaken.

8. Stage four is the deepest in this stage we don't even hear loud noises.

9. The most active type of sleep is called REM (rapid eye movement) sleep our eyes move back and forth quickly behind our eyelids.

10. REM sleep is only about as deep as stage one we do all our dreaming during the REM stage.

Source: Psychology: A Journey (Cengage, 2010)

Exercise 5

Correct the following run-on sentences using any of the methods studied in this section: adding punctuation or using dependent words to create dependent clauses. See the chart on page 86 if you need to review the methods.

1. White buffalos are very rare and they are extremely important in Native American folklore.

2. Many American Indian tribes feel a strong attachment to white buffalos they are viewed as omens of peace and prosperity.

3. One farm in Wisconsin is famous as a source of white buffalos three of them have been born on this farm since 1994.

4. The owners of the farm are Valerie and Dave Heider and they are as surprised as anyone about the unusual births.

5. The Heiders' first white buffalo was a female calf she was named Miracle.

6. Miracle became a local attraction visitors to the Heider farm raised tourism in the area by twenty-two percent in 1995.

7. A second white calf was born on the farm in 1996 however, it died after a few days.

8. Miracle survived until 2004 she lived for ten years.

9. In September of 2006, the Heider farm yielded a third white buffalo calf but it was a boy.

10. The odds against one white buffalo being born are high the odds against three being born in the same place are astronomical.

Source: http://www.denverpost.com/nationworld/ci_4836051

REVIEW OF FRAGMENTS AND RUN-ON SENTENCES

If you remember that all clauses include a subject and a verb, but only independent clauses can be punctuated as sentences (since only they can stand alone), then you will avoid fragments in your writing. And if you memorize these six ways to punctuate clauses, you will be able to avoid most punctuation errors.

PUNCTUATING CLAUSES

I am a student. I am still learning.	(two sentences)
I am a student; I am still learning.	(two independent clauses)
I am a student; *therefore,* I am still learning.	(two independent clauses connected by a transition such as *also, consequently, finally, furthermore, however, likewise, moreover, nevertheless, otherwise, then, therefore, thus)*
I am a student, *so* I am still learning.	(two independent clauses connected by a *fanboys: for, and, nor, but, or, yet, so)*
I am still learning *because I am a student.*	(dependent clause at end of sentence)
Because I am a student, I am still learning.	(dependent clause at beginning of sentence) Dependent words include *after, although, as, as if, because, before, even if, even though, ever since, how, if, since, so that, than, that, though, unless, until, what, whatever, when, whenever, where, whereas, wherever, whether, which, whichever, while, who, whom, whose,* and *why.*

It is essential that you study the previous chart to learn which of the italicized words transition between independent clauses and which of them create dependent clauses.

PROOFREADING EXERCISE

Rewrite the following student paragraph, making the necessary changes to eliminate fragments and run-on sentences.

With the focus on cleanliness lately in advertising for soaps and household cleaning products. People are surprised to hear that we may be too clean for our own good. This phenomenon is called the "hygiene hypothesis" and recent studies support its validity. For instance, one study showing the benefits of living with two or more pets. Babies may grow up with healthier immune systems and be less allergic if they live with a dog and a cat or two dogs or two cats. The old thinking was that young children would become more allergic living with many pets but they don't. Somehow the exposure to pets and all their "dirty" habits gives youngsters much-needed defenses. Maybe as much as a seventy-five percent lower allergy risk, according to this study.

Source: http://www.med.umich.edu/opm/newspage/2007/hmclean.htm

SENTENCE WRITING

Write a sample sentence of your own to demonstrate each of the six ways to punctuate two clauses. You may model your sentences on the examples used in the review chart on page 86.

Identifying Verb Phrases

Sometimes a verb is one word, but often the verb includes two or more words. Verbs made of more than one word are called *verb phrases*. Look at that following list of forms of the verb *speak,* for example. All but the first three of them are verb phrases, made up of the main verb (*speak*) and one or more *helping verbs* (*will, have, has, had, is, am, are, was, were, been, can, must, could, should, would*).

speak	is speaking	had been speaking
speaks	am speaking	will have been speaking
spoke	are speaking	is spoken
will speak	was speaking	was spoken
has spoken	were speaking	will be spoken
have spoken	will be speaking	can speak
had spoken	has been speaking	must speak
will have spoken	have been speaking	should have spoken

Note that certain adverbs may appear near a verb or in the middle of a verb phrase, but they are not part of the verb itself. For more about adverbs, see page 35.

They have *already* spoken to the landlord and will *also* speak with other tenants.

Here are the most common adverbs used to modify verbs and verb phrases:

already	ever	not	really
also	finally	now	sometimes
always	just	often	usually
probably	never	only	possibly

Two forms of *speak—speaking* and *to speak—*look like verbs, but neither form can ever be the only verb in a sentence. No *ing* word by itself or *to* _____ form of a verb can act as the main verb of a sentence.

Jeanine speaking French. (a fragment lacking a complete verb phrase)

Jeanine has been speaking French. (a sentence with a complete verb phrase)

And no verb with *to* in front of it can ever be the real verb in a sentence.

Ted to speak in front of groups. (a fragment without a real verb)

Ted <u><u>hates</u></u> to speak in front of groups. (a sentence with a real verb)

These two forms, *speaking* and *to speak,* may be used as subjects or other parts of a sentence.

<u>*Speaking*</u> on stage <u><u>is</u></u> an art. <u>*To speak*</u> on stage <u><u>is</u></u> an art. <u>Ted</u> <u><u>had</u></u> a *speaking*^{adj} part in that play.

E X E R C I S E S

Double underline the verbs or verb phrases in the following sentences. For now, you do not need to mark subjects. The sentences may contain independent *and* dependent clauses, so there may be several verbs and verb phrases. (Remember that *ing* verbs alone and the *to* _____ forms of verbs are never real verbs in sentences.)

Exercise 1

1. Scientists of all kinds have been learning a lot lately.
2. Those who study traffic safety have recently discovered a puzzling truth.
3. People drive more safely when they encounter fewer traffic signs and traffic lights.
4. The reason behind the "Shared Space" theory is easy to explain.
5. Drivers will regulate their speed and pay closer attention to other drivers when they are not told to do so by signs and lights.
6. Traffic signs and signals give drivers a false sense of security that often leads to recklessness.
7. When no signs or signals exist, drivers think about their own safety and drive more cautiously.
8. Many towns in Europe and America have already taken steps to test the truth of this theory.

9. In some cases, all lights, signs, and barriers have been removed so that all drivers and pedestrians must negotiate with each other to proceed through the town.

10. These changes have usually resulted in lower speeds, fewer accidents, and shorter travel times.

Sources: Discover, May 2007, and *International Herald Tribune,* January 22, 2005

Exercise 2

1. Have you ever felt a craving for art?

2. Have you said to yourself, "I need a new painting, or I will lose my mind"?

3. If you do find yourself in this situation, you can get instant satisfaction.

4. I am referring to Art-o-Mat machines, of course.

5. These vending machines dispense small pieces of modern art.

6. You insert five dollars, pull a knob on a refurbished cigarette dispenser, and out comes an original art piece.

7. The artists themselves get fifty percent of the selling price.

8. Art-o-Mat machines can be found at locations across the country.

9. Art-o-Mats are currently dispensing tiny paintings, photographs, and sculptures in twenty-eight states and in Canada and Austria.

10. The machines have sold the works of hundreds of contemporary artists.

Source: www.artomat.org

Exercise 3

1. During my last semester of high school, our English teacher assigned a special paper.

2. He said that he was becoming depressed by all the bad news out there, so each of us was asked to find a piece of good news and write a short research paper about it.

3. I must admit that I had no idea how hard that assignment would be.

4. Finally, I found an article while I was reading my favorite magazine.

5. The title of the article was a pun; it was called "Grin Reaper."

6. I knew instantly that it must be just the kind of news my teacher wanted.

7. The article explained that one woman, Pam Johnson, had started a club that she named The Secret Society of Happy People.

8. She had even chosen August 8 as "Admit You're Happy Day" and had already convinced more than fifteen state governors to recognize the holiday.

9. The club and the holiday were created to support people who are happy so that the unhappy, negative people around will not bring the happy people down.

10. As I was writing my essay, I visited the Society of Happy People Web site, *www.sohp.com*, and signed my teacher up for their newsletter.

Source: *Lawrence Journal World*, July 27, 1999

Exercise 4

1. I have always wondered how an Etch A Sketch works.

2. This flat TV-shaped toy has been popular since it first arrived in the 1960s.

3. Now I have learned the secrets inside this popular toy.

4. An Etch A Sketch is filled with a combination of metal powder and tiny plastic particles.

5. This mixture clings to the inside of the Etch A Sketch screen.

6. When the pointer that is connected to the two knobs moves, the tip of it "draws" lines in the powder on the back of the screen.

7. The powder at the bottom of the Etch A Sketch does not fill in these lines because it is too far away.

8. But if the Etch A Sketch is turned upside down, the powder clings to the whole underside surface of the screen and "erases" the image again.

9. Although the basic Etch A Sketch has not changed since I was a kid, it now comes in several different sizes.

10. Best of all, these great drawing devices have never needed batteries, and I hope that they never will.

Source: http://www.forbes.com/sites/alexknapp/2012/03/22/how-does-an-etch-a-sketch-work-anyway/

Exercise 5

1. Scientists successfully cloned a dog for the first time in 2005.

2. Cloning experts had been attempting to clone a dog for many years.

3. They had had success with horses, cats, and even rats before they could clone a dog.

4. The scientists who eventually succeeded were from Seoul National University in South Korea.

5. They named the cloned dog Snuppy as a tribute to the university where the accomplishment was made, and they pronounced the name "Snoopy."

6. Of course, Snuppy could thank his "parent" dog, a three-year-old Afghan hound, for all of his great physical features.

7. Both dogs had long glossy black fur that was accentuated by identical brown markings on their paws, tails, chests, and eyebrows.

8. Unfortunately, the cloning procedure does not guarantee that the clone of a dog will share the unique features of the original dog's personality.

9. Nevertheless, now that dog cloning has been achieved, many people have shown an interest in cloning their own dogs.

10. Although some people may not be happy with just a physical copy of a beloved pet, for others, a copy is better than nothing.

Source: Science News, August 6, 2005

REVIEW EXERCISE

To practice finding the sentence structures we have studied so far, mark the following paragraphs from a student essay. First, put parentheses around prepositional phrases; then underline verbs and verb phrases twice and their subjects once. Finally, put a broken line beneath dependent clauses. Start by marking the first paragraph and checking your answers. Remember that *ing* verbs alone and the *to* _____ forms of verbs are never real verbs in sentences, as explained on page 93–94. Also note that we have identified a few minor changes to the excerpt with brackets [ ] and ellipses (. . .). For more about their use, see page 232.

My brain feels like a computer's central processing unit. Information is continually pumping into its circuits. I organize the data, format it to my individual preferences, and lay it out in my own style. As I endlessly sculpt existing formulas, they become something of my own. When I need a solution to a problem, I access the data that I have gathered from my whole existence, even my preprogrammed DNA.

Since I am a student, teachers require that I supply them with specific information in various formats. When they assign an essay, I produce several paragraphs. If they need a summary, I scan the text, find its main ideas, and put them briefly into my own words. I know that I can accomplish whatever the teachers ask so that I can obtain a degree and continue processing ideas to make a living.

I compare my brain to a processor because right now I feel that I must work like one. As I go further into my education, my processor will be continually updated. And with any luck, I will end up with real, not artificial, intelligence.

Using Standard English Verbs

The next two discussions are for those who need to practice using Standard English verbs. Many of us grew up doing more speaking than writing. But in college and in the business and professional worlds, knowledge of Standard Written English is essential.

The following charts show the forms of four verbs as they are used in Standard Written English. These forms might differ from the way you use these verbs when you speak. Memorize the Standard English forms of these important verbs. The first verb (*talk*) is one of the regular verbs (verbs that all end the same way according to a pattern); most verbs in English are regular. The other three verbs charted here (*have, be,* and *do*) are irregular and are important because they are used not only as main verbs but also as helping verbs in verb phrases.

Don't go on to the exercises until you have memorized the forms of these Standard English verbs.

REGULAR VERB: TALK

PRESENT TIME		PAST TIME	
I		I	
you	talk	you	
we		we	talked
they		they	
he, she, it	talks	he, she, it	

IRREGULAR VERB: HAVE

PRESENT TIME		PAST TIME	
I		I	
you	have	you	
we		we	had
they		they	
he, she, it	has	he, she, it	

IRREGULAR VERB: BE

PRESENT TIME		PAST TIME	
I	am	I	was
you		you	
we	are	we	were
they		they	
he, she, it	is	he, she, it	was

IRREGULAR VERB: DO

PRESENT TIME		PAST TIME	
I		I	
you		you	
we	do	we	did
they		they	
he, she, it	·does	he, she, it	

Sometimes you may have difficulty with the correct endings of verbs because you don't actually hear the words correctly. Note carefully the *s* sound and the *ed* sound at the end of certain words. Occasionally, the *ed* is not clearly pronounced, as in "They tri*ed* to finish their essays," but most of the time you can hear it if you listen. Read the following sentences aloud, making sure that you exaggerate every sound:

1. He seems satisfied with his new job.

2. She likes saving money for the future.

3. It takes strength of character to control spending.

4. Todd brings salad to every party that he attends.

5. I used to know all of the state capitals.

6. They were supposed to sign both forms.

7. He recognized the suspect and excused himself from the jury.

8. The chess club sponsored Dorothy in the school's charity event.

Now read some other sentences aloud from this text, making sure that you say all the *s*'s and *ed*'s. Reading aloud and listening to others will help you use the correct verb endings automatically.

E X E R C I S E S

In these pairs of sentences, use the *present* form of the verb in the first sentence and the *past* form in the second. All the verbs follow the pattern of the regular verb *talk* except the irregular verbs *have, be,* and *do.* Keep referring to the charts if you're not sure which form to use. Check your answers.

Exercise 1

1. (end) Many new movies _____ too suddenly. The movie I saw yesterday _____ before I had finished my medium popcorn.

2. (do) Denise _____ her homework at the dinner table.
She _____ two hours of homework last night.

3. (be) I _____ now the president of the film club on campus.
I _____ just a member of the club last semester.

4. (vote) Patrick _____ in every election. He even _____ with an absentee ballot in the presidential election of 2008.

5. (have) The twins _____ similar ideas about the environment. Last year, they _____ a fund-raiser for their local wildlife preserve.

6. (shop) We _____ for almost everything online. We _____ for groceries online last week.

7. (be) They _____ finally satisfied with their living room. They _____ embarrassed by it before the remodeling.

8. (pick) I _____ the location of our seats whenever we go to a concert. Yesterday, I also _____ our seats on the plane for our upcoming vacation.

9. (do) We _____ what we can for the birds in winter. A few years ago, we _____ our best to save a nearly frozen sparrow.

10. (have) My twin sisters _____ the same teacher now. They _____ different teachers last year.

Exercise 2

1. (be)   She _____ a lawyer now. She _____ a law student last year.

2. (do)   They _____ their best work on the weekends. They _____ a great job last weekend.

3. (have)   I _____ a new education plan. I _____ originally a plan that would have taken too long to complete.

4. (ask)   She _____ for help when she needs it. She _____ her tutor for help with her latest essay.

5. (have)   I always _____ the flu at this time of year. I _____ the flu last year right on schedule.

6. (learn)   We _____ something about writing each week. Yesterday we _____ how to write a thesis.

7. (be)   Most of us _____ right handed. Therefore, we _____ not comfortable drawing with our left hands.

8. (do)   She _____ well on all of her assignments. She _____ very well on the term project.

9. (play)   He _____ the piano now. He _____ the guitar as his first instrument.

10. (be)   I _____ a natural comedian. However, last month I _____ too depressed to be funny.

Exercise 3

Circle the correct Standard English verb forms.

1. I (start, started) a new volunteer job last month, and so far I really (like, likes) it.

2. The organization (offer, offers) relief boxes to victims of crime or natural disasters around the world.

3. The other volunteers (is, are) all really nice, so we (has, have) a good work environment.

4. Yesterday, we (finish, finished) a project that (need, needed) lots of boxes.

5. The supervisors who (run, runs) the organization always (do, does) their best to explain the victims' situations to us.

6. And they (advise, advises) us to make sure that the boxes (comfort, comforts) the victims as much as possible.

7. I can tell that the supervisors (enjoy, enjoys) their work; they (is, are) always happy to see the relief on the victims' faces.

8. My fellow volunteers and I (complete, completed) our latest project in just one week even though the supervisor (expect, expected) it to take us two weeks.

9. We (has, have) our supervisors to thank for a smooth-running organization.

10. And I (thank, thanks) my coworkers for being my friends.

Exercise 4

Choose the correct Standard English verb forms.

1. My cousin Isabel and I (has, have) a lot in common.

2. We both (play, plays) many different sports.

3. She (play, plays) soccer, softball, and basketball.

4. I (play, plays) tennis, badminton, and golf.

5. However, Isabel (practice, practices) more often than I (does, do).

6. The result (is, are) that she (win, wins) more often, too.

7. I (is, am) as skilled as she (is, am), but I (is, am) a little bit lazy.

8. Our parents (remind, reminds) us about practicing all the time.

9. Isabel really (follow, follows) their advice.

10. We both (has, have) talent, but I (is, am) not as disciplined as she (is, am).

Exercise 5

Choose the correct Standard English verb forms to show the past.

1. Last semester, my drawing teacher (gave, give, gives) us a challenging assignment.

2. He (hands, handed, hand) each of us half a photograph taped to a whole piece of paper.

3. We (have, had, has) to imagine the missing half of the picture and draw it.

4. My half-image (shows, show, showed) parts of a subway tunnel.

5. There (was, were, are) half a stairway with a railing and a few people walking to their trains.

6. With all my creative energy, I (imagines, imagine, imagined) the rest of the image.

7. Then I (fills, filled, fill) in a rogue skateboarder heading down the stairway on top of the railing.

8. I (does, did, do) a great job on the realistic details of his hair, clothes, position, and board.

9. The full picture—with my additions—(look, looks, looked) dangerous and exciting.

10. For its impact and skill, my drawing (receives, received, receives) a perfect score.

PROOFREADING EXERCISE

Correct any sentences in the following paragraph that do not use Standard English verb forms.

Yesterday, when I walk on campus to go to my classroom, I notice a problem that needs to be fixed. Every morning, there is a long line of students in their cars waiting to enter the parking lots because the light at the corner do not change fast enough. It change too slowly, so cars start to stack up on the side streets. Anybody who walk to school is affected, too. Drivers get desperate when they are stuck in traffic. Many of them don't watch where they're going and almost run over people who is walking in the crosswalks and driveways.

SENTENCE WRITING

Write ten sentences about a problem on your campus. Check your sentences to be sure that they use Standard English verb forms. Try exchanging papers with another student for more practice.

Using Regular and Irregular Verbs

All regular verbs end the same way in the past form and when used with helping verbs. Here is a chart showing all the forms of some *regular* verbs and the various helping verbs with which they are used.

REGULAR VERBS				
BASE FORM	**PRESENT**	**PAST**	**PAST PARTICIPLE**	***ING* FORM**
(Use after *to, can, may, shall, will, could, might, should, would, must, do, does, did*.)			(Use after *have, has, had.* Some can be used after forms of *be.*)	(Use after forms of *be.*)
ask	ask (s)	asked	asked	asking
bake	bake (s)	baked	baked	baking
count	count (s)	counted	counted	counting
dance	dance (s)	danced	danced	dancing
decide	decide (s)	decided	decided	deciding
enjoy	enjoy (s)	enjoyed	enjoyed	enjoying
finish	finish (es)	finished	finished	finishing
happen	happen (s)	happened	happened	happening
learn	learn (s)	learned	learned	learning
like	like (s)	liked	liked	liking
look	look (s)	looked	looked	looking
mend	mend (s)	mended	mended	mending
need	need (s)	needed	needed	needing
open	open (s)	opened	opened	opening
start	start (s)	started	started	starting
suppose	suppose (s)	supposed	supposed	supposing
tap	tap (s)	tapped	tapped	tapping
walk	walk (s)	walked	walked	walking
want	want (s)	wanted	wanted	wanting

> **NOTE**—When there are several helping verbs, the one closest to the verb determines which form of the main verb should be used: They *should* finish soon; they could *have* finished an hour ago.

When do you write *ask, finish, suppose, use?* And when do you write *asked, finished, supposed, used?* Here are some rules that will help you decide.

Write *ask, finish, suppose, use* (or their *s* forms) when writing about the present time, repeated actions, or facts:

He *ask*s questions whenever he is confused.

They always *finish* their projects on time.

I *suppose* you want me to help you move.

Birds *use* leaves, twigs, and feathers to build their nests.

Write *asked, finished, supposed, used*

1. **When writing about the past:**

   He *asked* the teacher for another explanation.

   She *finished* her internship last year.

   They *supposed* that there were others bidding on that house.

   I *used* to study piano.

2. **When some form of *be* (other than the word *be* itself) comes before the word:**

   He was *asked* the most difficult questions.

   She is *finished* with her training now.

   They were *supposed* to sign at the bottom of the form.

   My essay was *used* as a sample of clear narration.

3. **When some form of *have* comes before the word:**

   The teacher has *asked* us that question before.

   She will have *finished* all of her exams by the end of May.

   I had *supposed* too much without any proof.

   We have *used* many models in my drawing class this semester.

All the verbs in the chart on page 105 are *regular.* That is, they're all formed in the same way—with an *ed* ending on the past form and on the past participle. But many verbs are irregular. Their past and past participle forms change spelling instead of just adding an *ed.* Here's a chart of some *irregular* verbs. Notice that the base, present, and *ing* forms end the same as regular verbs. Refer to this list when you aren't sure which verb form to use. Memorize all the forms you don't know.

IRREGULAR VERBS

BASE FORM	PRESENT	PAST	PAST PARTICIPLE	ING FORM
(Use after *to, can, may, shall, will, could, might, should, would, must, do, does, did.*)			(Use after *have, has, had.* Some can be used after forms of *be.*)	(Use after forms of *be.*)
be	is, am, are	was, were	been	being
become	become (s)	became	become	becoming
begin	begin (s)	began	begun	beginning
break	break (s)	broke	broken	breaking
bring	bring (s)	brought	brought	bringing
buy	buy (s)	bought	bought	buying
build	build (s)	built	built	building
catch	catch (es)	caught	caught	catching
choose	choose (s)	chose	chosen	choosing
come	come (s)	came	come	coming
do	do (es)	did	done	doing
draw	draw (s)	drew	drawn	drawing
drink	drink (s)	drank	drunk	drinking
drive	drive (s)	drove	driven	driving
eat	eat (s)	ate	eaten	eating
fall	fall (s)	fell	fallen	falling
feel	feel (s)	felt	felt	feeling
fight	fight (s)	fought	fought	fighting
find	find (s)	found	found	finding
forget	forget (s)	forgot	forgotten	forgetting
forgive	forgive (s)	forgave	forgiven	forgiving
freeze	freeze (s)	froze	frozen	freezing
get	get (s)	got	got or gotten	getting
give	give (s)	gave	given	giving
go	go (es)	went	gone	going
grow	grow (s)	grew	grown	growing
have	have or has	had	had	having
hear	hear (s)	heard	heard	hearing
hold	hold (s)	held	held	holding
keep	keep (s)	kept	kept	keeping
know	know (s)	knew	known	knowing
lay (to put)	lay (s)	laid	laid	laying

IRREGULAR VERBS

BASE FORM	PRESENT	PAST	PAST PARTICIPLE	ING FORM
lead (like "bead")	lead (s)	led	led	leading
leave	leave (s)	left	left	leaving
lie (to rest)	lie (s)	lay	lain	lying
lose	lose (s)	lost	lost	losing
make	make (s)	made	made	making
meet	meet (s)	met	met	meeting
pay	pay (s)	paid	paid	paying
read (pron. "reed")	read (s)	read (pron. "red")	read (pron. "red")	reading
ride	ride (s)	rode	ridden	riding
ring	ring (s)	rang	rung	ringing
rise	rise (s)	rose	risen	rising
run	run (s)	ran	run	running
say	say (s)	said	said	saying
see	see (s)	saw	seen	seeing
sell	sell (s)	sold	sold	selling
shake	shake (s)	shook	shaken	shaking
shine (give light)	shine (s)	shone	shone	shining
shine (polish)	shine (s)	shined	shined	shining
sing	sing (s)	sang	sung	singing
sleep	sleep (s)	slept	slept	sleeping
speak	speak (s)	spoke	spoken	speaking
spend	spend (s)	spent	spent	spending
stand	stand (s)	stood	stood	standing
steal	steal (s)	stole	stolen	stealing
strike	strike (s)	struck	struck	striking
swim	swim (s)	swam	swum	swimming
swing	swing (s)	swung	swung	swinging
take	take (s)	took	taken	taking
teach	teach (es)	taught	taught	teaching
tear	tear (s)	tore	torn	tearing
tell	tell (s)	told	told	telling
think	think (s)	thought	thought	thinking
throw	throw (s)	threw	thrown	throwing
wear	wear (s)	wore	worn	wearing
win	win (s)	won	won	winning
write	write (s)	wrote	written	writing

Be aware that verbs from the past participle column can work as adjectives to describe their subjects when these verbs come after forms of *be* (or other verbs that can also be linking verbs: *appear, seem, look, feel, get, act, become*). Here are several examples:

They <u>are</u> *educated*. ("Educated" is an *adjective* that describes them.)

They <u>*educated*</u> themselves. ("Educated" is a real *verb* here.)

You <u>appear</u> *shaken.*

He <u>seems</u> *contented.*

We <u>feel</u> *motivated.*

I <u>was</u> *embarrassed*. ("Embarrassed" is an *adjective* that describes me.)

I <u>get</u> *embarrassed* easily.

I <u>became</u> *embarrassed* at the party.

My friends <u>*embarrassed*</u> me by accident. (The word "embarrassed" is a *verb* here.)

For more about sentence patterns and linking verbs, see page 137–138.

As you can see, past participle forms can act as *adjectives* that describe subjects or as real *verbs* in sentences.

EXERCISES

Write the correct form of the verbs in the blanks. Refer to the columns and explanations on the preceding pages if you aren't sure which form to use after a certain helping verb. Check your answers after each exercise.

Exercise 1

1. (eat) People _____ a lot when they go to the movies.

2. (eat) I can _____ a whole bag of popcorn myself.

3. (eat) When someone else is _____ popcorn, the crunching sound drives me crazy.

4. (eat) Once I have _____ my dinner, I stay away from snacks.

5. (eat) My sister _____ a worm when she was in kindergarten.

6. (eat) My two-year-old nephew _____ everything; he is not picky.

7. (eat)   The apple in my lunch was half-_____.

8. (eat)   The people at the conference were _____ in silence.

9. (eat)   We _____ while we watched a documentary on television.

10. (eat)   If you want to pass a test, you should always _____ a good breakfast.

Exercise 2

1. (drive)   I always _____ my brother to school; in fact, I have _____ him to school for a whole year now.

2. (think)   The other day, I was _____ of new ways to get him there in the morning, but he _____ that they were all bad ideas.

3. (take)   He could _____ a school bus that stops nearby; instead he _____ me for granted.

4. (tell)   It all started when he _____ our mother that some of the other children were _____ him to stay out of their seats.

5. (write)   I _____ a note to the bus driver to see if she could help ease my brother's mind, but so far she hasn't _____ back.

6. (know)   When I was my brother's age, I _____ some tough kids at school, so I _____ how he must feel.

7. (teach)   But experiences like that _____ us how to get along with everyone; they sure _____ me.

8. (tear)   Now I am _____ between wanting to help him avoid the tough kids and wanting to _____ my hair out from having to take him to school every day.

9. (ride)   We have _____ together for so long that I might miss him if I _____ alone.

10. (make)   I have _____ up my mind. I will _____ the best of it while he still needs me. What else are big brothers for?

Exercise 3

1. (take, suppose)   My friend Brenda _____ a day off last week even though she was _____ to be working.

2. (do, earn)   She _____ not feel sick exactly; she just felt that she had _____ a day of rest.

3. (call, tell, feel)   So Brenda _____ her office and _____ her boss that she did not _____ well enough to work that day.

4. (think, be)   She never _____ that she would get caught, but she _____ wrong.

5. (leave, drive, see)   Just as Brenda was _____ the house to buy some lunch, her coworker _____ by and _____ her.

6. (feel, know, tell)   She _____ such panic because she _____ that he would _____ their boss that she looked fine.

7. (try, go)   Brenda _____ to explain herself when she _____ back to the office the next day.

8. (be, undo)   The damage had _____ done, however, and nothing could _____ it.

9. (wish, take)   Now Brenda _____ that she could _____ back that day.

10. (use, call, do)   She _____ to have a great relationship with her boss, but since the day she _____ in "sick," he _____ not trust her anymore.

Exercise 4

1. (use, put)   Many people _____ a direct deposit system that _____ their salary money directly into their bank accounts.

2. (do, do)   With such a system, the employer _____ not have to issue paychecks, and employees _____ not have to cash or deposit them.

3. (transfer, spend)   The employer's computer just _____ the money to the bank's computer, and the employee can _____ it as usual after that.

4. (be, like, choose)   Direct deposit _____ almost always optional, but so many people _____ the system that most people _____ it.

5. (do, want)   My uncle _____ not trust such systems; he _____ to have complete control over his cash.

6. (trust, be)   He barely even _____ banks to keep his money safe for him, so he _____ definitely suspicious of direct deposit.

7. (imagine, make)   I can _____ him as a pioneer in an old Western movie sleeping on a mattress stuffed with all of the money he has ever _____.

8. (talk, ask, worry)   I was _____ to my uncle about money the other day, and I _____ him why he always _____ about it so much.

9. (look, say, live,   He just _____ at me and _____, "If you had
    ever understand)   _____ without money, you would _____."

10. (wonder, be)   I _____ about my uncle's past experiences and hope that he _____ never without money again.

Exercise 5

1. (lie, fall)   I was _____ out in the sun last Sunday, and I _____ asleep.

2. (be, do)   That _____ the worst thing I could have _____.

3. (wear, shield)   I was _____ a pair of big dark sunglasses, which _____ my eyes from the light.

4. (lie, wake, realize, happen)   I must have _____ there for over an hour before I _____ up and _____ what had _____.

5. (feel, start)   At first I _____ fine, but then my skin _____ to feel really tight and thin.

6. (pass, turn, begin)   As the minutes _____, my skin _____ bright red, and the pain _____.

7. (describe, experience)   I can't even _____ how much pain I _____.

8. (be, feel, see)   Almost worse than the pain _____ the embarrassment I _____ as I _____ my face in the mirror.

9. (look, tape, be, protect, wear)   Around my eyes, it _____ as if someone had _____ the shape of white glasses to my face, but that _____ just the skin that had been _____ by the sunglasses I was _____.

10. (have, feel)   The people at work _____ a big laugh the next day at my expense, but then they just _____ sorry for me.

PROGRESS TEST

This test covers everything you've studied so far. One sentence in each pair is correct. The other is incorrect. Read both sentences carefully before you decide. Then write the letter of the incorrect sentence in the blank. Try to name the error and correct it if you can.

1. _____ **A.** No one was left in the classroom except the teacher and me.

   _____ **B.** As soon as I finish the test, the bell rang.

2. _____ **A.** Textbooks available online.

   _____ **B.** They can be less expensive than the ones in stores.

3. _____ **A.** Our class took a field trip to the museum and I loved it.

   _____ **B.** I asked the teacher if I could do some extra credit there.

4. _____ **A.** My research paper will probably be late.

   _____ **B.** I should of gone to the library sooner.

5. _____ **A.** We were suppose to lock the door after class.

   _____ **B.** We forgot and had to drive back to school.

6. _____ **A.** Adam and Tracy have finished all of their school work.

   _____ **B.** Their going away for spring break, and I'm staying at home.

7. _____ **A.** The package had no official label, only a handwritten address.

   _____ **B.** We were surprise that it was delivered on time.

8. _____ **A.** In my math class, we've already took three quizzes.

   _____ **B.** We'll have six more quizzes before the final exam.

9. _____ **A.** The bus driver tried to start the bus after it stalled.

   _____ **B.** Nothing worked so we all got off the bus and waited for another one.

10. _____ **A.** Although I don't like the taste of grapefruits or lemons.

    _____ **B.** I do like cleaning products with citrus scents.

Maintaining Subject-Verb Agreement

As we have seen, the subject and verb in a sentence work together, so they must always agree. Different subjects need different forms of verbs. When the correct verb follows a subject, we call it subject-verb agreement.

The following sentences illustrate the rule that *s* verbs follow most singular subjects but not plural subjects.

One student studies.   Two students study.

The bell rings.   The bells ring.

A democracy listens to the people.   Democracies listen to the people.

One person writes the dialogue.   Many people write the dialogue.

The following sentences show how forms of the verb *be* (*is, am, are, was, were*) and helping verbs (*be, have,* and *do*) are made to agree with their subjects. We have labeled only the verbs that must agree with the subjects.

This puzzle is difficult.   These puzzles are difficult.

I am amazed.   You are amazed.

He was studying.   They were studying.

That class has been canceled.   Those classes have been canceled.

She does not want to participate.   You do not want to participate.

The following words are always singular and take an *s* verb or the irregular equivalent (*is, was, has, does*):

one	anybody	each
anyone	everybody	
everyone	nobody	
no one	somebody	
someone		

Someone feeds my dog in the morning.

Everybody was at the party.

Each does her own homework.

Remember that prepositional phrases often come between subjects and verbs. You should ignore these interrupting phrases, or you may mistake the wrong word for the subject and use a verb form that doesn't agree.

Someone from the apartments feeds my dog in the morning. (*Someone* is the subject, not *apartments.*)

Everybody on the list of celebrities was at the party. (*Everybody* is the subject, not *celebrities.*)

Each of the twins does her own homework. (*Each* is the subject, not *twins.*)

However, the words *some, any, all, none,* and *most* are exceptions to this rule of ignoring prepositional phrases. These words can be singular or plural, depending on the words that follow them in prepositional phrases. Again, we have labeled only the verbs that must agree with the subjects.

Some of the *information* is helpful.

Some of the *facts* are convincing.

Does any of the *furniture* come with the apartment?

Do any of the *chairs* and *tables* come with the apartment?

All of her *work* has been published.

All of her *poems* have been published.

None of the *jewelry* was missing.

None of the *jewels* were missing.

On July 4th, most of the *country* celebrates with a picnic or a party.

On July 4th, most of the *citizens* celebrate with a picnic or a party.

When a sentence has more than one subject joined by *and,* the subject is plural:

The teacher *and* the tutors eat lunch at noon.

A doughnut *and* a bagel were sitting on the plate.

However, when two subjects are joined by *or,* then the subject *closest* to the verb determines the verb form:

Either the teacher *or* the *tutors* eat lunch at noon.

Either the tutors *or* the *teacher* eats lunch at noon.

A doughnut *or* a *bagel* was sitting on the plate.

In most sentences, the subject comes before the verb. However, in some cases, the subject follows the verb, and subject-verb agreement needs special attention. Study the following examples:

Over the building flies a solitary flag. (flag flies)

Over the building fly several flags. (flags fly)

There is a good reason for that deadline. (reason is)

There are good reasons for that deadline. (reasons are)

EXERCISES

Circle the correct verbs in parentheses to maintain subject-verb agreement in the following sentences. Remember to ignore prepositional phrases, unless the subjects are *some, any, all, none,* or *most.* Check your answers after the first exercise.

Exercise 1

1. There (is, are) a Web site that (has, have) been rating movies since 1997 based on how accurately they (portray, portrays) the laws of physics.

2. "Insultingly Stupid Movie Physics" (is, are) the name of the site.

3. Examples of bad physics in movies (include, includes) bullets that (spark, sparks) on contact and laser beams that (is, are) visible to the naked eye.

4. The reviewers at Intuitor.com (give, gives) movies one of the following ratings: GP, PGP, PGP-13, RP, XP, or NR.

5. These labels (rank, ranks) the physics in a particular movie from "good physics" [GP] to "pretty good physics" [PGP] to "totally unbelievable physics" [XP], such as those in *Star Trek 2009, Armageddon*, and *Avatar*.

6. The recent classic films *Titanic, Casino Royale*, and *The Terminator* (has, have) all received GP or PGP ratings.

7. A movie that (get, gets) the PGP-13 rating—such as *King Kong* in 2005—is one that (has, have) flaws in portraying the laws of physics, but the movie (is, are) so convincing that it may lead children to believe that it (is, are) scientifically accurate.

8. The NR label (signify, signifies) that movies like *The Hulk* and *Spider-Man* (is, are) "not rated" because of their obvious focus on imaginative, not scientific, possibilities.

9. RP, the lowest of the site's ratings, (is, are) given to movies with such bad physics that they (make, makes) the reviewers "retch."

10. The RP rating (has, have) been given to *10,000 BC, The Abyss, Independence Day*, and to two of *The Matrix* movies.

Source: http://www.intuitor.com/moviephysics/

Exercise 2

1. An old rhyme about sneezing (give, gives) a sneeze on each day of the week special meaning.

2. The poem (sound, sounds) a lot like the one that (begin, begins) "Monday's child (is, are) full of woe."

3. This poem about sneezing also (connect, connects) Monday with a negative outcome.

4. It (say, says) that a sneeze on Monday (mean, means) "danger."

5. A Tuesday sneeze (forecast, forecasts) a meeting with a "stranger."

6. Wednesday and Thursday (is, are) days when sneezes (mean, means) we will receive a "letter" or "something better," respectively.

7. There (is, are) no TGIF celebrations for sneezes on Friday, for they (foretell, foretells) "sorrow."

8. But a sneeze on Saturday (mean, means) the visit of a loved one "tomorrow."

9. Sunday sneezes (is, are) left out of the poem altogether.

10. Such day-of-the-week rhymes from the past (seem, seems) to reveal a lot about us.

Source: *Schott's Original Miscellany* (Bloomsbury, 2003)

Exercise 3

1. There (is, are) new risks for kids in this technological age; these risks primarily (involve, involves) their wrists.

2. Many adults already (suffer, suffers) from carpal tunnel syndrome.

3. And now children (is, are) also coming down with similar conditions, called repetitive stress injuries (RSIs).

4. From the use of computers and video games (come, comes) unnatural body positions that (lead, leads) to health problems.

5. The child's wrists, neck, and back (start, starts) to hurt or feel numb after he or she (work, works) or (play, plays) on the computer for a long time.

6. The problem (start, starts) with computer furniture.

7. The chairs, desks, and screens (is, are) usually not at the proper height to be used comfortably by children.

8. Straining and repetition often (cause, causes) reduced circulation and even nerve damage.

9. Often RSI damage to the wrists (is, are) irreversible.

10. Experts in the field of RSI (warn, warns) parents to teach children how to avoid these injuries.

Source: *healthychildren.org* ("Repetitive Stress Injury")

Exercise 4

1. Many people (is, are) trying to find ways to save fuel and lower the emissions from cars.

2. Robin Chase (has, have) created a carpooling Web site called GoLoco.org.

3. GoLoco.org's design and mission (is, are) simple.

4. Its design (is, are) the same as other social-networking sites.

5. Its mission (involve, involves) filling cars with passengers so that the gas, expenses, and emissions (is, are) not wasted on just one person.

6. Potential carpoolers (enter, enters) their information at the site.

7. Members' information (include, includes) such things as musical preferences, languages spoken, and even recordings of their voices.

8. Passengers (set, sets) up accounts, and drivers (receive, receives) payments through the site for each trip with members on board.

9. This carpooling method (has, have) become an especially popular way to travel to sporting events and concerts since all of the riders (has, have) the same interest in seeing the event and saving the planet.

10. Of course, one of the most popular benefits (is, are) the time saved by using carpool lanes.

Source: The Boston Globe, April 23, 2007

Exercise 5

1. A group of scientists (is, are) looking into the sensation that we (call, calls) déjà vu.

2. Déjà vu (is, are) the feeling that we (is, are) repeating an experience that (has, have) happened in exactly the same way before.

3. Part of the odd sensation (is, are) that we (is, are) aware of the illogical part of déjà vu while it (is, are) happening.

4. Scientists (has, have) developed a new profile of a person who (is, are) likely to experience this particular sensation.

5. People who (is, are) most prone to déjà vu (is, are) between fifteen and twenty-five years old.

6. Regardless of age, however, anyone who (experience, experiences) déjà vu probably (has, have) a vivid imagination.

7. Stress and fatigue (is, are) often factors because the mind (function, functions) differently under these conditions.

8. Education level and income also (determine, determines) a person's susceptibility to déjà vu.

9. The phenomenon of déjà vu (seem, seems) to require an open mind.

10. Since political leanings (affect, affects) open-mindedness, liberals (tend, tends) to have more déjà vu experiences than conservatives.

Source: Psychology Today, March/April 2005

PROOFREADING EXERCISE

Find and correct the ten subject-verb agreement errors in the following paragraph.

Unfortunately, tension between members of the public are common these days. When two people at a movie theater irritates each other or have a disagreement, the whole audience suffer. Everyone who is sitting around the troublemakers want to move immediately to another section. However, if anyone get up to sit somewhere else, then everyone else start to get nervous. So most people just waits until one of the two fighting people calm down. After that, the members of the audience forgets about the disturbance and enjoy the rest of the movie. The same pattern repeat itself in stadiums and ballparks, too.

SENTENCE WRITING

Write ten sentences in which you describe the shoes that you are wearing today. Have fun writing about their smallest details! Use verbs in the *present* tense since they are the ones that can go wrong if they don't agree. As you write your sentences, underline the verbs twice and their subjects once. Then check these two parts carefully to be sure they agree. Refer to the explanations whenever necessary.

For example, you might write, "One of the laces on my left shoe is broken." After ignoring the prepositional phrases in this example, "(of the laces)(on my left shoe)," the subject and verb that must agree are "one is." The word "broken" is an adjective to describe "one of the laces on my left shoe." See page 109 for more about verbs used as adjectives.

And remember, whether you write about shoes or Shakespeare, your sentences will use similar patterns and structures. For example, in a literature class in the future, you might write, "One of the lines in Hamlet's speech is truncated" and know with confidence that your subject and verb agree!

Avoiding Shifts in Time

People often worry about using different time frames in writing. Let common sense guide you. If you begin writing a paper in past time, don't shift back and forth to the present unnecessarily; and if you begin in the present, don't shift to the past without good reason. In the following paragraph, the writer starts in the present and then shifts to the past, then shifts again to the present:

> In the novel *To Kill a Mockingbird,* Jean Louise Finch is a little girl who lives in the South with her father, Atticus, and her brother, Jem. Everybody in town calls Jean Louise "Scout" as a nickname. When Atticus, a lawyer, defended a black man against the charges of a white woman, some of their neighbors turned against him. Scout protected her father by appealing to the humanity of one member of the angry mob. In this chapter, five-year-old Scout turns out to be stronger than a group of adult men.

All the verbs should be in the present:

> In the novel *To Kill a Mockingbird,* Jean Louise Finch is a little girl who lives in the South with her father, Atticus, and her brother, Jem. Everybody in town calls Jean Louise "Scout" as a nickname. When Atticus, a lawyer, defends a black man against the charges of a white woman, some of their neighbors turn against him. Scout protects her father by appealing to the humanity of one member of the angry mob. In this chapter, five-year-old Scout turns out to be stronger than a group of adult men.

This sample paragraph discusses only the events that happen within the novel's plot, so it needs to maintain one time frame—the present, which we use to write about literature and repeated actions.

However, sometimes you will write about the present, the past, and even the future together. Then it may be necessary to use these different time frames within the same paragraph, each for its own reason. For example, if you were to give biographical information about Harper Lee, author of *To Kill a Mockingbird,* within a discussion of the novel and its influence, you might need to use all three time frames:

> Harper Lee grew up in Alabama, and she based elements in the book on experiences from her childhood. Like the character Atticus, Lee's father was a lawyer. She wrote the novel in his law offices. *To Kill a Mockingbird* is Harper Lee's most famous work, and it received the Pulitzer Prize for fiction in 1961. Lee's book turned fifty years old in the year 2010. It deals with the effects of prejudice unforgivingly, and it will always remain one of the most moving and compassionate novels in American literature.

The previous paragraph uses past (*grew, based, was, wrote, received, turned*), present (*is, deals*), and future (*will remain*) in the same paragraph without committing the error of unnecessary shifting. A shift in time occurs when the writer changes time frames *inconsistently* or *for no reason,* confusing the reader (as in the first example given).

PROOFREADING EXERCISES

Which of the following paragraphs shift *unnecessarily* back and forth between time frames? In those that do, change the verbs to maintain one time frame, thus making the entire paragraph read smoothly. One of the paragraphs is correct, even though it includes multiple time frames, because those time frames make sense.

1. Back in the early 1900s, Sears Roebuck sold houses through the mail. In the famous Sears catalog, these mail-order houses are listed along with the rest of the products. The house kits arrived in thousands of pieces, and people can put them together themselves, or they hire a builder to help them. In 1919, one company, Standard Oil, placed an order for an entire town's worth of homes for its employees. The house kits even include the paint that the homeowners use to paint the houses when they finish. The ability to order a whole house from the Sears catalog ended in 1940, but thousands of these houses are still standing in communities across America.

Source: CBS News Sunday Morning, May 18, 2003

2. No one knows for certain who the model for Leonardo da Vinci's *Mona Lisa* was. However, recent studies have discovered some new information. Dutch scientists used a computer program that is capable of "emotion recognition" to find out how the model felt at the time of the painting. Their results show that she was primarily happy. But her expression also registers tiny bits of anger, fear, and disgust. Another expert, Japanese forensic scientist Dr. Matsumi Suzuki, has created an actual voice for *Mona Lisa.* Using measurements of her head and hands,

Dr. Suzuki has determined that she was approximately five-and-a-half feet tall and had a deep voice. A recording of what Mona Lisa might have sounded like can be heard on the Web.

Source: Renaissance Magazine, Issue #50 (2006)

3. Plastic surgery helps many people look better and feel better about themselves. Of course, there were stories of unnecessary surgeries and even heartbreaking mistakes. People make their own decisions about whether plastic surgery was right for them. Dogs, however, can't communicate what they wanted. Nevertheless, some people took their dogs in for cosmetic surgeries, such as tummy tucks and face-lifts. Just like humans, dogs sometimes needed surgery to correct painful or unhealthy conditions. A dog with a low-hanging tummy could get an infection from scratches that were caused by rocks on the ground. And another dog may need a face-lift to help it stay clean when it ate. Animal lovers were worried that some canine plastic surgeries were done without good reasons.

Source: Newsweek, March 21, 2005

Recognizing Verbal Phrases

As explained in the previous sections, the main job of verbs and verb phrases is to join with subjects to form clauses, both independent and dependent. However, some forms of verbs get to take a vacation from their normal job and play a different part of speech in a sentence. When a verb acts as a noun, adjective, or adverb—*not a real verb*—in a sentence, it is called a *verbal*.

A verbal can act as a noun subject:

Skiing is my favorite sport. (*Skiing* is a noun. Here, it is the subject of the sentence, not the verb. The real verb in the sentence is *is*.)

A verbal can act as a noun object:

I like *to ski* during the winter. (*To ski* is a noun object; it is *what I like*. I could similarly write, "I like *cocoa* during the winter." The real verb in both sentences is *like,* and the two objects are *to ski,* a verbal as a noun, and *cocoa,* a regular noun.) For more about sentence patterns with objects, see page 138.

A verbal can act as an adjective:

My *bruised* ankle healed quickly. (*Bruised* is an adjective that describes the noun, ankle. The real verb in the sentence is *healed*.)

A verbal can also act as an adverb:

My ankle swelled quickly, *doubling* in size. (*Doubling* is an adverb, adding to the verb *swelled*.)

Verbals also link up with other words to form *verbal phrases*. To see the difference between a real verb phrase and a verbal phrase, look at these two sentences:

I was bowling with my best friends. (*Bowling* is the main verb in a verb phrase. Along with the helping verb *was,* it shows the action of the sentence.)

I enjoyed *bowling* with my best friends. (Here the real verb is *enjoyed*. *Bowling* is not the verb; it is the object, and it links up with a prepositional phrase to form a verbal phrase—*bowling with my best friends*—which is the whole *activity* I *enjoyed*.)

THREE KINDS OF VERBALS

1. *ing* verbs used without helping verbs, such as *running, thinking,* and *baking*
2. verbs in the *to* ____ form, such as *to walk, to eat,* and *to educate*
3. *ed, en,* or *t* forms (past participles) such as *tossed, taken,* and *lost*

Look at the following sentences using all of the examples from the box on page 125 as verbals and verbal phrases:

Running is great exercise. (real verb = is)

She spent two hours *thinking of a title for her essay.* (real verb = spent)

We had such fun *baking those cherry vanilla cupcakes.* (real verb = had)

I like *to walk around the zoo by myself.* (real verb = like)

To eat exotic foods takes courage. (real verb = takes)

They wanted *to educate themselves.* (real verb = wanted)

He *served* us a *tossed* salad with artichoke hearts. (real verb = served)

Taken in Spanish, the class made even more sense to me. (real verb = made)

I found my *lost* watch on the windowsill. (real verb = found)

EXERCISES

Each of the following sentences contains at least one verbal or verbal phrase. Double underline the real verbs or verb phrases and put brackets around the verbals and verbal phrases. Locate the verbals first (*winning, graded, to sleep . . .*) and include any word(s) that go with them (*winning a race, graded online, to sleep through the night*). Remember that real verbs will never be inside verbal phrases. Check your answers after each set to make the most progress.

Example: They tried [to help] by [cooking a meal of [frozen] leftovers].

Exercise 1

1. Mark Twain lived to become one of the most admired Americans of his time.

2. Traveling across the U.S. and to countries around the world, Twain formed unwavering opinions, both favorable and unfavorable, of the people and places he visited.

3. Twain began to write his autobiography in the last years before he died in 1910.

4. Hoping to be honest and thorough, he decided to dictate his thoughts as they struck him.

5. However, he knew that it might be impossible to be as honest as he wanted to be.

6. Being truthful meant including statements that could hurt or upset the people that he knew, and he knew almost everyone.

7. Twain thought of a way to avoid causing that potential pain or embarrassment.

8. He decided not to publish his autobiography until 100 years after his death.

9. In that way, Twain did not need to hold back any of his strong opinions.

10. In 2010, the first volume of *The Autobiography of Mark Twain* was finally released, making it one of the most anticipated books of all time.

Source: http://www.nytimes.com/2010/07/10/books/10twain.html

Exercise 2

1. The idea of home-schooling children has become more popular recently.

2. Many parents have decided to teach kids themselves instead of sending them to public or private school.

3. There are many different reasons to choose home-schooling.

4. In Hollywood, for instance, child actors often must use home-schooling due to their schedules.

5. The home-schooling option allows for one of their parents, or a special teacher, to continue to instruct them on the set.

6. Other parents simply want to be directly involved in their child's learning.

7. Many school districts have special independent study "schools," offering parents the structure and materials that they need to provide an appropriate curriculum on their own.

8. Children do all of their reading and writing at home, with their parents guiding them along the way.

9. The family meets with the independent study school's teacher regularly to go over the child's work and to clarify any points of confusion.

10. Many parents would like to have the time to home-school their children.

Source: http://www.lausd.net/City_of_Angels/programhighlights.html

Exercise 3

1. Philippe Halsman was a well-known portrait photographer working in the twentieth century.

2. Halsman's photographs were good enough to appear on the cover of *Life* magazine 101 times.

3. Capturing the essence of famous people on film was Halsman's specialty.

4. The list of celebrities that Halsman was asked to photograph included Marilyn Monroe, Albert Einstein, and Winston Churchill.

5. Halsman found that taking good pictures of such powerful people was not easy.

6. He often tried to find new ways to loosen them up.

7. In 1952, Halsman asked one of his elite clients to jump in the air while being photographed.

8. Halsman loved the results, and he started a series of jumping pictures.

9. Who doesn't like to see famous people like Richard Nixon jumping up like a little boy in a photograph?

10. Halsman gathered the best of the jumping photographs in a book called *Philippe Halsman's Jump Book*.

Source: Smithsonian, October 2006

Exercise 4

1. Some travelers want to know how to behave in other countries.

2. *Behave Yourself!* is a book written to help such people.

3. It outlines what to do and what not to do in different countries around the world.

4. In Austria, for example, cutting your food with a fork is more polite than cutting it with a knife.

5. In Egypt, nodding the head upward—not shaking the head from side to side—means "no."

6. In the Netherlands, complimenting people about their clothes is not a good idea.

7. An Italian diner will fold lettuce into a bite-size piece with the fork and knife instead of cutting it.

8. A common mistake that people make in many countries is to stand with their hands on their hips.

9. This posture and pointing at anything with the fingers are thought to be very rude and even threatening.

10. Travelers should study any country before visiting it in order to avoid confusing or offending anyone.

Source: *Behave Yourself!* (Globe Pequot, 2005)

Exercise 5

1. John Steinbeck, author of *The Grapes of Wrath,* was the first native of California to receive the Nobel Prize for literature.

2. Calling his hometown of Salinas "Lettuceberg," Steinbeck's writing made the area famous.

3. At the time, not everyone liked the attention brought by his portrayals of life in *Cannery Row* and other works.

4. Steinbeck's father was the treasurer of Monterey County for ten years, working also for the Spreckels company.

5. John Steinbeck tried to find satisfaction in his birthplace, enrolling in and quitting his studies at Stanford University many times.

6. Finally, Steinbeck moved to New York, distancing himself from his California roots.

7. Steinbeck won the Nobel Prize in 1962, revealing the literary world's esteem for his work.

8. Not writing anything of the caliber of the Salinas stories while living in New York, Steinbeck did return to California before he died in 1968.

9. In 1972, the Salinas library changed its name, to be known thereafter as the John Steinbeck Library.

10. The house Steinbeck was born in became a restaurant and then a full-fledged museum chronicling the life of Salinas' most celebrated citizen.

Source: *California People* (Peregrine Smith, 1982)

PARAGRAPH EXERCISE

Double underline the real verbs or verb phrases, and put brackets around the verbals and verbal phrases in the following paragraphs from the popular book *An Incomplete Education: 3,684 Things You Should Have Learned but Probably Didn't,* by Judy Jones and William Wilson.

CHRISTO AND JEANNE-CLAUDE (1935-, 1935-)

It started as an obsession with wrapping. The Bulgarian-born artist Christo spent years swaddling bicycles, trees, storefronts, and women friends before moving on to wrap a section of the Roman Wall, part of the Australian coastline, and eventually all twelve arches, plus the parapets, sidewalks, streetlamps, vertical embankment, and esplanade, of Paris' Pont Neuf. And yes, together they did wrap the Reichstag. But Christo and his wife/manager/collaborator Jeanne-Claude are quick to insist that wrappings form only a small percentage of their total oeuvre. There were, for instance, those twenty-four and a half miles of white nylon, eighteen feet high, they hung from a steel cable north of San Francisco; the eleven islands in Biscayne Bay, Florida, they "surrounded"—not wrapped, mind you—with pink polypropylene fabric; and the 3,100 enormous blue and yellow "umbrellas" they erected in two corresponding valleys in California and Japan. Not to mention their 2005 blockbuster, "The Gates," 7,503 sixteen-foot-tall saffron panels they suspended, to the delight of almost everybody, over twenty-three miles of footpaths in New York's Central Park.

So, what's their point? Rest assured, you're not the first to ask. And no one is more eager to tell you than the artist formerly known as Christo (now, officially, "Christo and Jeanne-Claude") whose art is nothing if not Open to the Public.

In fact, taking art public—that is, taking it away from the Uptown Museum Gallery Complex by making it too big to fit in studios, museums, or galleries—was part of the original idea. Christo and Jeanne-Claude will tell you that their point is, literally, to rock your world. By temporarily disrupting one part of an environment, they hope to get you to "perceive the whole environment with new eyes and a new consciousness."

SENTENCE WRITING

Write ten sentences that contain verbal phrases. Use the ten verbals listed here to begin your verbal phrases: *thinking, folding, skiing, marking, to take, to get, to paste, to exercise, planned, given.* The last two may seem particularly difficult to use as verbals. You'll find sample sentences listed in the Answers. But first, try to write your own sentences containing verbals so that you can compare the two.

Correcting Misplaced or Dangling Modifiers

To modify something means to change whatever it is, usually by adding to it. You might modify a normal car, for example, by adding a special roof rack. In English, *modifiers* are words, phrases, and clauses working as adjectives and adverbs to *add* information to part of a sentence. To do its job properly, a modifier must be in the right spot—as close to the word(s) it adds something to as possible. Putting a roof rack underneath the car instead of where it belongs would cause the roof rack to be *misplaced*. In the following example, the verbal phrase *Swinging from tree to tree* is too far away from the word that it modifies, *monkeys*. The phrase seems to describe Jonathan instead. Therefore, like our misplaced roof rack under the car, *Swinging from tree to tree* is a *misplaced modifier* in this sentence:

Swinging from tree to tree, Jonathan watched the monkeys at the zoo.

To correct this misplaced modifier, move it so that it's right next to the monkeys.

At the zoo, Jonathan watched the monkeys swinging from tree to tree.

In the next example, there is no word for the phrase *At the age of eight* to modify:

At the age of eight, my family finally bought a dog.

Obviously, the family was not eight when it bought a dog. And the dog was not eight. *At the age of eight* is a *dangling modifier* with no word to attach itself to, no word for it to modify. To correct this dangling modifier, we can change it to *When I was eight,* a dependent clause with its own subject and verb.

When I was eight, my family finally bought a dog.

Now the meaning of the whole sentence is clear. Here's another dangling modifier:

The train pulled into the station after a two-hour nap.

Can you identify the dangling modifier? You're right if you think it is *after a two-hour nap*. Did the train or the station take a two-hour nap? Who did? Here is a correction with the addition of *I took,* a subject and verb to clarify who took the nap:

The train pulled into the station after I took a two-hour nap.

E X E R C I S E S

Carefully rephrase any of the following sentences that contain misplaced or dangling modifiers. Note that many misplaced and dangling modifiers sound comical because of the confusion about what's happening in the sentence. Some sentences are correct.

Exercise 1

1. I noticed an iPad on the ground walking to my car.
2. They located the auditorium by asking a security guard for directions.
3. Full of 360-degree loops, people will wait for hours to ride the new roller coaster.
4. Being just six years old, the flight attendant helped the little boy find his seat.
5. As soon as the tutor stopped talking, the students started asking questions.
6. We have found several travel bargains shopping on the Internet.
7. Hidden by the long curtains, Angelica finally spotted her lost keys.
8. After getting help from a specialist, her knee began to improve.
9. With a low-cost data plan, I can't use my phone very often to go online.
10. Faded from direct sunlight, students couldn't read the bulletin board.

Exercise 2

1. Loaded with explosions and special effects, the new movie is a hit.
2. Before asking for an extension, the teacher gave us a few extra days to turn in our papers.
3. They spotted a hawk and its babies looking through their binoculars.
4. After I finished my audition, the director released everyone else.
5. I called the doctor on the roof.
6. We sat on the lawn and waited for further instructions on how to prune the roses.

7. Screeching to a stop, I got on the bus and grabbed a seat.

8. Without pickles, I can't eat a hamburger.

9. Given as a token of friendship, that ring means a lot to me.

10. We had to write a paragraph about the weather in our notebooks.

Exercise 3

1. Lying under the table for a week, they finally found their lost credit card.

2. She located the door to the auditorium walking down the hall.

3. They bought a hammer at the hardware store.

4. After taking an aspirin, my doctor told me to drink extra water.

5. He always brings a calculator to school in his backpack.

6. Our mail carrier tripped and fell on a crack in the sidewalk.

7. Arguing nonstop, the road trip was not as much fun as we hoped it would be.

8. Now that she has finished her math classes, she can focus on her major.

9. Seeing her new granddaughter's picture for the first time, our mother cried.

10. Smiling nicely at everyone, the students immediately liked their substitute teacher.

Exercise 4

1. Taken before surgery, that medicine can help your recovery.

2. Filled with the perfect amount of air, I enjoyed the way the new tires made my car handle on the road.

3. After three weeks of waiting, the textbooks that I bought online finally arrived.

4. He cooked all of his meals in his slippers.

5. The class watched the video with the door open.

6. While driving past the park, a ball bounced into the street between two parked cars.

7. Torn into tiny pieces, I didn't even want the scraps of that quiz paper near me.

8. I will take the test again tomorrow.

9. Trying to look happy, the runner-up applauded too loudly.

10. Walking in the cracks of the sidewalk, I saw an army of ants.

Exercise 5

1. Feeling the thrill of a day at the amusement park, my blisters didn't bother me.

2. Full of touching scenes, my friends and I saw the new tearjerker.

3. My classmates and I always turned our essays in on time.

4. Practicing for an hour a day, her piano has improved.

5. Gasoline prices fluctuate with politics.

6. Sitting on a bench all day, an idea came to her.

7. On the road to their cousins' house, they discovered a new outlet mall.

8. He felt the pressure of trying to get a good job from his parents.

9. I enjoy talking to new people at parties.

10. Written in chalk, the notes on the board were hard to read.

PROOFREADING EXERCISE

Find and correct any misplaced or dangling modifiers in the following paragraph.

I love parades, so last year my family and I traveled to Pasadena, California, to see one of the biggest parades of all—the Tournament of Roses Parade on New Year's Day. It turned out to be even more wonderful than I expected.

Arriving one day early, the city was already crowded with people. Lots of families were setting up campsites on Colorado Boulevard by nightfall. We didn't want to miss one float in the parade, so we found our own spot and made ourselves at home. When the parade began, I had as much fun watching the spectators as the parade itself. I saw children pointing at the breathtaking horses and floats sitting on their fathers' shoulders. Decorated completely with flowers or plant material, I couldn't believe how beautiful the floats were and how good they smelled.

The crowd was overwhelmed by the sights and sounds of the parade. Marching and playing their instruments with perfect precision, everyone especially enjoyed hearing the school bands. They must have practiced for the whole year to be that good.

My experience didn't end with the parade, however. After the last float had passed by, I found a twenty dollar bill walking down Colorado Boulevard. Now hanging on my wall at home, I framed it as a souvenir of my trip to the Rose Parade.

SENTENCE WRITING

Write five sentences that contain misplaced or dangling modifiers; then revise those sentences to put the modifiers where they belong or to clarify their meaning. Use the examples in the explanations as models. For more practice, exchange papers with another student and correct each other's misplaced or dangling modifiers.

Following Sentence Patterns

Sentences are built according to a few basic patterns. For proof, rearrange each of the following sets of words to form a complete statement (not a question):

apples a ate raccoon the

classes have many together taken we

your in am partner I lab the

school was to she walking

in wonderful you look scrubs

There are only one or two possible combinations for each due to English sentence patterns. Either *A raccoon ate the apples,* or *The apples ate a raccoon,* and so on. But in each case, the verb or verb phrase makes its way to the middle of the statement, and the nouns and pronouns take their places as subjects and objects.

To understand sentence patterns, you need to know that every verb performs one of three jobs. Note that the focus is on the *double-underlined* verbs below.

The Three Jobs of Verbs

1. Verbs can show actions:

A raccoon ate the apples.

We have taken many classes together.

She was walking to school.

2. Verbs can link subjects with nouns, pronouns, or adjectives that describe them:

I am your partner in the lab.

You look wonderful in scrubs.

3. Verbs can help other verbs form verb phrases:

We have taken many classes together. (Without the help of *have,* the main verb would be *take* or *took.*)

She was walking to school. (Without *was,* the main verb would be *walked.*)

Look at these sentences for more examples:

> Mel grabbed a scholarship application. (The verb *grabbed* shows Mel's action.)

> His pen was empty. (The verb *was* links *pen* with its description as *empty.*)

> Mel had been waiting for his grades. (The verbs *had* and *been* help the main verb *waiting* in a verb phrase.)

Knowing the three jobs a verb can perform will help you gain an understanding of the three basic sentence patterns:

SUBJECT + ACTION VERB + OBJECT PATTERN

Some action verbs must be followed by an object (a person, place, thing, or idea) that receives the action.

> S   AV   Obj
> Sylvia completed her degree. (*Sylvia completed* makes no sense unless it is followed by the object that she completed—*her degree.*)

SUBJECT + ACTION VERB (+ NO OBJECT) PATTERN

At other times, the action verb itself completes the meaning and needs no object after it.

> S   AV
> She celebrated at home with her family. (*She celebrated* makes sense alone.
> It does not need the two prepositional phrases—*at home* and *with her family,* which simply tell where and how she celebrated.)

SUBJECT + LINKING VERB + DESCRIPTION PATTERN

A special kind of verb that does *not* show an action is called a *linking verb.* The linking verb acts like an equal sign in a sentence: "I am student" means "I = a student" means "A student = I." These verbs link the subject with a word that describes the subject. The description can be a noun, a pronoun, or an adjective. Learn to recognize the most common linking verbs: *is, am, are, was, were, seem, feel, appear, become,* and *look.* Even the verbs *taste* and *smell* can be linking verbs at times.

> S LV   Desc
> Sylvia is a natural writer. (*Sylvia* equals *a natural writer.*)

> S   LV   Desc
> Sylvia seems very happy. (*Very happy* describes *Sylvia.*)

> **NOTE**—As explained on page 93, a verb phrase includes a main verb and its helping verbs. Note that helping verbs can help main verbs in any of the sentence patterns.

      S   AV

Sylvia is moving to Seattle. (Here the verb *is* does not link Sylvia with a description but helps the verb *moving,* an action verb with no object followed by the prepositional phrase *to Seattle.*)

The following chart outlines the patterns using short easy-to-memorize examples:

THREE BASIC SENTENCE PATTERNS

S   +   AV   +   Obj

Stephanie adopted a dog.

S + AV + (no object)

The dog barks (at strangers).

S + LV +   Desc

The dog is a mixed breed.

The dog looks sweet and harmless.

These are the basic patterns, the grammatical backbone, for most of the clauses used in English sentences. Knowing them can help you control your sentences and improve your phrasing.

EXERCISES

First, put parentheses around any prepositional phrases in the following sentences. Next, underline the verbs or verb phrases twice and their subjects once. Then mark the correct sentence pattern above the words: S + AV + Obj, S + AV, or S + LV + Desc. Remember that these patterns *never* mix or overlap. For example, you won't find "She took tall," which mixes an action verb (AV) with a description of the subject (Desc). However, if there are two clauses, each one may have a different pattern. Check your answers after each set to make the most progress.

Exercise 1

1. Sleep is an important part of life.

2. Animals and humans use sleep as a vacation for their brains and bodies.

3. Some facts about sleep might surprise people.

4. Large animals require less sleep than small animals do.

5. A typical cat will sleep for twelve hours in a day.

6. An ordinary elephant will sleep for only three hours.

7. Smaller animals use their brains and bodies at higher rates.

8. Therefore, they need many hours of sleep.

9. The reverse is true for large animals.

10. Humans fall between cats and elephants for their sleep requirements.

Exercise 2

1. Erasto Mpemba is a big name in science.

2. In the early 1960s, he observed an odd phenomenon.

3. At the time, he was a high school student in Tanzania.

4. Mpemba made ice cream for a school project.

5. He boiled the milk and mixed it with the other ice cream ingredients.

6. Then he put this boiling hot mixture directly into the freezer.

7. He discovered that the hot liquid froze very fast.

8. Mpemba told his teachers and fellow students about his discovery.

9. They laughed at the idea of hot liquid freezing quickly.

10. Now all scientists call this phenomenon the "Mpemba effect."

Sources: Current Science, September 8, 2006, and *physicsweb.org,* April 2006

Exercise 3

1. In late September, the Stade de France in Paris hosted an unusual spectacle.
2. Hundreds of actors, stunt people, and extras reenacted the famous chariot race from the classic film *Ben-Hur*.
3. The same show included live gladiator fights and a galley ship assault.
4. Promoters also encouraged participation from the audience.
5. Many of the 60,000 audience members attended in traditional Roman costumes.
6. The stadium sold toga-like robes in advance along with the tickets.
7. Obviously, the live chariot race was the highlight of the show.
8. Participants in the dangerous race rehearsed for nine months.
9. The chariot race lasted for fifteen minutes.
10. It was the final event of the night.

Source: npr.org, Weekend Edition Saturday, September 23, 2006

Exercise 4

1. Horatio Greenough was a sculptor in the 1800s.
2. Greenough created a controversial statue of George Washington.
3. The statue weighed twelve tons, but its weight was not the reason for the controversy.
4. The controversial aspect of the statue involved Washington's clothes.
5. The statue portrayed Washington in a toga-like garment.
6. His stomach, chest, and arms were bare and very muscular.
7. One part of the toga draped over the statue's raised right arm.
8. The bare-chested statue of Washington stood in the rotunda of the Capitol for only three years.
9. Officials moved the statue many times.
10. In 1962, it arrived in its final home at the American History Museum.

Source: Smithsonian, February 2005

Exercise 5

1. Charles Osgood is a writer, TV host, and radio personality.
2. He is also the editor of a book about letters.
3. The book's title is *Funny Letters from Famous People.*
4. In his book, Osgood shares hilarious letters from history.
5. Thomas Jefferson wrote to an acquaintance about rodents eating his wallet.
6. Benjamin Franklin penned the perfect recommendation letter.
7. Franklin did not know the recommended fellow at all.
8. Beethoven cursed his friend bitterly in a letter one day.
9. In a letter the following day, Beethoven praised the same friend excessively and asked him for a visit.
10. Osgood ends the book with a letter by Julia Child; it includes her secrets for a long life.

Source: Funny Letters from Famous People (Three Rivers Press, 2004)

PARAGRAPH EXERCISE

Label the sentence patterns in the following paragraph from the book *The First Men on the Moon: The Story of Apollo 11,* by David M. Harland. It helps to put parentheses around prepositional phrases first to isolate them from the words that make up the sentence patterns—the subjects, the verbs, and any objects after action verbs or any descriptive words after linking verbs (*is, was, were, seem, appear,* and so on). This paragraph describes Neil Armstrong's first moments on the moon.

Armstrong released his grip on the handrail of the ladder and stepped fully off the foot pad. Walter Cronkite proudly told his CBS audience that a 38-year-old American was now standing on the surface of the Moon. When Armstrong scraped his foot across the surface, he noticed that the dark powdery material coated his overshoe. "The surface is fine and powdery. I can kick it up loosely with my toe. It adheres in fine layers like powdery charcoal to the sole and sides of my boots." Although his boots only slightly impressed the surface, the material preserved the imprint of his boots very well. "I only go in a small fraction of an inch—maybe one-eighth of an inch—but I can see the prints of my boots and the treads in the fine, sandy particles."

SENTENCE WRITING

Using Neil Armstrong's descriptions of the moon's surface as models, write ten sentences describing the weather today and how it feels to be living in it. Keep the sentences short to allow your sentence patterns to flow naturally. Then find and label the sentence patterns you have used. For extra practice, exchange papers with another student and label each other's sentence patterns.

Avoiding Clichés, Awkward Phrasing, and Wordiness

CLICHÉS

A *cliché* is an expression that has been used so often it has lost its originality and effectiveness. Whoever first referred to the most important result of something as "the bottom line" had thought of an original way to express it, but today that expression is worn out. Most of us use occasional clichés when speaking, but in writing, clichés are missed opportunities to express an idea or detail in your own way.

Here are a few examples of clichés. Think of more you could add to the list:

too little too late

older but wiser

last but not least

in this day and age

different as night and day

out of this world

white as a ghost

sick as a dog

tried and true

at the top of his lungs

the thrill of victory

one in a million

busy as a bee

easier said than done

better late than never

Clichés lack freshness because the reader always knows what's coming next. Can you complete these expressions?

the agony of . . .

breathe a sigh of . . .

lend a helping . . .

odds and . . .

raining cats and . . .

as American as . . .

been there . . .

worth its weight . . .

Clichés are expressions that too many people use. Try to avoid them in your writing.

AWKWARD PHRASING

Unlike clichés, the problem of *awkward phrasing* comes from writing sentence structures that *no one* else would use because they break basic sentence patterns, omit necessary words, or use combinations of words without clear meaning. Like clichés, awkward sentences might *sound* acceptable when spoken, but not when written. Here is an example:

> There should be greater efforts (in communication) (between students and their academic advisors).

Who is doing *what* here? Efforts should be? The words that could form a much better clause are hiding in prepositional phrases: *students, communication,* and *advisors*. Here's the sentence again after revision to eliminate the awkward phrasing:

> Students and their advisors should communicate more often.

Basically, awkward phrasing results in sentences that leave readers wondering:

> During the experiment, the use of key principles was essential to ensure the success of it.

Similar to the previous example, these sixteen words don't actually say very much because the phrasing of *the use. . . was essential to ensure* makes little sense. What do you think it is trying to say? Here is a revision to clarify one possible meaning:

> To ensure success, we carefully followed key principles in the experiment.

WORDINESS

Good writing is concise writing. Effective writers don't use twenty words if they can say it better in ten. "In today's society" isn't as effective as "today," and it's a cliché. "At this point in time" could be "presently" or "now." For proof, look at a piece of writing that you have recently enjoyed reading. You'll find that most of its sentences are relatively short. When a longer sentence shows up, it's there for a good reason.

One kind of wordiness comes from saying something twice. There's no need to write "in the month of August" or "9 a.m. in the morning" or "my personal opinion." August *is* a month, 9 a.m *is* morning, and everyone's opinion *is* personal. All you need to write is "in August," "9 a.m.," and "my opinion."

Another type of wordiness comes from using words that add nothing to the meaning of the sentence. "The point is that we can't afford it" says no more than "We can't afford it." Here is a sample wordy sentence:

The construction company worked long and hard on that building, off and on, for a period of six full months.

And here it is after eliminating the extra words:

The construction company worked on that building intermittently for six months.

Of course, naming the *construction company* and *that building* would be even better. Including real details in your sentences is often the best way to avoid wordiness.

WORDY WRITING	CONCISE WRITING
advance planning	planning
an unexpected surprise	a surprise
at a later date	later
basic fundamentals	fundamentals
green in color	green
but nevertheless	but (or nevertheless)
combine together	combine
completely empty	empty
down below	below
end result	result
fewer in number	fewer
free gift	gift
in order to	to
in spite of the fact that	although
large in size	large
new innovation	innovation
on a regular basis	regularly
past history	history
rectangular in shape	rectangular
refer back	refer
repeat again	repeat
serious crisis	crisis
sufficient enough	sufficient (or enough)
there in person	there
two different kinds	two kinds
very unique	unique

PROOFREADING EXERCISES

The following student paragraphs contain examples of clichés, awkward phrasing, and wordiness. Revise the paragraphs so that they are concise examples of Standard Written English. When you're done, compare your revisions with the sample answers.

1. I've been trying to help my small son finish his first-grade homework every night, but that's easier said than done. Of course, I think that he is the smartest kid in the world, but getting him to show it takes a lot of hard work. When I do get him to sit down in front of his workbooks, he will work for a few minutes on them and then run off as soon as my back is turned. I try to tell him that when I was his age, I got in big trouble if I didn't do my homework. Unfortunately, my son's teacher just doesn't give him a sticker for that day if he doesn't do his. Stickers don't do the trick as motivators. I hope with all my heart that my son will learn the value of keeping up in school.

2. In today's society, many shoppers at the supermarkets are on the lookout for organic meats, fruits, and vegetables. In fact, they don't draw the line at fresh foods; these same shoppers' eyes light up whenever they see an organic label on a box, can, or any other package. I know this for a fact since I work as an employee at the supermarket in the middle of the busiest section of town. It's not only people with a lot of money that want the foods grown without pesticides and hormones. It's just about everybody that walks in the door. I guess that what's going on is that people are taking a good long look at their lives and caring about their children's eating habits too. I do have to admit that the organic eggs I buy taste pretty good when you get right down to it. Knowing that the eggs come from happy, free-ranging chickens makes me feel good about eating them. Of course, the bottom line for some people will always be price. If organic foods cost more than traditionally grown foods, some of the shoppers are going to keep passing them by on the supermarket shelves.

3. I have a friend who used to be one of those struggling actors who couldn't find a steady job, but now she has become a professional house sitter, and it has really paid off in more ways than one. First of all, she joined a house sitters' organization that is supposed to find out about all of the house-sitting opportunities that are available at any one time and match house sitters up with each of them. Then she landed her first house-sitting job at a house in Malibu. You're not going to believe this, but she got paid to live in a house on the beach in Malibu and even got her meals and movie rentals for free. All she had to do to do the job she was paid for was to watch out for the house and feed one cat. The cat was even an indoor cat. Now my friend is house sitting in Sedona, watching a house for friends of the same people who own the Malibu house. Well, I'll tell you, I want a job like that and am thinking seriously about trying it out for myself.

Correcting for Parallel Structure

Your writing will be clearer and more memorable if you use parallel structure. That is, when you write two pieces of information or any kind of list, put the items in similar form. Look at this sentence, for example:

My favorite movies are comedies, romantic, and sci-fi fantasies.

The sentence lacks parallel structure. The second item in the list, an adjective, doesn't match the other two, which are nouns. Here's a revision to make them parallel:

My favorite movies are comedies, love stories, and sci-fi fantasies.

Now the items are parallel; they are all nouns. Or you could write the following:

I like movies that make me laugh, make me cry, and make me wonder.

In this new sentence, the three items are parallel *predicates* (verbs and the words that go with them) within one dependent clause. Here are a few more examples. Note how much easier it is to read the sentences with parallel structure.

WITHOUT PARALLEL STRUCTURE	WITH PARALLEL STRUCTURE
I like hiking, skiing, and to go for a sail.	I like hiking, skiing, and sailing. (all *"ing"* verbals)
The office has run out of pens, paper, ink cartridges, and we need more toner, too.	The office needs more pens, paper, ink cartridges, and toner. (all nouns)
They decided that they needed a change, that they could afford a new house, and wanted to move to Arizona.	They decided that they needed a change, that they could afford a new house, and that they wanted to move to Arizona. (all dependent clauses)

The parts of an outline should always be parallel. Following are two brief outlines about food irradiation. The parts of the outline on the *left* are not parallel. The first subtopic (I.) is a question; the other (II.) is just a noun. And the supporting points (A., B., C.) are written as nouns, verbs, and even clauses. The parts of the outline on the *right* are parallel. Both subtopics (I. and II.) are plural nouns, and all details (A., B., C.) are action verbs followed by objects.

NOT PARALLEL	PARALLEL
Food Irradiation	Food Irradiation
I. How is it good?	I. Benefits
A. Longer shelf life	A. Extends shelf life
B. Using fewer pesticides	B. Requires fewer pesticides
C. Kills bacteria	C. Kills bacteria
II. Concerns	II. Concerns
A. Nutritional value	A. Lowers nutritional value
B. Consumers are worried	B. Alarms consumers
C. Workers' safety	C. Endangers workers

Using parallel structure will make your writing more effective. Note the parallelism in these well-known quotations:

A place for everything and everything in its place.

Isabella Mary Beeton

Ask not what your country can do for you; ask what you can do for your country.

John F. Kennedy

We hold these truths to be self-evident, that all men are created equal, that they are endowed by their creator with certain unalienable rights, that among these are Life, Liberty, and the pursuit of Happiness.

Thomas Jefferson

EXERCISES

In the following exercises, rephrase any sentences that do not contain parallel structures.

Exercise 1

1. Preparing for emergencies involves two steps: planning for anything and to gather certain supplies.

2. When planning for emergencies, ask yourself the following questions.

3. What kinds of emergencies have occurred or might occur in your area?

4. Where would you go, and what method of transportation would you use to get there?

5. Have you made a list of phone contacts within the area and outside it, too?

6. Do the adults, teenagers, and do the children in the family carry those phone numbers with them?

7. Are the most important supplies ready at hand, including water, food, flashlight, radio, and are there batteries as well?

8. Have you assembled your own first-aid kit, or maybe you have bought a ready-made one?

9. Do you stay prepared by reading and understanding your important insurance policies; also, do you remember to update them?

10. By planning for anything and if you stock up on the right supplies, you can prepare yourself and your family for emergencies.

Exercise 2

1. Taking driving lessons was exciting, but I also found it nerve-wracking.

2. At first, I learned how to start the car, steer it, and eventually how to make the car stop smoothly.

3. Between driving lessons, I studied the manual, watched videos about driving, and I even practiced the hand signals that people use in emergencies.

4. My instructors taught me, tested me, and were encouraging to me.

5. Each of my teachers had a special tip or two to share about driving.

6. Finally, my teachers decided that I had learned enough, and I was probably ready to take the test for my driver's license.

7. I arrived at the testing location, waited in the lobby for a few minutes, and then I heard someone call my name.

8. During the test, I changed lanes, made right and left turns, and even showed that I could parallel park like a professional driver.

9. The man who tested me said that I knew the rules and kept telling me that I must have had good teachers.

10. I got my driver's license and sent a box of chocolates to my driving school to thank everyone who helped me.

Exercise 3

1. The Internet is full of information about new gadgets and using the latest technology.

2. People want to have the coolest phones, the clearest photos, and travel accessories that are the best quality.

3. One of these high-tech inventions is a new kind of wedding ring.

4. The ring doesn't use technology to help people do something more easily or living more comfortably.

5. Instead, it helps people avoid doing something, and that is not to forget their anniversary.

6. The "Remember Ring" is designed for people who love gadgets, but they tend to forget special occasions.

7. It includes several hi-tech features: a perpetually charging battery, a clock run by a microchip, and a tiny element that heats up.

8. The built-in heating element activates at a preprogrammed time and reminding the wearer about an upcoming anniversary.

9. One day before the anniversary, the ring starts to heat up to 120 degrees for ten seconds once every hour.

10. The Remember Ring comes in seven styles in both white gold and the regular yellow kind.

Source: news.cnet.com, June 10, 2013

Exercise 4

Rephrase the following list to improve the use of parallel structures. The list includes instructions on how to begin searching for ancestors—in other words, how to create a "family tree." Try to maintain similar phrasing at the beginning of the instructions and in any pairs or lists within them.

1. To begin, decide which person or the family you want to focus on.

2. Making a blank chart that includes spaces for all of a person's important information will help.

3. Then visit a relative who knows a lot of family history and hopefully someone who saves papers and mementos.

4. You should plan to spend a lot of time with any such valuable resource.

5. It is best to gather information from one individual at a time and about one person.

6. Ask about every part of the person's life—marital status, children, believing in religion, working, and travel.

7. As you talk with your resources, thank them for providing you with valuable information.

8. Visit the attics or even going into the dusty old cupboards of anyone who has documents relating to your family.

9. Don't forget the local records office in the town where a relative grew up.

10. To make your family tree come together faster, you can purchase books that provide preprinted worksheets and family tree templates.

Exercise 5

Revise the following sentences to make them a list of clear suggestions using parallel structures. You may want to add transitions like *first* and *finally* to help make the steps clear.

1. Experts give the following tips to get the most out of a visit to the doctor.

2. Avoid getting frustrated after a long wait in the reception area or if you have to wait a long time in the exam room.

3. You should always answer the doctor's questions first; then asking the doctor your own questions might be a good idea.

4. It's smart to inquire about a referral to a specialist if you think you need one.

5. Finding out if there are other treatments besides the one the doctor first recommends can't hurt.

6. Ask about any tests that the doctor orders, and you might wonder what the results mean, so you probably want to get in touch with the doctor after the results come back.

7. Prescriptions are often given quickly and with little explanation, so ask about side effects and optional medicines if one doesn't work.

8. When discussing these things with your doctor, try not to be nervous.

9. The final step is to be prepared to wait in a long line at the pharmacy.

10. If you follow these suggestions when visiting a doctor, you will be more informed and also you can feel involved in your own treatment.

PROOFREADING EXERCISE

Proofread the following paragraph about William Shakespeare, and revise it to correct any errors in parallel structure.

The world knows relatively little about the life of William Shakespeare. Stanley Wells' book *Is It True What They Say about Shakespeare?* addresses the questions that people continue to have about the famous poet and playwright. Because of Shakespeare's talent and the reputation that his works have earned, everyone wants to know when he was born, the schools he went to, his travels, who his friends or lovers were, the way he looked, as well as the method and date he wrote each of his poems and plays. Wells starts with the basic question, "Is it true that . . .?" Throughout the book, he identifies commonly held beliefs about Shakespeare, discusses the historical evidence, and then he judges each belief to be "true," "untrue," or something in between. Wells even examines the numerous theories that someone else wrote the works of Shakespeare, but there is no evidence that he finds strong enough to convince him of their validity.

SENTENCE WRITING

Write ten sentences that include parallel structures. You may choose your own subject, or you may describe the process you go through (or tips that you could give someone else) when studying for an important test. Be sure to include pairs and lists of objects, actions, locations, or ideas.

Using Pronouns

Nouns name people, places, things, and ideas—such as *students, school, computers,* and *literacy. Pronouns* take the place of nouns to avoid repetition and to clarify meaning. The pronouns *they* or *them* could replace *students* and *computers;* the pronoun *it* could replace *school* and *literacy.* Personal pronouns that replace people's names or descriptions vary depending on gender and number.

Of the many kinds of pronouns, the personal pronouns cause the most difficulty because they often include two ways of identifying the same person (or people) as either a subject or an object. Although only one form is technically "correct" in a given situation, modern usage sometimes allows for relaxed adherence to these rules about subject and object pronouns.

SUBJECT GROUP	OBJECT GROUP
I	me
we	us
you	you
he	him
she	her
they	them
it	it

To follow standard rules, use a pronoun from the Subject Group in two instances:

1. Before a verb as a subject (even if the verb is missing at the end):

He is my cousin. (*He* is the subject of the verb *is.*)

He is older than *I.* (Here a second verb is missing at the end, but it is implied. The sentence means "*He is* older than *I am.*" *I* is the subject of the understood verb *am.*)

Whenever you see *than* used to compare two items in a sentence, ask yourself whether a verb has been left off the end of the sentence. Add the verb, and you'll automatically use the correct pronoun. Instead of informally writing, "She's taller than *me,*" write, "She's taller than *I am*" if you want to use the proper pronoun.

2. After a linking verb (*is, am, are, was, were*) as a pronoun that renames the subject:

The ones who should apologize are *we.* (*We are the ones who should apologize.* Therefore, the pronoun from the Subject Group is used.)

The winner of the lottery was *she.* (*She was the winner of the lottery.* Therefore, the pronoun from the Subject Group is used.)

Modern usage allows some exceptions to this rule, however. For example, it's common to hear people say *It's me* or *I am taller than her* (instead of the grammatically correct *It is I* and *I am taller than she*).

Use pronouns from the Object Group for all other purposes. In the following sentence, *me* is not the subject, nor does it rename the subject. It is the object of a preposition; therefore, it comes from the Object Group.

My boss went to lunch with Jenny and *me.*

A good way to tell whether to use a pronoun from the Subject Group or the Object Group is to leave out any extra name (and the word *and*). By leaving out *Jenny and,* you will say, *My boss went to lunch with me.* You would never say, *My boss went to lunch with I,* would you?

My father and *I* play chess on Sundays. (*I* play chess on Sundays.)

She and her friends rented a movie. (*She* rented a movie.)

It is up to *us* students to find a solution. (It is up to *us* to find a solution.)

The coach asked Craig and *me* to carry the trophy. (The coach asked *me* to carry the trophy.)

Pronoun Agreement

Just as subjects and verbs must agree, pronouns should agree with the words they refer to. If the word referred to is singular (for example, *parrot*), the pronoun referring to it should also be singular (*its*): The *parrot* sat on *its* perch. Likewise, if the noun is plural (parrots), the pronoun referring to it should be plural (*their*): The *parrots* sat on *their* perches. Here are two more examples:

Each classroom has its own chalkboard.

The pronoun *its* refers to the singular noun *classroom* and therefore is singular.

Both classrooms have their own chalkboards.

The pronoun *their* refers to the plural noun *classrooms* and therefore is plural.
The same methods to maintain subject and verb agreement also apply to pronoun agreement. For instance, ignore any prepositional phrases that come between a word and the pronoun that refers to it.

That *box* of supplies arrived with a huge dent in *its* side.

Boxes of supplies often arrive with huge dents in *their* sides.

The *player* with the best concentration usually beats *her* opponent.

Players with the best concentration usually beat *their* opponents.

When a pronoun refers to more than one word joined by *and,* the pronoun is plural:

> The *teacher* and the *tutors* eat *their* lunches at noon.

However, when a pronoun refers to more than one word joined by *or,* then the word closest to the pronoun determines its form:

> Either the teacher or the *tutors* eat *their* lunches in the classroom.

> Either the tutors or the *teacher* eats *his* lunch in the classroom.

It is tempting to avoid gender bias by using pairs of pronouns that include both singular forms—*he or she, his or her, him or her.* The results are wordy and awkward:

> As an actor, *he or she* must share *his or her* emotions with an audience.

> If anybody calls, tell *him or her* that I'll be back soon.

> Somebody left *his or her* cell phone in the classroom.

Here are a few better ways to eliminate gender bias and wordiness *without* using pairs of pronouns:

> As actors, *they* must share *their* emotions with an audience. (use plurals)

> Tell *anybody* who calls that I'll be back soon. (use general pronouns)

> Somebody left *a* cell phone in the classroom. (use articles—*a, an, the*)

Finally, to be clear, a pronoun must refer to only *one* element in a sentence:

> Before backing up my essay folder on the flash drive, I deleted everything in *it.*

> Did you delete everything in your *essay folder* or *flash drive?* The pronoun "*it*" could refer to either one, making the sentence unclear. Here's a revision that clarifies the meaning and eliminates the need for a pronoun:

> Before backing up my *essay folder,* I deleted everything on *the flash drive.*

E X E R C I S E S

Exercise 1

Circle the correct pronouns in the following sentences. Remember the trick of leaving out any extra name and the word *and* to help you choose the correct pronoun. For example, "Send the e-mail to ~~Lee and~~ (I, *me*)." Refer to the examples whenever necessary, and check your answers after each set to make the most progress.

1. My friend Kate and (I, me) took our third field trip to a museum last week.

2. I usually enjoy these museum visits more than (she, her).

3. Last time, however, (she and I, me and her) both enjoyed it.

4. Since Kate is less of an art lover than (I, me), at first she didn't feel comfortable just standing and looking at a painting or a sculpture.

5. The first two times that (she and I, her and me) had gone museum-hopping, the gallery and choice of collection were made by (I, me).

6. The one who made the choices this time was (she, her).

7. Kate may not get into art as much as (I, me), but she sure picked a great place to visit—a beautiful new gallery on a nearby university campus.

8. Since no one else chose this gallery, Kate and (I, me) had the sun-filled rooms lined with paintings all to ourselves.

9. They were lovely in the natural light, and one huge painting even drew (she and I, her and me) to sit by it for a long time before moving on.

10. When Kate comes with (I, me) again, I will leave all decisions up to (she, her).

Exercises 2–5

Circle the correct pronoun or pair of pronouns. If the correct answer is *he or she, his or her,* or *him or her,* revise the sentence to avoid gender bias *and* wordiness (as explained on page 157). Check your answers as you go through the exercise.

1. I live a long way from the city center and don't own a car, so I use public transportation and rely on (its, their) stability.

2. Based on my experiences, I'd say the city's system of buses has (its, their) problems.

3. Each of the bus routes that I travel on my way to work falls behind (its, their) own schedule.

4. Many of the other passengers also transfer on (his or her, their) way to work.

5. One day last week, each of the passengers had to gather (his or her, their) belongings and leave the bus, even though it had not reached a scheduled stop.

6. Both the driver and the mechanic who came to fix the bus offered (his, their) apologies for making us late.

7. Once the bus was fixed, the passengers were allowed to bring (his or her, their) things back on board.

8. Everyone did (his or her, their) best to hide (his or her, their) annoyance from the driver because he had been so nice.

9. As every passenger stepped off the bus at the end of the line, the driver thanked (him or her, them) for (his or her, their) patience and understanding.

10. Sometimes it is the people within a system that makes (it, them) work after all.

Exercise 3

1. The teacher gave my classmates and (I, me) very specific instructions for the essay.

2. My brother was surprised to learn that Bruce Lee was taller than (he, him).

3. (She and he, Her and him) are working on the same topic for their speeches.

4. Each of the dentists received (his or her, their) gift bags full of toothbrushes and dental floss.

5. Mobile phone companies are usually very competitive in (its, their) pricing.

6. I confess that the person responsible for ordering those flowers was (I, me).

7. Everyone in the audience had (his or her, their) opinion of the performances and expressed it with (his or her, their) applause.

8. Only the jury knows all of the factors involved in (its, their) decision.

9. No one understands your feelings better than (I, me).

10. I talked to my academic counselor; it was (she, her) who called this morning.

Exercise 4

1. My friend asked, "Are you taking as many classes as (I, me) this semester?"

2. When it comes to organic farming methods, no one knows more than (she, her).

3. At work, I always answer the phone correctly by saying, "This is (she, her)" when someone asks, "May I speak to the manager?"

4. A little boy and girl were opening (his or her, their) presents when you arrived.

5. We asked the parking enforcement office to waive (its, their) fees for the event.

6. Everyone must use (his or her, their) own password to enter the network.

7. Purchase orders can be signed by my boss or (I, me).

8. The winners of the scholarships were Justin and (she, her).

9. Those two actors have given the best performance of (his or her, their) lives.

10. The judge sent the lawyers and (we, us) jurors a message.

Exercise 5

1. The university representative gave my friends and (I, me) a brochure of the campus.

2. Each of the students will buy (his or her, their) own materials for the jewelry class.

3. The top players in last year's poker tournament have finished (his or her, their) first game in this year's competition.

4. I can't remember—was it you or (I, me) who asked for a raise first?

5. Due to the holiday, everyone was allowed to turn (his or her, their) essay in late.

6. It was (she, her) who loaned him the money for a vacation.

7. There is no one more interested in bats and other flying creatures than (he, him).

8. You and (I, me) drive the same kind of car, but mine is an automatic.

9. I can't believe that the tutors helped you and (I, me) for over an hour.

10. According to Max and (she, her), the deadline for applications is today.

PROOFREADING EXERCISE

The following paragraph contains several incorrect or unclear pronouns. Find and correct the errors.

Rude drivers have one thing in common. Whether they are male or female, they they all think that they know how to drive better than anybody else. The other day, as my friends and me were driving to school, we stopped at an intersection. A very old man who used a cane started to walk across it in front of my friends and I just before the light was ready to change. So we waited. But while we waited for him, an impatient driver behind us started to honk his horn since he couldn't see him. I wondered, "Does he want us to hit him, or what?" Finally, it was clear. He pulled his car up beside ours, opened his window, and yelled at us before he sped away. The old man reached the other side safely, but he hardly noticed.

SENTENCE WRITING

Write ten sentences in which you compare yourself to someone else in terms of athletic ability or creativity. Then check that your pronouns are grammatically correct, that they agree with the words they replace.

Avoiding Shifts in Person

To understand what "person" means when using pronouns, imagine a conversation between three people. The *first* person would speak using "I." That person would call the *second* person "you." And when those two talked of a *third* person, they would use "he, she, or they." Here are more personal pronouns arranged by person:

First person—*I, me, my, we, us, our, mine*

Second person—*you, your, yours*

Third person—*he, him, his, she, her, they, them, their, one, anyone, it, its*

Although it is possible (and at times necessary) to use all three groups of pronouns in a paper, most writers try not to shift from one group to another without a good reason. Such errors are called shifts in person.

The following paragraph includes unnecessary shifts in person:

Few people know how to manage *their* time. *We* don't need to be efficiency experts to realize that *everyone* could get a lot more done by budgeting *his* or *her* time more wisely. Nor do *you* need to work very hard to become more organized.

To correct the shifts in person, you could use only *first-person* pronouns:

Few of *us* know how to manage *our* time. *We* don't need to be efficiency experts to realize that *we* could get a lot more done by budgeting *our* time more wisely. Nor do *we* need to work very hard to become more organized.

Or you could address the reader directly and use only *second-person* pronouns:

You are not alone if you don't know how to manage *your* time. *You* don't need to be an efficiency expert to realize that *you* could get a lot more done by budgeting *your* time more wisely. Nor do *you* need to work very hard to become more organized.

Finally, you could correct the shifts by using only *third-person* pronouns:

Few people know how to manage *their* time. *One* does not need to be an efficiency expert to realize that *everyone* could get a lot more done by budgeting *his* or *her* time more wisely. Nor does *anyone* need to work very hard to become more organized. (Note that "*his* or *her*" could then be deleted to avoid using this wordy pair of pronouns. See page 157.)

PROOFREADING EXERCISES

Which of the following student paragraphs shift *unnecessarily* between first, second, and third person? In those that do, revise the sentences to eliminate such shifting. One of the paragraphs is already correct.

1. Scientists and others are working on several inventions that have not been perfected yet. Some of these developments seem like complete science fiction, but they're not. Each of them is in the process of becoming a real new technology. It's hard to imagine eating meat grown on plants or in petri dishes. Scientists will feed the plants artificially made "blood." Researchers are also working to produce animals (perhaps even humans) grown in artificial wombs. The most interesting development is selective amnesia (memory loss). Patients will be able to ask their doctors to erase painful memories as a mental-health tool. And, of course, computers will gain more and more personality traits to become more like human beings.

Source: The Futurist, August–September 1998, and *Current Science,* April 6, 2007.

2. I was reading about superstitions for my psychology class, and I learned that a lot of these beliefs concern brooms and sweeping. One superstition says that, whenever you change your residence, you should get a new broom. People should not take their old brooms with them because the brooms might carry any bad luck that was swept up at the old place and bring it to the new one. Also, if you sweep dirt out an open door, make it the back door so that the bad luck will depart forever. If you sweep dirt out the front way, the same bad luck will come right back in again. Finally, I learned never to walk across a fallen broomstick unless I never want to get married, for that is the fate for anyone who steps over a broomstick. I bet most people would be surprised by how many things can go wrong when you pick up a broom.

3. Most of us in America could use more vacation time. We hear about citizens of other countries getting several weeks—and sometimes even months—off every year to rest their bodies, recharge their energies, and lift their spirits. But in the United States, we have to fight for and often forfeit our one-week or two-week vacations. In fact, if we complain too loudly about needing a break, we could be the newest person on the unemployment line. It's time for all of us to stand up for our right to sit down and take a rest.

REVIEW OF SENTENCE STRUCTURE ERRORS

One sentence in each pair contains an error. Read both sentences carefully before you decide. Then write the letter of the *incorrect* sentence in the blank. Try to name the error and correct it if you can. You may find any of these errors:

awk	awkward phrasing
cliché	overused expression
dm	dangling modifier
frag	fragment
mm	misplaced modifier
pro	incorrect pronoun
pro agr	pronoun agreement
ro	run-on sentence
shift	shift in time or person
s-v agr	subject-verb agreement error
verb	incorrect verb form
wordy	wordiness
//	not parallel

1. _____ **A.** Family cruises have become a very popular way of taking a vacation.

   _____ **B.** They're suppose to be relaxing for parents and exciting for children.

2. _____ **A.** My speech professor is much luckier than me.

   _____ **B.** She has won two big prizes in the lottery.

3. _____ **A.** Community colleges offer day, night, and weekend classes.

   _____ **B.** I have taken day and night classes but never give up my weekends.

4. _____ **A.** As the teacher entered the classroom, he removed his headphones and his backpack.

   _____ **B.** He put them on the podium and he immediately started lecturing.

5. _____ **A.** We always lock the door to the language lab.

   _____ **B.** Because too many people wander in if we don't.

6. _____ **A.** In today's society, people usually mind their own business.

   _____ **B.** If I see someone who really needs help, I will get involved.

7. _____ **A.** The library renewed the books that my friend and me had checked out.

   _____ **B.** Now we have enough time to finish our research papers.

8. _____ **A.** The store was offering a free gift of a coffee maker.

   _____ **B.** My uncle gave the coffee maker as a gift for his son's wedding.

9. _____ **A.** My essay is full of interesting details and had a strong thesis.

   _____ **B.** I don't understand why I have to revise it.

10. _____ **A.** The band members arrived in a stretch limo and took their guitars out of the trunk.

    _____ **B.** Everyone at the party had a shocked look on their faces.

11. _____ **A.** Some of the new furniture have scratches on it already.

    _____ **B.** The delivery company should have been more careful.

12. _____ **A.** Water bottles come in all sizes now.

_____ **B.** From the size of a baby bottle to the size of a magnum of champagne.

13. _____ **A.** We walked around the park before dinner last night.

_____ **B.** Hanging from the top of a tree, we saw a beautiful metallic kite.

14. _____ **A.** Shawn and Sharon are twin cousins of mine; they are both talented musicians.

_____ **B.** However, there is one big difference between them Shawn is not as ambitious as Sharon is.

15. _____ **A.** Whenever I plan a whole meal around a single specific in-gredient, the different dishes themselves don't always taste good.

_____ **B.** For example, I like the flavor of curry with chicken but not with vegetables.

PROOFREADING EXERCISE

Find and correct the sentence structure errors in the following essay.

LET'S GET TECHNICAL

In my child development classes, I'm learning about ways to keep girls interested in technology. Studies shows that girls and boys begin their school years equally interested in technology. After elementary school is the time that computers are less of an interest for girls. Because boys keep up with computers and other technology throughout their educations more than girls, they get ahead in these fields. Experts have come up with some suggestions for teachers and parents of girls to help them.

Girls need opportunities to experiment with computers. Girls spend time on computers, but they usually just do their assignments then they log off. Since computer games and programs are often aimed at boys. Parents and teachers need to buy computer products that will challenge girls not only in literature and art, but also in math, science, and business is important.

Another suggestion is to put computers in places where girls can socialize. One reason many boys stay interested in technology is that it is something he can do on his own. Girls tend to be more interested in working with others and to share activities. When computer terminals are placed close to one another, girls work at them for much longer periods of time.

Finally, parents and teachers need to be aware that nothing beats positive role models. Teach them about successful women in the fields of business, scientific, and technology. And the earlier we start interesting girls in these fields, the better.

P A R T 3

Punctuation

Periods, Question Marks, Exclamation Points, Semicolons, Colons, Dashes

Punctuation is a written code. As part of this code, each piece of punctuation works to clarify meaning. This section covers six pieces of punctuation: periods, question marks, exclamation points, semicolons, colons, and dashes. Commas will be explained in the two sections that follow.

You learned very early as a writer to put a period, question mark, and exclamation point (. ? !) at the end of a sentence. The main use of semicolons (;) you learned when you studied independent clauses on page 84 and the ways to avoid run-on sentences on page 86. You may be unfamiliar, however, with the uses of colons (:) and dashes (—). Here is an explanation of all of the uses of periods, question marks, exclamation points, semicolons, colons, and dashes:

Use a period (.) at the end of sentences that make statements or mild commands and after most abbreviations.

> Heavy rain will be causing delays on Highway 101. (statement)
>
> Take a different route if you can. (mild command)
>
> Fwy.   Sept.   in.   pgs.   ft.   Ave.   Tues. (abbreviations)

Use a question mark (?) after direct questions but not after indirect questions.

> Has online registration already started? (direct question)
>
> I wonder if online registration has already started. (indirect question)

In a sentence with quotation marks, put the question mark *outside* the quote marks if the sentence itself is a question but *inside* if the quotation or title is a question.

> Have you actually said, "I quit"? (The sentence is a question.)
>
> I asked my boss, "Do you want me to quit?" (The quotation is a question.)
>
> Did they play "Who Let the Dogs Out?" (Sentence and song title are questions.)

Use an exclamation point (!) after expressions or quotations that convey strong emotions or loud sounds. Exclamations appear most often in informal writing.

> Let's see a movie. I need a break from reality!

> The heavy box landed with a thud!

The same rules about using quotation marks with question marks apply to using them with exclamation points.

> Someone yelled, "I can't believe I got an A!" (Quotation is an exclamation.)

> I finally memorized "The Road Not Taken"! (Poem title is not an exclamation.)

Use a semicolon (;) between two independent clauses in a sentence when they are *not* joined by one of the *fanboys* (*for, and, nor, but, or, yet, so*).

> My brother co-signed for a loan; now I have a car of my own.

> She volunteered her house as a polling place; however, its rooms were too small to qualify.

To be sure that a semicolon is correct, try replacing it with a period and capital letter.

> My brother co-signed for a loan. Now I have a car of my own.

> She volunteered her house as a polling place. However, its rooms were too small to qualify.

Aside from its main use to separate two independent clauses, a semicolon can also act as a "*super comma*" within a list to separate items that already contain commas.

> I enjoy cooking, my hobby; biking, my passion; and screen-printing, my job.

Use a colon (:) after a set-up clause—a complete statement that sets up an expectation in the reader's mind. Imagine that the colon is a *fence*, and you're setting the reader up to *look over the fence*. Then, after the colon, include the word, list, explanation, or quotation that the reader is expecting.

> The company announced its Employee of the Month: Lee Jones.

> That car comes in the following colors: red, black, blue, and white.

> I gave my boss a simple explanation: I need more time with my family.

> Hamlet asks the ultimate question: "To be, or not to be?"

The previous examples all contain complete set-up clauses before the colons. Now look at a few sentences that do *not* require colons because they do *not* include complete set-up clauses.

> The company announced that Lee Jones is its Employee of the Month.
>
> That car comes in red, black, blue, and white.
>
> I explained to my boss that I need more time with my family.
>
> Hamlet asks, "To be, or not to be?"

Note that, in the last example, the signal phrase *Hamlet asks* leads directly into the quotation without including the words *the ultimate question* to complete the set-up clause. Therefore, no colon—just a comma—comes between them. See page 232 for more about punctuating quotations and signal phrases.

Use dashes (—) in place of other punctuation to emphasize information or to isolate phrasing that includes its own punctuation. Dashes are optional and should be used sparingly. They can replace commas, semicolons, or colons.

> Lee Jones—Employee of the Month—quit yesterday. (Dashes replace commas.)
>
> I love Bollywood movies—my sister hates them. (Dash replaces a semicolon.)
>
> We have exciting news for you—we're moving! (Dash replaces a colon.)
>
> The new club members—Jan, Ted, and Anne—arrived. (Dashes isolate a list.)

EXERCISES

Exercises 1 and 2

Add the necessary end punctuation (periods, question marks, and exclamation points) to the following sentences. Any punctuation marks used *within* the sentences are correct and do not need to be changed. Pay attention to the other punctuation marks, however, to help you understand their uses while you are adding the end punctuation.

Exercise 1

1. Do you know how many resources go into making the jeans that we all love to wear

2. Here are a couple of the details: the dyeing process uses about a pound of harsh chemicals and 15 dye baths to create a single pair of jeans

3. Would you believe that it also takes 2,500 gallons of water to finish that one pair

4. Of course, each movement of the jeans through the process requires electricity

5. Luckily, textile scientists in Switzerland have come up with a "greener" method of jeans production

6. The result is called Advanced Denim, and its environmental benefits are staggering

7. The scientific and environmental communities are excited, and who wouldn't be

8. This new denim requires only one trip through a dye vat and finishes the fabric with eco-friendly substances

9. The Advanced Denim process uses 30 percent less energy and over 90 percent less water than traditional denim

10. Can you imagine the positive effects it could have when multiplied by the 2 billion pairs of jeans produced each year

Source: Science Daily, June 19, 2012 (http://www.sciencedaily.com/releases/2012/06 /120619123753.htm)

Exercise 2

1. Have you noticed that light bulbs don't last as long as they used to

2. Some seem to burn out after only a month or two

3. Would you believe that one light bulb has lasted for 110 years

4. Well, it's true—believe it or not

5. At a fire station in Livermore, California, the same bulb has been burning since 1901

6. The now famous light bulb is treated like a celebrity by the firefighters

7. They are proud of its history, and who wouldn't be

8. The famous bulb doesn't get cleaned or covered by any type of shade; no one wants to risk damaging it or making it burn out after so many years

9. The Livermore Light Bulb, as it's called, has even made it into the *Guinness Book of World Records* as the longest running light bulb

10. Anyone who wants to see this famous bulb in action can visit its 24-hour Web cam online

Source: www.centennialbulb.org

Exercises 3 and 4

Add any necessary semicolons, colons, and dashes to these sentences. The commas and end punctuation do not need to be changed. Some sentences are already correct.

Exercise 3

1. Have you ever heard of Vinnie Ream?

2. This young woman a very controversial figure in Washington, D.C. began her career as a sculptor in 1863 at the age of sixteen.

3. Miss Ream was a student of the famous sculptor Clark Mills he is perhaps best known for his statue of Andrew Jackson located across from the White House.

4. Vinnie Ream started to work with Mills in his studio in the basement of the Capitol building soon members of Congress were volunteering to sit for Miss Ream, and she sculpted busts of them.

5. Her fame and reputation grew in the late 1860s that's when she was awarded a $10,000 commission to create a life-size statue of Abraham Lincoln.

6. Vinnie Ream had known Lincoln in fact, before his assassination, President Lincoln would allow Miss Ream to sit in his office within the White House and work on a bust of him as he carried out the business of running the country.

7. Ream's intimate observation of Lincoln at work affected her design of Lincoln's posture and facial expression for her statue of him.

8. Vinnie Ream's relationships and the works she produced were not accepted by everyone Ream's youth and physical beauty led to much of this harsh criticism.

9. Some people questioned her motives others even questioned her abilities.

10. Ream prospered in spite of the jealous accusations of others and often demonstrated her sculpting abilities in public to prove that she did her own work.

Source: Smithsonian, August 2000

Exercise 4

1. Thunderstorms are spectacular demonstrations of nature's power.

2. Do you know where the safest places are during a thunderstorm?

3. One relatively safe place is inside a building that has plumbing pipes or electrical wires those channels can absorb the electrical energy unleashed by lightning.

4. Of course, once inside such a building, people should stay away from the end sources of plumbing and wiring faucets, hoses, phone receivers, and computer terminals.

5. Buildings without pipes or wires are not safe shelters during lightning strikes these might include pergolas, dugouts, and tents.

6. Outside, lightning can move over the ground therefore, you should be aware of a position that emergency officials call the "lightning squat."

7. This emergency position involves curling up into the smallest ball you can while balancing on the balls of your feet and covering your ears.

8. That way, there is less of you in contact with the ground if lightning strikes.

9. Lightning is electrical energy consequently, it can travel far from the actual storm clouds.

10. In fact, lightning has struck as far as twenty miles away from the storm that caused it.

Source: Current Health, October 2003

Exercise 5

Add the necessary periods, question marks, exclamation points, semicolons, colons, and dashes. Any commas in the sentences are correct and should not be changed.

1. What do math and origami Japanese paper folding have to do with each other

2. Erik Demaine and other origami mathematicians would answer, "Everything"

3. If you have never heard of the field of origami mathematics, you're not alone

4. Origami math is a relatively new field back in 2003, Demaine won a "genius" award partly due to his work with origami and its applications in many fields

5. The MacArthur Foundation awarded Demaine more than just the title "genius" it awarded him half a million dollars

6. At twenty, Demaine was hired as a professor by the Massachusetts Institute of Technology he became the youngest professor MIT has ever had

7. Erik Demaine has his father to thank for much of his education Martin Demaine home-schooled Erik as the two of them traveled around North America

8. Erik was always intensely interested in academic subjects during his travels, he and his father would consult university professors whenever Erik had questions that no one else could answer

9. Erik Demaine continues to investigate one area in particular the single-cut problem

10. This problem involves folding a piece of paper then making one cut the result can be anything from a swan to a star, a unicorn, or any letter of the alphabet

Source: New York Times, February 15, 2005

PROOFREADING EXERCISE

Find and correct the punctuation errors in this paragraph. All of the errors involve periods, question marks, exclamation points, semicolons, colons, and dashes. Any commas used within the sentences are correct and should not be changed.

Who hasn't seen one of those inflatable jumping rooms at a park or in the front yard of a house hosting a child's birthday party. These jumpers are popular for several reasons; children can have fun playing with their friends—adults can keep an eye on many children at once, and everyone gets a lot of exercise. In 2007, a freak accident occurred on a beach in Hawaii it involved an inflated castle-shaped bouncer, a few brave adults, and several lucky children. As the kids bounced around as usual, a strong gust of wind—a whirlwind, according to one witness; lifted the castle straight up into the air and knocked all but two of the children out instantly. Then the castle bounced on the sand once before flying fifty yards out into the ocean. As the castle flew, another child dropped out of it luckily, he was unhurt. Many adults both lifeguards and others jumped in to save the two-year-old girl who remained inside the castle. One man was able to reach her incredibly, she was not seriously injured.

Source: *The Honolulu Advertiser,* June 10, 2007

SENTENCE WRITING

Write ten sentences of your own that use periods, question marks, exclamation points, semicolons, colons, and dashes correctly. Imitate the sample sentences or any of the exercises.

Commas Used to Separate Elements

Commas guide the reader through your sentence structures in the same way that signs guide people on the highway. Imagine what effects misplaced or incorrect road signs would have. From now on, try not to use a comma without a good reason for it.

Commas serve two purposes in the written code of punctuation: they separate elements or enclose elements. This section covers the first function of commas—to separate one part of a sentence from another. The next section will explain how commas are used to enclose sentence structures.

Use a comma to separate two independent clauses joined by one of the fanboys (for, and, nor, but, or, yet, so).

> We all brought our final drafts to class, and the teacher congratulated us.
>
> My art history book will be very expensive, but I'll look for a good deal online.

If you use a comma without a *fanboys* between two independent clauses, the result is an error called a **comma splice.**

> Dogs are people's best friends, people are cats' best friends. (comma splice)
>
> Dogs are people's best friends, *and* people are cats' best friends. (corrected)

Before using a comma, be sure one of the *fanboys* actually connects two independent clauses and not just two words or phrases. The following sentence contains only one independent clause with two verbs. Because no subject follows the *fanboys,* the sentence does not require a comma:

> My dog curled up under my chair and waited for me to finish my essay.

Now compare the previous sentence with this one that does require a comma:

> My cat was hungry, and she meowed for me to finish my essay.

Use commas to separate items in a series, date, or address.

> Students in literature classes read short stories, poems, and plays.
>
> Today I walked to school, biked to work, and took a train to the movies.

Some writers leave out the comma before the *and* connecting the last two items in a series, but this comma is needed to separate all of the items clearly and equally.

> My favorite sandwiches are tuna, turkey, and ham and cheese.
>
> My favorite composers are Mozart, Beethoven, Chopin, and Shubert.

In a full date or an address including city and state (or country), put a comma after each item, including the last.

> He was born on August 21, 1961, in Clitheroe, England, but later moved to Paris.
>
> Our old house at 212 Eden Street, Denver, Colorado, has become a bakery.

When only the month and year are used in a date, no commas are needed.

> My aunt graduated from Yale in May 2011.

Use a comma to separate an introductory word, phrase, or dependent clause from the beginning of a sentence. The complete sentence begins *after* the introduction.

> Finally, he got through to his insurance company. (introductory word)
>
> During her last performance, the actress broke her leg. (introductory phrase)
>
> Whenever I finish my homework, I feel so satisfied. (introductory dependent clause)

Use a comma to separate a tag question, contrast, comment, or description from the end of a sentence. The complete sentence ends *before* the tag.

> The new chairs aren't very comfortable, are they? (tag question)
>
> I wanted a full refund, not an exchange. (tag contrast)
>
> My professor said he needed to "ruminate," whatever that means. (tag comment)
>
> We sat all day at the beach, enjoying the waves and sunshine. (descriptive tag)

As these examples show, a tag is a kind of afterthought. Note that most prepositional phrases and dependent clauses at the ends of sentences are not tags and do *not* require commas.

> "Ruminate" means to think about something for a long time. (prepositional phrase)
>
> I feel so satisfied when I finish my homework. (dependent clause)

E X E R C I S E S

Add commas according to the specific directions for each exercise. Any other punctuation already in the sentences is correct. Refer to the examples whenever necessary, and check your answers often.

Exercise 1

Add commas to the following sentences to separate two independent clauses joined by a *fanboys*. Remember that some *fanboys* link other parts of a sentence, not independent clauses, and may *not* require commas. Look for the *fanboys* that have a subject and verb before *and* after them to find the ones that join independent clauses.

1. The young actor named Sabu began his career in 1937 and he became famous for his unique background and abilities.

2. He had an amazing rapport with animals and an athletic and energetic acting style.

3. An American filmmaker discovered Sabu as a young boy in Southern India and asked him to be in a film about elephants.

4. In real life, Sabu understood elephants very well for his father owned and trained elephants.

5. *The Elephant Boy* was Sabu's first film and it made him an instant celebrity.

6. He went on to star in fantasy films like *The Thief of Bagdad* and *Arabian Nights.*

7. The special effects in these two films matched today's standards and in some ways exceeded them.

8. In his most celebrated role, Sabu played Mowgli in the live-action 1942 film of Rudyard Kipling's *The Jungle Book.*

9. Sabu's version of *The Jungle Book* was made twenty-five years before Disney's animated version but it captured the essence of the mysterious jungle even more vividly with its real actors and animals.

10. In one scene, Sabu rode into the village on a galloping water buffalo and calmly slid off the animal to deliver his dialogue.

Source: http://www.imdb.com/name/nm0754942/

Exercise 2

Add commas to the following sentences to separate items in a series, date, or address. Some sentences may not need any commas.

1. I finished high school on June 23 2012 after moving here from Houston Texas.

2. My favorite English teacher was young enthusiastic and highly motivated.

3. We read essays stories poems novels and research articles in her class.

4. My group even opted to read a play memorize all of its parts and perform it for everyone.

5. One of Ms. Kern's best assignments involved writing a complaint letter.

6. She taught us how to argue fairly and how to modify what she called the "tone of voice" in our writing.

7. We each wrote a letter of complaint about a product a service or an experience that was unsatisfactory to us.

8. Then we sent copies of our letter to the company's business address to our home address and to Ms. Kern's school address.

9. Ms. Kern assured us that we would receive a response from the company if we described our dissatisfaction clearly asked for a reasonable solution and used a respectful tone.

10. My company replied to my letter with a note of apology a bumper sticker and an impressive gift card to use at any of the company's stores.

Exercise 3

Add commas after introductory words, phrases, or dependent clauses in the following sentences. Some sentences may not need any commas.

1. As if people don't have enough to worry about Melinda Muse wrote a book called *I'm Afraid, You're Afraid: 448 Things to Fear and Why.*

2. In her book Muse points out the dangers of common places, objects, foods, months, days, and activities.

3. If people go to Vegas regularly they should worry because paramedics can't reach people as quickly in large crowds or huge buildings.

4. Another dangerous spot is the beauty parlor; people can suffer a stroke from leaning their heads back too far into the shampoo sink.

5. In the comfort of our homes unwashed new clothes may transfer dangerous chemicals to people's eyes, skin, and lungs.

6. Among the foods to avoid grapefruit juice can interfere with certain medications' effectiveness.

7. Thanks to Independence Day celebrations and outdoor picnics July ranks highest of all the months in accidental injuries and food poisonings.

8. Being linked with more suicides and heart attacks than any other weekday Mondays are the most dangerous days of the week.

9. Believe it or not singing in a choir can even permanently damage people's ears.

10. After reading *I'm Afraid, You're Afraid* it's possible to be afraid of almost everything.

Source: *I'm Afraid, You're Afraid: 448 Things to Fear and Why* (Hyperion, 2000)

Exercise 4

Add commas before tag questions, contrasts, comments, or descriptions in the following sentences. Some sentences may not need any commas.

1. The United States introduced the Susan B. Anthony dollar in 1979 making her the first woman on a circulating coin.

2. No one deserved this honor more than Susan B. Anthony having led the fight for women's voting rights in America.

3. The Anthony dollar quickly became unpopular however.

4. People disliked certain features of the coin not the person on the coin.

5. This dollar coin was too much like a quarter nearly the same size and color with the same rough edge around it.

6. People mistakenly put Anthony dollars in machines that called for quarters.

7. In 1999, the government stopped issuing Susan B. Anthony dollars preferring to introduce a new golden dollar coin instead.

8. The new coin portrayed the image of a famous American woman just as the Anthony dollar did.

9. The Sacagawea "golden dollar" has suffered from its own lack of popularity unfortunately.

10. Women haven't had much luck as images on coins have they?

Source: http://womenshistory.about.com/od/anthonysusanb/a/anthony.htm

Exercise 5

Use commas to separate all of the necessary elements in the following sentences.

1. Fish may be considered "brain food" but I've never liked it.

2. While everyone is saying how delicious a big salmon steak is or how yummy the shrimp tastes you'll find me grimacing and munching on the bread.

3. Part of the problem with fish is the smell but my friends who love to eat fish also love the smell of fish cooking.

4. I always thought that was strange but it makes sense doesn't it?

5. If someone hates the taste of onions that person probably also hates the smell of onions cooking.

6. Come to think of it my husband hates to eat sweets and doesn't like the smell of them either.

7. When we walk into a bakery together he practically has to hold his nose the way I would in a fish market.

8. To me that's odd but my aversion to fish must seem weird to someone who loves it.

9. Our daughter adores the taste of bacon but she hates the smell of bacon frying.

10. So I guess there are always exceptions.

PARAGRAPH EXERCISE

Use commas to separate all of the necessary elements in the following paragraph. Try to identify the elements you are separating. Check your answers often to make the most progress.

There I was in the pilot's seat of a small airplane. I had signed up for a course in flying at the aviation school but I didn't really expect to get my pilot's license. Learning the instruments took the most time. Once we began training in the cockpit the instructor told us what to do and we did it. When I turned the yoke to the right the plane banked right. When I turned it to the left the plane went left. Actually it was very similar to driving a car only much more fun. I'm exaggerating about it being easy of course. My favorite type of practice involved landings bringing the plane in softly and safely. After many hours of supervised flying my time to solo came and I was nervous but excited. I covered my checklist on the ground took off without any problems and landed smoothly in the middle of the runway. On a cold day in October 2012 I became a licensed pilot. Now I can work toward my next dream of becoming a private pilot for a rock star.

SENTENCE WRITING

For more practice using commas to separate elements in sentences, combine the following sets of details in different ways to create sentences that include two independent clauses with *fanboys* or an introductory element, a list, or a tag. Refer to the examples in the explanations whenever necessary. Feel free to reorder these details and add to or alter the phrasing. If you include a list, be sure to use parallel structure (see page 149). You'll find sample combinations in the Answers, but try not to look at them before writing your own.

I like to watch golf and tennis.
I love to play baseball and soccer.

Tutors do not correct students' essays.
They can explain how to clarify ideas.
They will also show how to add stronger details.
They may even offer tips on improving organization.

My parents grew up in the 1960s.
Most cars in the 1960s had seatbelts.
There were no car seats for children.
Air bags had not been introduced yet.

Commas Used to Enclose Elements

The second function of commas is to enclose "scoopable" elements in sentences. Scoopable elements are extra words, phrases, and clauses that can be scooped out of the middle of a sentence because they are not necessary to understand its meaning. Have you noticed that a comma **(,)** is shaped like the tip of an ice cream scoop? Let this similarity help you remember to use commas to enclose *scoopable* elements. Use two commas, like the ones used here**,** to show where each scoopable element begins and ends.

Use commas to enclose the name of a person being spoken to in a sentence.

> Did you know, Danielle, that you left your backpack at the library?
>
> We regret to inform you, Mr. Davis, that your policy has been canceled.

Use commas to enclose transitions or expressions that interrupt the flow of the sentence (such as *however, moreover, therefore, of course, by the way, on the other hand, I believe,* or *I think*).

> I know, of course, that I have missed the deadline.
>
> They will try, therefore, to use the rest of their time wisely.
>
> Today's exam, I think, was only a practice test.

Read the previous examples *aloud,* and you'll hear how these expressions surrounded by commas stand out as interruptions. Sometimes such expressions flow smoothly in the sentence and do not need commas around them.

> Of course he checked to see if there were any rooms available.
>
> We therefore decided to stay out of it.
>
> I think you made the right decision.

Remember, when a word like *however* comes between two independent clauses, you should use a semicolon to separate them, as explained on page 169. In such sentences, *however* functions as an introductory word for the second independent clause, as explained in the previous section about commas that separate elements.

> Voter turnout was low; however, the election results were definitive.
>
> She has started to like architecture; therefore, she plans to change her major.
>
> I spent hours studying for the test; finally, I felt prepared.

Thus, you've seen words like *however, therefore,* and *finally* used in several ways:

1. as introductory words or tag comments (use a comma to separate them from the rest of the sentence, as explained on page 177)

2. as "scoopable" words that interrupt the flow of the sentence (use two commas to enclose them)

3. as words that flow smoothly within the sentence (use no punctuation)

4. as transitions between two independent clauses (use a semicolon before and a comma after them)

Use commas to enclose extra or unnecessary information in the middle of a sentence. These are the most common forms of "scoopables."

Here's an example of a sentence that includes additional information about its subject:

Maxine Taylor, who organized the fund-raiser, will introduce the candidates.

The clause *who organized the fund-raiser* is scoopable information in the sentence. Without it, we still know exactly who the subject is and what she is going to do: "Maxine Taylor will introduce the candidates." Therefore, the additional information is enclosed by commas to show that it is scoopable. Now read the following sentence:

The person who called the police apologized to everyone at the party.

Of the two—*the person* and *who called the police*—can you tell which information is more specific? You're right if you think *who called the police* is more specific. Without it, the generic subject would be totally unclear: "The person apologized to everyone at the party." The reader would have no idea *which person* it was. The clause *who called the police* is required to identify the person, so there are no commas around it. Here's another example:

<u>Avatar</u>, James Cameron's film, was nominated for Best Picture.

The additional identification *James Cameron's film* is scoopable. It could be left out without making the subject unclear: "<u>Avatar</u> was nominated for Best Picture." Therefore, two commas enclose the scoopable information to show that it piece of extra identification. Here is the same sentence with the information reversed:

James Cameron's film <u>Avatar</u> was nominated for Best Picture.

In this sentence, the title of the movie is not additional, but necessary. Without it, the sentence would read, "James Cameron's film was nominated for Best Picture."

The reader would not know which of Cameron's many films was nominated for Best Picture. Therefore, *Avatar* is necessary identification, and commas should not be used around it.

Occasionally, scoopable elements show up at the end of the sentence, and when they do, the period acts as the end of the scoop. We might even call these "scoopable tags." See page 177 for more about using commas with tags.

We drove to Las Vegas with Siobhan, our neighbor from Ireland.

E X E R C I S E S

Use commas to enclose any "scoopable" elements in the following sentences. Some sentences may not need commas. Refer to the explanations and examples whenever necessary. Check your answers often to make the most progress.

Exercise 1

1. The first person who guessed correctly won a trip to the Grand Canyon.

2. Professor Jones who guessed correctly won a trip to the Grand Canyon.

3. Cookies that contain nuts may be harmful to people with allergies.

4. My cookie recipe which does not contain nuts is safe for people with allergies.

5. Students who take the train to school catch a shuttle from the station to campus.

6. Melissa who takes the train to school catches a shuttle from the station to campus.

7. The teacher explained the answer to the question that everyone missed.

8. The teacher explained the answer to question 14 which everyone missed.

9. The gorilla an animal on many endangered species lists has an average lifespan of 30 to 50 years.

10. Koko the gorilla who became famous for learning to communicate through sign language turned 42 years old in July 2013.

Source: koko.org (for Koko information)

Exercise 2

1. We hope of course that people will honor their summons for jury duty.

2. Of course we hope that people will honor their summons for jury duty.

3. People who serve as jurors every time they're called deserve our appreciation.

4. Thelma and Trevor Martin who serve as jurors every time they're called deserve our appreciation.

5. We should therefore be as understanding as we can be about the slow legal process.

6. Therefore we should be as understanding as we can be about the slow legal process.

7. A legal system that believes people are innocent until proven guilty must offer a trial-by-jury option.

8. The U.S. legal system which believes people are innocent until proven guilty offers a trial-by-jury option.

9. With that option, we hope that no one will receive an unfair trial.

10. With that option, no one we hope will receive an unfair trial.

Exercise 3

1. The story of Dracula the frightening Prince Vlad Tepes has been fascinating people across the world for hundreds of years.

2. He was held as a prisoner in Bran Castle a medieval fortress in Transylvania in the 15th century.

3. Bran Castle also called Dracula's Castle has become a popular tourist attraction.

4. For the past forty years, people who traveled to Romania have been visiting the museum at Bran Castle.

5. The towers and Transylvanian charm of the castle have also made it the perfect setting for many Dracula movies.

6. The owners of Dracula's Castle have changed throughout the years.

7. It was given to Marie Queen of Romania in 1920.

8. But the political landscape changed, and the castle became national property in 1948.

9. A law that was passed in 2005 returned Bran Castle to the ancestors of the Romanian royal family.

10. Queen Marie's grandson Dominic von Habsburg now owns the castle, along with his two sisters Maria Magdalena and Elizabeth.

Source: Renaissance Magazine, Issue #51 (2006)

Exercise 4

1. Arthur S. Heineman a California architect designed and built the world's first motel in the 1920s.

2. He chose the perfect location the city of San Luis Obispo which was midway between Los Angeles and San Francisco.

3. Heineman an insightful man of business understood the need for inexpensive drive-in accommodations on long motor vehicle trips.

4. Hotels which required reservations and offered only high-priced rooms within one large structure just didn't fulfill the needs of motorists.

5. Heineman envisioned his "Motor Hotel" or Mo-Tel as a place where the parking spaces for the cars were right next to separate bungalow-style apartments for the passengers.

6. Heineman's idea was so new that when he put up his "Motel" sign several residents of the area told him to fire the sign's painter who couldn't even spell the word *hotel.*

7. Heineman had the sign painter place a hyphen between *Mo* and *Tel* to inform the public of a new kind of resting place.

8. Heineman's Milestone Mo-Tel the world's first motel opened in San Luis Obispo in 1925.

9. Before Heineman's company the Milestone Interstate Corporation could successfully trademark the name "Mo-Tel," other builders adopted the style and made *motel* a generic term.

10. Some of the original Milestone Mo-Tel building now called the Motel Inn still stands on the road between Los Angeles and San Francisco.

Source: Westways, May/June 2000

Exercise 5

1. I bought a book The Story of the "Titanic" because I am interested in famous events in history.

2. This book written by Frank O. Braynard is a collection of postcards about the ill-fated ocean liner.

3. The book's postcards four on each page can be pulled apart and mailed like regular ones.

4. The postcards have images of *Titanic*-related people, places, and events on one side.

5. The blank sides where messages and addresses go include brief captions of the images on the front of the cards.

6. The book's actual content the part written by Braynard offers a brief history of each image relating to the *Titanic.*

7. One of my favorite cards shows the ship's captain Edward Smith and its builder Lord Pirrie standing on the deck of the *Titanic* before it set sail.

8. Another card is a photograph of *Titanic* passengers on board the *Carpathia* the ship that rescued many survivors.

9. There is also a picture of two small children survivors themselves who lost their father in the disaster but were later reunited with their mother.

10. The most interesting card a photo of the ship's gymnasium shows that one of the pieces of exercise equipment for the passengers was a rowing machine.

Source: The Story of the "Titanic" (Dover, 1988).

PARAGRAPH EXERCISE

Use commas to enclose any extra or unnecessary ("scoopable") elements in the following paragraph. Remember to add a pair of commas, one to begin the scoop and another to end it, unless the scoopable element ends at the period.

Do you know Ryan that there is a one-unit library class that begins next week? It's called Library 1 Introduction to the Library and my friends recommended it. The librarians who teach it will give us an orientation and a series of assignment sheets. Then whenever we finish the assignments we turn them in to the librarians for credit. Ms. Kim the librarian that I spoke with said that the course materials cover really valuable library skills. These skills such as finding books or articles in our library and using the Internet to access other databases are the ones universities will expect us to know. I therefore plan to take this class, and you I hope will take it with me.

SENTENCE WRITING

Combine the following sets of sentences in different ways with scoopables in mind. Try to combine each set in a way that needs commas and in a way that doesn't need commas. In other words, try to make an element "scoopable" in one sentence and not "scoopable" in another. You may reorder the details and change the phrasing as you wish. Sample responses are provided in the Answers, but try to write your own before looking at them.

Samantha Jones is a great boss.
A great boss recognizes hard work and rewards dedicated employees.

She plans to buy herself an expensive watch.
It is sold by Tag Heuer.
Tag Heuer is her favorite brand.

Only two people were in the store when the commercial was filmed.
One was the manager.
The other was an actor.

REVIEW OF THE COMMA

USES OF THE COMMA

1. Use a comma to separate two independent clauses joined by one of the *fanboys (for, and, nor, but, or, yet, so).*
2. Use a comma to separate items in a series, date, or address.
3. Use a comma after an introductory word, phrase, or dependent clause.
4. Use a comma before a tag question, contrast, comment, or description.
5. Use commas around the name of a person being spoken to.
6. Use commas around interrupting words and expressions.
7. Use commas around extra, unnecessary ("scoopable") information.

COMMA REVIEW EXERCISE

Add the missing commas, and identify which one of the seven comma uses applies in the brackets at the *end* of each sentence (see the box on page 189 for a numbered list). Each of the seven sentences illustrates a different rule.

I am writing you this note Melanie to ask you to do me a favor. [ ] Before you leave for work today would you take the chicken out of the freezer? [ ] I plan to get started on the appetizers drinks and desserts as soon as I wake up. [ ] I will be so busy however that I might forget to thaw out the chicken. [ ] It's the first time I've cooked all the food for a party by myself and I want everything to be perfect. [ ] The big oval baking pan the one that is in the cupboard above the refrigerator will be the best place to keep the chicken as it thaws. [ ] Wish me luck seriously! [ ]

Thanks for your help.

SENTENCE WRITING

Write at least one sentence of your own to demonstrate each of the seven comma uses. You could write your sentences in the form of a note to a friend, like the one in the Comma Review Exercise. Be sure to think of a new situation that the note could explain. Exchange notes or sentences with a classmate and check each other's commas.

Quotation Marks and Italics/Underlines

Knowing the code of punctuation is crucial when you include quotations of other people's words and ideas or the titles of other people's work.

Use quotation marks around direct quotations (the exact words of a speaker or writer) but not around paraphrases or an indirect quotations. For more about "Choosing and Using Quotations," see pages 230–233.

> In his first speech as president, Franklin D. Roosevelt said the famous words, "The only thing we have to fear is fear itself." (a direct quotation)
>
> In his first speech as president, Franklin D. Roosevelt reassured the nation and told people not to be afraid. (a paraphrase)
>
> The officer said, "Please show me your driver's license." (a direct quotation)
>
> The officer asked to see my driver's license. (an indirect quotation)

If the writer or speaker continues for two or more sentences, use just one set of quotation marks around them.

> She said, "One of your brake lights is out. You need to take care of the problem right away."

If the quotation begins the sentence, the words telling who is speaking (called the signal phrase) are set off with a comma unless the quotation ends with a question mark or an exclamation point. See page 232 for more about signal phrases.

> "I didn't even know it was broken," I said.
>
> "Do you have any questions?" she asked.
>
> "You mean I can go!" I answered excitedly.
>
> "Yes," she said, "consider this just a warning."

Notice that most of the previous quotations begin with a capital letter. But when a quotation is interrupted by a signal phrase, the second part doesn't begin with a capital letter unless the second part is a new sentence.

> "If you knew how much time I spent on the essay," the student explained, "you would give me an A."
>
> "An artist might work on a painting for years," the teacher replied. "That doesn't mean that the result will be a masterpiece."

Use quotation marks to identify the titles of short works: poems, essays, articles, chapters, songs, short stories, Web pages, and TV or radio episodes.

> We read George Orwell's essay "A Hanging" in my speech class.
>
> I couldn't sleep after I read "The Lottery," a short story by Shirley Jackson.
>
> My favorite Woodie Guthrie song is "This Land Is Your Land."
>
> Jerry Seinfeld's troubles in "The Puffy Shirt" episode are some of the funniest moments in TV history.
>
> "The Writer's Almanac" is a Web page with daily updates about famous writers and other interesting information.

Use italics or underlines to identify the titles of long works: books, newspapers, magazines, plays, albums or CDs, Web sites, movies or DVDs, and TV or radio series.

Italicize the appropriate titles whenever you write using a computer.

> *The Host* is a film based on the novel by Stephanie Meyer, author of *Twilight*.
>
> I read about the latest discovery of dinosaur footprints on *CNN.com*.
>
> Many people found the series finale of *The Sopranos* to be a perfect ending.
>
> My mother loves to read the archives on *The Writer's Almanac* Web site.

When handwriting a paper, use underlines, the low-tech equivalent of italicizing.

> The Host is a film based on the novel by Stephanie Meyer, author of Twilight.
>
> I read about the latest discovery of dinosaur footprints on CNN.com.
>
> Many people found the series finale of The Sopranos to be a perfect ending.
>
> My mother loves to read the archives on The Writer's Almanac Web site.

EXERCISES

Correctly punctuate quotations and titles in the following sentences by adding quotation marks or italics/underlines.

Exercise 1

1. A film crew was setting up in the park by my house, and I saw a sign that said, Extras holding.

2. I found someone who didn't look too busy and asked, Are you looking for extras?

3. Yes, she answered, if you want to be in a crowd scene, just fill out the paperwork and sit over there.

4. I didn't even think twice and told her, Sure, I'd love to be in it.

5. I found out from another extra that we were filming the pilot for a new TV comedy series along the lines of Desperate Housewives.

6. When I asked what I was supposed to do, he said, They'll give you a picket sign, and you'll wave it. That's it.

7. I held my sign that said, No more cuts to education! and waved it when I was told to.

8. While it was happening, I kept telling myself, You're going to be on TV—just try not to look stupid.

9. I heard someone ask, Did anyone else hear that the title of the series is going to be Tangle Square?

10. We all shook our heads; then I added, But that's an interesting title, if it's true.

Exercise 2

1. I am reading a book called Don't: A Manual of Mistakes & Improprieties More or Less Prevalent in Conduct and Speech.

2. The book's contents are divided into chapters with titles such as At Table, In Public, and In General.

3. In the section about table don'ts, the book offers the following warning: Don't bend over your plate, or drop your head to get each mouthful.

4. The table advice continues by adding, Don't bite your bread. Break it off.

5. This book offers particularly comforting advice about conducting oneself in public.

6. For instance, it states, Don't brush against people, or elbow people, or in any way show disregard for others.

7. When meeting others on the street, the book advises, Don't be in a haste to introduce. Be sure that it is mutually desired before presenting one person to another.

8. In the section titled In General, there are more tips about how to get along in society, such as Don't underrate everything that others do, and overstate your own doings.

9. The Don't book has this to say about books, whether borrowed or owned: Read them, but treat them as friends that must not be abused.

10. And one can never take the following warning too much to heart: Don't make yourself in any particular way a nuisance to your neighbors or your family.

Exercise 3

1. Emilie Buchwald once noted, Children are made readers on the laps of their parents.

2. Have you read Mark Twain's book The Adventures of Tom Sawyer?

3. I took a deep breath when my counselor asked, How many math classes have you had?

4. Let's start that again! shouted the dance teacher.

5. Last night we watched the Beatles' movie Help! on DVD.

6. Books, wrote Jonathan Swift, are the children of the brain.

7. Voltaire stated in A Philosophical Dictionary that Tears are the silent language of grief.

8. Why do dentists ask questions like How are you? as soon as they start working on your teeth?

9. Did you say, I'm sleepy or I'm beeping?

10. My favorite essay that we have read this semester has to be The Pie by Gary Soto.

Exercise 4

1. Women's Wit and Wisdom is the title of a book I found in the library.

2. The book includes many great insights that were written or spoken by women throughout history.

3. England's Queen Elizabeth I noted in the sixteenth century that A clear and innocent conscience fears nothing.

   4. Nothing is so good as it seems beforehand, observed George Eliot, a
       female author whose real name was Mary Ann Evans.

   5. Some of the women's quotations are funny; Alice Roosevelt Longworth,
       for instance, said, If you don't have anything good to say about anyone,
       come and sit by me.

   6. If life is a bowl of cherries, asked Erma Bombeck, what am I doing in
       the pits?

   7. Some of the quotations are serious, such as Gloria Steinem's statement,
       The future depends on what each of us does every day.

   8. Maya Lin, the woman who designed Washington D.C.'s Vietnam
       Veterans Memorial, reminded us that, as she put it, War is not just a
       victory or a loss. . . . People die.

   9. Emily Dickinson had this to say about truth: Truth is such a rare thing, it
       is delightful to tell it.

  10. Finally, columnist Ann Landers advised one of her readers that The
       naked truth is always better than the best-dressed lie.

Exercise 5

   1. In Booker T. Washington's autobiography Up from Slavery, he describes
       his early dream of going to school.

   2. I had no schooling whatever while I was a slave, he explains.

   3. He continues, I remember on several occasions I went as far as the
       schoolhouse door with one of my young mistresses to carry her books.

   4. Washington then describes what he saw from the doorway: several
       dozen boys and girls engaged in study.

   5. The picture, he adds, made a deep impression upon me.

   6. Washington cherished this glimpse of boys and girls engaged in study.

   7. It contrasted directly with his own situation: My life had its beginning
       in the midst of the most miserable, desolate, and discouraging
       surroundings.

   8. I was born, he says, in a typical log cabin, about fourteen by sixteen
       feet square.

9. He explains, In this cabin I lived with my mother and a brother and sister till after the Civil War, when we were all declared free.

10. As a slave at the door of his young mistress's schoolhouse, Booker T. Washington remembers, I had the feeling that to get into a schoolhouse and study in this way would be about the same as getting into paradise.

Source: Great Americans in Their Own Words (Mallard Press, 1990)

PARAGRAPH EXERCISE

Correctly punctuate quotations and titles in the following paragraph by adding quotation marks or underlining (*italics*).

We were allowed to choose a book to review in our journals last week. The teacher specified that it should be a short nonfiction book about something of interest to us. I found a great book to review. It's called Tattoo: Secrets of a Strange Art. Albert Parry breaks the contents down into chapters about tattoo legends, techniques, and purposes. A few of the chapter titles are The Art and Its Masters, The Circus, Identification, and Removal. The book also includes illustrations and photographs of tattoo designs and tattooed people and animals throughout history, including Miss Stella: The Tattooed Lady, The Famous Tattooed Cow, and Georgius Constantine. Parry describes Constantine's tattoos in the following way: the most complete, elaborate, and artistic tattooing ever witnessed in America or Europe. Parry continues, There was almost no part of his body, not a quarter-inch of the skin, free from designs. Needless to say, since I love tattoos, I loved Parry's book about them.

Source: Tattoo: Secrets of a Strange Art (Dover, 2006)

SENTENCE WRITING

Write ten sentences that list and discuss your favorite films, books, TV shows, characters' expressions, and so on. Be sure to punctuate quotations and titles correctly. Refer to the explanations and examples whenever necessary.

Capital Letters

Capital letters are an essential part of the code of punctuation. Without capitals, we couldn't start a sentence or distinguish between the generic name of a plant (fern) and the specific name of friend (Fern).

Capitalize the first word of every sentence.

Peaches and nectarines taste best when they are cold.

I think every piece of fruit is work of art.

Capitalize the first word of a sentence-length quotation.

The college president asked, "What can we do for our students today?"

"The labs tools are a little dangerous," Zoe said, "but I am always careful." (The *but* is not capitalized because it does not begin a new sentence.)

"I love my art classes," she added. "Maybe I'll change my major." (*Maybe* is capitalized because it begins a new sentence within the quoted material.)

Capitalize the first, last, and main words in a title. Don't capitalize prepositions (*in, of, at, with, about…*), fanboys (*for, and, nor, but, or, yet, so*), or articles (*a, an,* or *the*). See page 250 for more about titles.

I found a copy of Darwin's book *The Origin of Species* at a yard sale.

Our class read the essay "How to Write a Rotten Poem with Almost No Effort."

Shakespeare in Love is a tribute to the life and work of William Shakespeare.

Capitalize specific names of people, places, languages, and nationalities.

English	Shah Rukh Khan	Cesar Chavez
Inuit	Danish	Hindi
Ryan White	Philadelphia	Shanghai

Capitalize names of months, days of the week, and special days, but not the seasons.

March	Fourth of July	spring
Monday	Valentine's Day	summer
Earth Day	Labor Day	fall

Capitalize a title of relationship if it takes the place of the person's name. If *my* (or *your, her, his, our, their*) is in front of the word, a capital is not used.

I think Mom wrote to him.	*but*	I think my mom wrote to him.
We visited Aunt Sophie.	*but*	We visited our aunt.
They spoke with Grandpa.	*but*	They spoke with their grandpa.

Capitalize names of particular people or things, but not general terms.

I admire Professor Washborne.	*but*	I admire my professor.
We saw the famous Danube River.	*but*	We saw the famous river.
Are you from the South?	*but*	Is your house south of the mountains?
I will take Philosophy 4 and English 100.	*but*	I will take philosophy and English.
She graduated from Sutter High School.	*but*	She graduated from high school.
They live at 119 Forest St.	*but*	They live on a beautiful street.
We enjoyed the Long Beach Aquarium.	*but*	We enjoyed the aquarium.

E X E R C I S E S

Add all of the necessary capital letters to the sentences that follow.

Exercise 1

1. i have always wanted to learn another language besides english.

2. recently, i have been watching a lot of films from india.

3. some people call them "bollywood movies."

4. whatever they are called, i love to watch them.

5. one part of these movies that i love is their main language: hindi.

6. i have to use english subtitles to understand the dialogue most of the time.

7. but sometimes i can catch what's happening without the subtitles.

8. because of my intense interest in hindi-language films, i plan to take a hindi class.

9. i have already bought a book that explains the devanagari writing system.

10. now i will enroll in a class and learn hindi as a second language.

Exercise 2

1. when people think of jazz, they think of *down beat* magazine.

2. *down beat*'s motto may be "jazz, blues & beyond," but some people think that the magazine has gone too far "beyond" by including two guitarists in the *down beat* hall of fame.

3. the two musicians in question are jimi hendrix and frank zappa.

4. jimi hendrix was inducted into the hall of fame in 1970.

5. *down beat* added frank zappa to the list in 1994.

6. since then, readers and editors have been debating whether hendrix and zappa belong in the same group as duke ellington, john coltrane, and miles davis.

7. those who play jazz guitar have some of the strongest opinions on the subject.

8. russell malone, mark elf, and john abercrombie all agree that hendrix and zappa were great guitarists but not jazz guitarists.

9. others like steve tibbetts and bill frisell don't have any problem putting hendrix on the list, but tibbetts isn't so sure about including zappa.

10. it will be interesting to see who *down beat*'s future inductees will be.

Source: Down Beat, July 1999

Exercise 3

1. many consider *the diary of anne frank* to be one of the most important books of the twentieth century.

2. anne frank wrote her famous diary during the nazi occupation of holland in world war ii.

3. the building in amsterdam where the frank family and several others hid during the two years before their capture is now a museum and has been recently renovated.

4. visitors to the anne frank house can stand before her desk and see pictures of movie stars like greta garbo on her wall.

5. they can climb the stairs hidden behind a bookcase that led to the annex where anne lived with her mother, edith; her father, otto; and her sister, margot.

6. one of the others hiding with the franks was peter van pels, who was roughly the same age as anne.

7. anne writes of her relationship with peter in her diary.

8. visitors to the museum can enter the room where peter gave anne her first kiss just a few months before the nazis discovered their hiding place in 1944.

9. anne's family and peter's were both sent to concentration camps in germany.

10. only anne's father lived to see the anne frank house open as a museum for the first time on may 3, 1960.

Source: Smithsonian, October 2001

Exercise 4

1. i recently saw the movie *v for vendetta,* and i wanted to learn more about it.

2. i found out that it's based on an extensive series of comic books.

3. they were written by alan moore and illustrated by david lloyd.

4. the original episodes of *v for vendetta* were published in black and white within a british comic series called *warrior.*

5. once the series caught on in the united states, dc comics began to publish it.

6. at that time, the creators added color to the drawings.

7. the letter v in the title *v for vendetta* stands for the main character, a mysterious costumed figure who calls himself v.

8. however, many other connections between the letter v and the roman numeral 5, which is written as a v, come up throughout the story.

9. v wears a mask that people in the united kingdom refer to as a guy fawkes mask.

10. guy fawkes was an english historical figure famous for his involvement in the gunpowder plot, which failed on the fifth of november in 1605.

Exercise 5

1. when my art teacher asked the class to do research on frida kahlo, i knew that the name sounded familiar.

2. then i remembered that the actress salma hayek starred in the movie *frida,* which was about this mexican-born artist's life.

3. frida kahlo's paintings are all very colorful and seem extremely personal.

4. she painted mostly self-portraits, and each one makes a unique statement.

5. one of these portraits is called *my grandparents, my parents, and i.*

6. kahlo gave another one the title *the two fridas.*

7. but my favorite of kahlo's works is *self-portrait on the borderline between mexico and the united states.*

8. in an article i read in *smithsonian* magazine, kahlo's mother explains that after frida was severely injured in a bus accident, she started painting.

9. kahlo's mother set up a mirror near her daughter's bed so that frida could use herself as a model.

10. in the *smithsonian* article from the november 2002 issue, kahlo is quoted as saying, "i never painted dreams. i painted my own reality."

REVIEW OF PUNCTUATION AND CAPITAL LETTERS

Apply the full code of punctuation to the following sentences by adding the appropriate periods, question marks, exclamation points, semicolons, colons, dashes, commas, quotation marks, italics/underlines, and capital letters. Apostrophes have already been added to the sentences for contractions (page 41) and possessives (page 47). Compare your answers carefully with those at the back of the book. Sentences may require several different pieces of punctuation or capital letters.

1. we couldn't leave san anonio texas without visiting its most famous site the alamo

2. my teacher asked have you ever seen the first episodes of the simpsons

3. the bridges have remodeled their garage now their son uses it as an apartment

4. when eric my older brother gets a traffic ticket he always goes to traffic school

5. we have refunded your money ms jones and have sent you a confirmation

6. one of the teachers who visited the library left his wallet on the checkout counter

7. the united parcel service better known as ups was hiring on campus yesterday

8. even though i am enjoying my latin class i wish i had taken chinese instead

9. you always misremember the date of my birthday you think it's in may

10. pink normally a calming color can have the opposite effect when it's neon

11. stopping by woods on a snowy evening is a famous poem by robert frost

12. finding a good deal for a new car online takes time patience and luck

13. my friend is reading the play taming of the shrew in her women's studies class

14. i wonder how much my history of textiles book will cost

15. the foreign film club needs people to pass out flyers let's volunteer

COMPREHENSIVE TEST

Proofread the following sentences to catch errors in word use, sentence structure, and punctuation. Try to identify the error in the blank before each sentence, and then correct the error if you can.

adj	incorrect adjective
adv	incorrect adverb
apos	apostrophe
awk	awkward phrasing
c	comma needed
cap	capitalization
cliché	overused expression
cs	comma splice
dm	dangling modifier
frag	fragment
mm	misplaced modifier
p	punctuation
pro	incorrect pronoun
pro agr	pronoun agreement
ro	run-on sentence
shift	shift in time or person
sp	misspelled word
s-v agr	subject-verb agreement
verb	incorrect verb form
wordy	wordiness
ww	wrong word
//	not parallel

A perfect—or nearly perfect—score will mean you've mastered the essential skills covered in first three parts of this book: Word Use, Sentence Structure, and Punctuation.

1. _____ I wonder if I can get an earlier registration date?

2. _____ The bookstore has updated it's checkout system again.

3. _____ Kids' movies and the TV shows for children usually have better stories than the ones made for adults.

4. _____ The fencing coach gives great advise to help students improve quickly.

5. _____ "Welcome, the teacher said to all of us, are we ready to begin?"

6. _____ Depending of the price of gasoline at the time, I either ride my bike to school or drive my car to school.

7. _____ Both math and english require intense concentration.

8. _____ Reunions seem like a good idea but they seldom live up to expectations.

9. _____ When I put my lunch in the microwave, it blew a fuse.

10. _____ We volunteered to read books to children at the library, it was really fun.

11. _____ Students often throw their notes away when you should always keep them.

12. _____ Either the employees or the company have to take a cut in earnings.

13. _____ We ordered business cards with are new logos printed on them.

14. _____ Each of the candidates receive the questions in advance.

15. _____ As we stepped outside the sunlight hurt our eyes.

16. _____ She felt badly when her sister didn't get a scholarship.

17. _____ Our group only studied for an hour; that's why we failed.

18. _____ The critique of our sculpture projects took much longer then I expected.

19. _____ An error occurring while uploading the video on YouTube.

20. _____ Their going to pack their boxes on Wednesday and move on Friday.

P A R T 4

Writing

What Is the Least You Should Know about Writing?

"Unlike medicine or the other sciences," William Zinsser points out, "writing has no new discoveries to spring on us. We're in no danger of reading in our morning newspaper that a breakthrough has been made in how to write [clearly]. . . . We may be given new technologies . . . to ease the burdens of composition, but on the whole we know what we need to know."

One thing is certain: people learn to write by *writing*—not by reading long discussions about writing. Therefore, the explanatory sections in Part 4 are as brief as they can be, and they include samples by both professional and student writers.

Understanding the basic structures and learning the essential skills covered in these sections will help you become a better writer.

Writing as Structure

Aside from the basics of word use, sentence structure, and punctuation, what else do you need to understand to write better? Just as sentences are built according to accepted patterns, so are the larger "structures" in writing—paragraphs and essays, for example.

Think of writing as a system of structures, beginning small with words that connect to form phrases, clauses, and sentences. Then sentences connect to form paragraphs and essays. Each level has its own set of "blueprints." To communicate clearly in writing, words must be chosen and spelled correctly. Sentences must have a subject, a verb, and a complete thought. Paragraphs must be indented and should contain a main idea supported with sufficient detail. Essays should explore a valuable topic in several coherent paragraphs, usually including an introduction, a body, and a conclusion.

Not everyone approaches writing as a structure, however. It is possible to write better without thinking about structure at all. A good place to start might be to write what you care about and to care about what you write. You can make an amazing amount of progress by simply being *genuine,* being who you are naturally. No one has to tell you to be yourself when you speak, but you might need encouragement to be yourself in your writing.

First-Person and Third-Person Approaches

You may have identified—and your professors may have pointed out—two main approaches to writing: the first-person approach (using *I, me, we, us*) and the third-person approach (using *one, he, she, it, they, them*). Note that the second-person pronoun—*you*—serves a special purpose, not commonly required in college papers. Writers use *you* to guide the reader through a process or to teach the reader how to do something, just as we use *you* in this book to teach "the least you should know about English." Unless you are writing a "how-to" paper of some kind, it's best to avoid using *you*. Let's focus, then, on first person vs. third person.

What are the benefits of the first-person approach? First-person pronouns allow you to express yourself directly ("I agree with Isaac Asimov.") and to connect with readers by including them in your observations. Here is an example from Browning's essay about the concept of "home" on page 212: "Nesting. Why do we do it, why does it matter? Why do we care so much?" The first-person approach establishes a direct connection between the writer, the information, and the reader.

How does the third-person approach compare? The third-person point of view presents information about people and ideas more objectively. For example, you'll find this sentence in Vanderbilt's excerpt about traffic on page 214: "So much time is spent in cars in the United States, studies show, that drivers (particularly men) have higher rates of skin cancer on their left sides. . . ." The third-person approach creates a comfortable distance between the writer, the information, and the reader.

Most writers don't consciously restrict themselves to one approach, but in some cases they do. As an example, Geoff Colvin adheres to the third-person approach in his excerpt about Mozart on page 230. However, it is possible to use more than one approach when necessary. Professional writers often successfully blend first and third person (sometimes even first, second, and third person). On page 130, Judy Jones and William Wilson mix second- and third-person approaches in their excerpt about the controversial artist team of Christo and Jeanne-Claude: "So what's their point? Rest assured, you're not the first to ask." Being aware of your options will help you grow as a writer.

Learning to write well is important, and confidence is the key. The Writing sections will help you build confidence, whether you are expressing your own ideas or presenting and responding to the ideas of others. Like the Sentence Structure sections, the Writing sections are best taken in order. However, each one discusses an aspect of writing that you can review on its own at any time.

Basic Structures

I. THE PARAGRAPH

A paragraph is unlike any other structure in English. It has its own visual profile: the first line is indented about five spaces, and sentences continue to fill the space between both margins until the paragraph ends (which may be in the middle of the line):

_____

_____

_____

_____

_____

_____.

As a beginning writer, you may forget to indent your paragraphs, or you may break off in the middle of a line within a paragraph, especially when writing in class. You must remember to indent whenever you begin a new paragraph and fill the space between the margins until it ends. (Note: In business writing, paragraphs are not indented but double-spaced in between.)

Defining a Paragraph

A paragraph usually develops one idea, often phrased as a topic sentence from which all the other sentences in the paragraph radiate. The topic sentence does not need to begin the paragraph, but it most often does, and the other sentences support it with specific details. (For more on topic sentences and organizing paragraphs, see page 224.) Paragraphs usually contain several sentences, though no set number is required. A paragraph can stand alone, but more commonly paragraphs are part of a larger composition, an essay. There are different kinds of paragraphs, based on the jobs they do.

Types of Paragraphs

SAMPLE PARAGRAPHS IN AN ESSAY

Introductory paragraphs begin essays. They provide background information about the topic and usually include the thesis statement or main idea of the essay. (See page 222 for information on how to write a thesis statement.) Here is the introductory paragraph of a brief student essay about the impact of movies in our lives:

> We all love a good movie, whether it is action, drama, romance, or comedy, we just can't get enough of it. Movies are as important in our lives as food, it seems. And like food, we usually take them for granted. Why is that? The way I see it, movies can be like fast food or full, satisfying meals. Either way, we enjoy them.

In this opening paragraph, the student introduces the main idea that "Movies are as important in our lives as food" but that "we take them for granted" and sets up a two-part organization for the essay to show how some movies are "like fast food" and others "full, satisfying meals."

Body paragraphs are those in the middle of essays. Each body paragraph contains a topic sentence and presents detailed information about one idea or aspect that relates directly to the essay's thesis. (See page 224 for more information on organizing body paragraphs.) Here are the body paragraphs of the same essay:

> In the same way that we eat fast food on the run, a good movie can take us on a journey. We don't question it; we just go, and we eat it with gusto. These movies focus on action and fantasy because they give us that edge in life. They take us to a dream or even nightmare place that we don't want to wake up from. They put us directly into the superhero's or alien hunter's shoes. In other words, they give us ordinary people that kick in life that we might not have. Like french fries, these films keep us wanting more until, eventually, we get sick of them.
>
> When we are not looking for mindless adventure, we set our eyes to something more serious and satisfying—movies that fortify us like a good meal. Documentaries and crime movies come to mind. We want these movies to inform, challenge, or expand our thoughts. Documentaries can bring us up to date on a world problem, our favorite rock band, or an important person that we might not know about. Crime stories and mysteries have us questioning every part of a complex puzzle, using logic and critical thinking. At the end of these films of substance, we earn the satisfaction of having learned or solved something new.

Notice that each body paragraph develops one of the two types of movies brought up in the thesis statement.

Concluding paragraphs are the final paragraphs in essays. They bring the discussion to a close and share the writer's final thoughts on the subject. (See page 209 for more about concluding paragraphs.) Here is the conclusion of the sample essay:

> Most people enjoy a little bit of everything when it comes to movies. But I think the majority of us prefer the journey of fast-food films, full of action and fantasy. Whether we're slouching on the couch or sitting upright in front of a huge movie screen, these movies make us want to be there, saving the earth and stopping the bad guys. These films take us with them, and we go, no questions asked.

In this concluding paragraph, the student shares his final thoughts about the impact of movies, which ones seem to please us the most, and why.

SAMPLE OF A SINGLE-PARAGRAPH ASSIGNMENT

Single-paragraph writing assignments may be given in class or as homework. They test your understanding of the unique structure of a paragraph. They may ask you to react to a reading or provide details about a limited topic. Here is a sample paragraph-length reaction following the class's reading of an essay called "What Is Intelligence, Anyway?" by Isaac Asimov. In his essay, Asimov explains that there are other kinds of intelligence besides just knowledge of theories and facts. This student shares Asimov's ideas about intelligence and uses personal experiences to support her reaction:

> I agree with Isaac Asimov. Intelligence doesn't only belong to Nobel Prize winners. I define "intelligence" as being able to value that special skill a person has been born with. Not everyone is a math genius or a brain surgeon. For example, ask a brain surgeon to rotate the engine in a car. It isn't going to happen. To be able to take a certain skill that someone has inherited and push it to its farthest limits I would call "intelligence." Isaac Asimov's definition is similar to mine. He believes that academic questions are only correctly answered by academicians. He gives the example of a farmer. Questions on a farming test would only be correctly answered by a farmer. Not everyone has the same talent; we are all different. When I attend my math classes, I must always pay attention. If I don't, I end up struggling with what I missed. On the other hand, when I'm in my music classes, I really don't have to work hard because reading music, playing the piano, and singing all come easily to me. I see other students struggling with music the way I do with math. This is just another example of how skills and talents differ. Some people are athletic; others are brainy. Some people can sing; others can cook. It really doesn't matter what the skill might be. If it's a talent, to me that's a form of intelligence.

These shorter writing assignments help students practice presenting information within the limited structure of a paragraph. If this had been an essay-length reaction, the writer would have included more details about her own and other people's types of intelligence. And she may have wanted to quote from Asimov's essay and discuss his most important points at length.

II. The Essay

Like the paragraph, an essay has its own profile, usually including a title and several paragraphs.

Title

_____

_____
_____
_____
_____.

_____
_____
_____
_____

_____.

_____
_____
_____
_____
_____
_____.

_____
_____
_____
_____
_____.

_____
_____
_____
_____.

While the paragraph is the single building block of text used in almost all forms of writing (essays, magazine articles, letters, novels, newspaper stories, e-mails, and so on), an essay is a larger, more complex structure.

The Five-Paragraph Essay and Beyond

The student essay analyzed on pages 208–209 illustrates the different kinds of paragraphs within essays. Many people like to include five paragraphs in an essay: an introductory paragraph, three body paragraphs, and a concluding paragraph. However, an essay can include any number of paragraphs. Three is a comfortable number of body paragraphs to start with—it is not two, which makes an essay seem like a comparison even when it isn't; and it is not four, which may be too many subtopics for the beginning writer to organize clearly.

An essay should be long enough to explore and support its topic without leaving unanswered questions in the reader's mind. As you become more comfortable with the flow of your ideas and gain confidence in your ability to express yourself, you can write longer essays. As with many skills, learning about writing begins with basic structures and then expands to include all possibilities.

Defining an Essay

There is no such thing as a typical essay. Essays may be serious or humorous, but the best of them present thought-provoking information or opinions. Try looking up the word *essay* in a dictionary right now. Some words used to define an essay might need to be explained themselves:

An essay is *prose* (meaning it is written in the ordinary language of sentences and paragraphs).

An essay is *nonfiction* (meaning it deals with real people, factual information, actual opinions and events).

An essay is a *composition* (meaning it is created in parts that make up the whole, several paragraphs that explore a single topic or issue).

An essay is *personal* (meaning it shares the writer's unique perspective, even if only in the choice of topic, method of analysis, and details).

An essay is *analytical* and *instructive* (meaning it examines the workings of a subject and shares the results with the reader).

An essay may be *argumentative* (meaning it tries to convince the reader to accept an opinion or take action).

A Sample Professional Essay

For an example of a brief piece of writing that fits the above definition, read the following essay, in which professional writer Dominique Browning explains how hard it is to define the word *home*.

Wandering Home

Every morning for weeks this spring I was awakened at five by the gentle, persistent cooing of a dove. Such a soft, lovely song, yet each day it was able to penetrate my dreams and lure me from my bed onto the balcony. I would search through the treetops for a glimpse of her until the damp chill sent me back indoors, and then finally one day I spotted her. She had built a nest on the trellis right over my door, wedged in amid a looping tangle of wisteria. I didn't dare go out onto the balcony again, for fear of disturbing her. Several days later the cooing stopped, and I suppose she became serious about laying and hatching her eggs, or why else would she sit so still and silent in her new home?

Nesting. Why do we do it, why does it matter? Why do we care so much? This has been on my mind lately, because I recently met a real wanderer, someone who is defiantly, dogmatically, devotedly nomadic. He isn't selfishly drifting; homeless by choice, he has spent the past 20 years living all over the world, doing good. Home for him is a provisional thing. I was so struck by the marked contrast to the way my friends and I have hunkered down, sent out roots, gathered treasure, gotten anchored. Maybe got stuck, who knows? I have always thought of making a home as one of those basic desires, but why should it be?

It is too easy to say home is where the heart is, where your loved ones sleep. Your loved ones can go with you, wherever you roam, and your loved ones can just as well be scattered to all corners of the world. We grow up (most of us) and ruthlessly leave behind the first homes of our childhood. And we often leave with the thought that the home we make for ourselves will be markedly different from the one made by our parents.

Some of us end up finding home in the town where we were raised. Some of us have ancestral homes, where generations of the family have been raised—places dear enough to draw everyone back. Some of us simply choose a place, or, if we are lucky, we feel the place chooses us. For some of us, a home is as large as a country—"I'm at home in France," one friend will say, or "I felt like I had come home when I got to Ireland"—and for others, a home is as small as the four walls of a room. Some of us move restlessly from house to house; others are restless within the house, rearranging the furniture, circling toward some approximation of beauty, serenity. And then some of us are so settled that our bodies creak to leave the sofa.

Maybe home is one of those subjects over which much of the world is divided: those who care about it passionately and those who don't give it a second thought. Maybe some of us are the fixed points of the compass: we're home, so others can twirl in circles around the globe. Some of us need the foundation of a home because our thoughts, dreams, emotions are constantly wheeling, wandering. And for some of us, there is the great adventure of making a home— you know, that thing about the world in a grain of sand or, dare I say, a smear of paint, a dab of plaster, the twinkle of a chandelier, the gleam of that old pearwood commode. The adamant wanderer finally confessed to having a warehouse full of stuff collected over the years, so even a nomad isn't immune to fantasies of home, however delayed the gratification of making one might turn out to be.

As for the dove: after a few quiet weeks, I noticed on the ground beneath her nest what I first took to be a bright curl of Styrofoam and of course turned out to be the fragment of an eggshell. One down. One untimely flight, one tiny lost soul. But still the dove sits, home for the time being.

Now that you have learned more about the basic structures of the paragraph and the essay, you are ready to practice the skills necessary to write them.

Writing Skills

III. Writing in Your Own Voice

All writing speaks on paper. And the person listening is the reader. Some beginning writers forget that writing and reading are two-way methods of communication, just like spoken conversations between two people. When you write, your reader hears you; when you read, you also listen.

When speaking, you express a personality in your choice of phrases, your movements, your tone of voice. Family and friends probably recognize your voice mail messages without your having to identify yourself. Would they also be able to recognize your writing? They would, if you extended your *voice* into your writing.

Writing should not sound like talking, necessarily, but it should have a personality that comes from the way you decide to approach a topic, to develop it with details, to say it *your* way.

The beginning of this book discusses the difference between spoken English, which follows the looser patterns of speaking, and Standard Written English, which follows accepted patterns of writing. Don't think that the only way to add voice to your writing is to use the patterns of spoken English. Remember that Standard Written English does not have to be dull or sound academic. Look at this example of Standard Written English that has a distinct voice, part of the book *Traffic: Why We Drive the Way We Do (and What It Says about Us)* by Tom Vanderbilt:

> Traffic has even shaped the food we eat. "One-handed convenience" is the mantra, with forkless foods like Taco Bell's hexagonal Crunchwrap Supreme, designed "to handle well in the car." I spent an afternoon in Los Angeles with an advertising executive who had, at the behest of that same restaurant chain, conducted a test, in actual traffic, of which foods were easiest to eat while driving. The main barometer of success or failure was the number of napkins used. But if food does spill, one can simply reach for Tide to Go, a penlike device for "portable stain removal," which can be purchased at one of the more than twelve hundred (and growing) CVS drugstores that feature a drive-through window. . . . Car commuting is so entrenched in daily life that National Public Radio refers to its most popular segments as "driveway moments," meaning that listeners are so riveted to a story they cannot leave their cars. . . . So much time is spent in cars in the United States, studies show, that drivers (particularly men) have higher rates of skin cancer on their left sides—look for the opposite effect in countries where people drive on the left.

Vanderbilt's examination of traffic's effect on us illustrates Standard Written English at its liveliest—from its sentence structures to its precise use of words. But more importantly, Vanderbilt's clear voice speaks to us and involves us in his fascination with traffic. You can involve your reader, too, by writing in your own voice. Here is an example of a student response to a brief assignment that asked her to describe a person who had recently made an impression on her.

> Sitting at the kids' play area of my local mall one afternoon last week, I glanced over at another parent paying closer attention to his Blackberry than to his son. Enclosed in an oval-shaped ring with cushioned benches lining the edges, shoppers' kids ran around and played as their parents caught their breaths. In the middle of the play area lay an array of toys: boats, turtles, and small mounds of plastic for kids to crawl on and cylinders for them to crawl through. The workaholic looked up occasionally, making sure his son was still there. His thick brimmed glasses sat loosely on the bridge of his nose. His straight, jet-black hair was about a month overdue for a cut. In his late thirties, he was obviously concentrating more on his career and business than on his family in its youth. As I watched my own daughter run and play, I looked over to see the workaholic diligently typing away. I wasn't sure if he was checking e-mail, responding to e-mail, or updating his calendar, but his small brown eyes squinted, and this gave a pained look to his face; half deep in thought, the other half confused and stressed. Alternately leaning forward and slouching back, he caused his khaki pants to wrinkle and crease. His plaid shirt, unevenly tucked in, was held in place by an old and fading brown belt. His professional successes hadn't translated into any sense of style. Even on what might have been a rare day off, he couldn't escape the electronic leash that dominated his life. While his son grew up right in front of his eyes, his vision seemed way out of focus.

Notice that both professional and student writers can engage readers by telling stories (narration) and painting pictures with words (description). Narration and description require practice, but once you master them, you will strengthen and clarify your voice and increase interest in your writing.

Narration

Narrative writing tells a story or stories from the writer's personal experience. Since most of us like to tell stories, it is a good place to begin writing in your own voice. Effective narration allows readers to experience events with the writer. Since we all see the world differently and feel unique emotions, the purpose of narration is to take readers with us through our experiences. As a result, the writer gains a better understanding of the events, and readers get to live other lives momentarily.

A Sample Student Essay

Listen to the *voice* of this student writer using narration and description to support her private definition of "home." The student wrote this in-class (timed) essay in response to a reading prompt from Browning's essay "Wandering Home" on page 212:

Missing Home

Dominique Browning's idea of home is a place where people feel safe, and every city, country, and room can feel like "home" to someone. People think differently when it comes to being at home somewhere. Browning notes that some people like to live in the place they are born or raised. Others move "from house to house" or from country to country to find a home. After reading Browning's essay, I figure that the true meaning of "home" depends on the person who's defining it.

I don't have or feel that I have a place I can call home, but I can tell you of a place where I used to have that feeling—my grandmother's house. My parents moved around like gypsies when I was growing up. They always rented the places we lived in, and the longest we stayed in one was ten years. That was a record. But I never felt at home in any of the places we lived.

Every summer, I would spend one week by myself at my grandma's place. I loved it. I always felt welcomed and warm in her house. Even though it was summer vacation, we didn't do anything exciting like spend a day at the beach or go to Disneyland. I just hung around in her kitchen while she made my favorite foods, what she called "poor man's dinners" of tacos, fried potatoes with hot dogs, or hamburger patties and corn. She always watched her "novellas" (Spanish soap operas) on TV when I was there. I didn't know how to speak Spanish (still don't), so she would translate for me. Before I knew it, I was getting into the stories with her, and each one led to a good conversation. She shared bits of how she and her family struggled though the great depression and how she met my grandfather.

Grandma's house was a duplex, not too big inside, and it was always clean, never dirty. The mantle over

the fireplace was crammed with pictures of her children,
grandchildren, and great-grandchildren. Her home had one
bedroom and one bathroom and was more narrow than wide.
The kitchen was kind of small, but it carried the scent
of her strong cooking. Through its back door, we could
look out into the shady yard and watch the squirrels
flick their tails in the sun.

I felt at home at my grandmother's house because it
was quiet and filled with care and concern all the time.
I was relaxed and knew that I could depend on her. I felt
peace in her house, and I didn't feel that anywhere else
(still don't). To me, that's the feeling of "home."

See page 234 for more about "Writing in Response to a Reading" and page 237
for a chart of helpful "Tips for In-Class Writing."

Description

Descriptive writing paints pictures with words that appeal to the reader's five
senses—sight, sound, touch, taste, and smell. The writer of the description often
uses comparisons (figures of speech) to help readers picture one thing by imagining
something else. For example, on page 212, Browning compares some people to
"the fixed points of the compass," and Vanderbilt describes the stain-remover Tide
to Go as a "penlike device" in his excerpt about traffic on page 214 to help the
reader *picture* the object.

Here is an example of a descriptive paragraph in which a student describes
her car door's remote control device by comparing it to a robot:

My Robot

My car door's remote control looks like a small robot's head. The front

of it resembles a human face to me. It has two droopy eyes, a nose, and a

mouth—but the eyes cannot see, the nose cannot smell, and the mouth

cannot open because of a strip of shiny old tape that covers my robot's face

like an uncomfortable mask and secures it to a flat piece of leather on my key

chain. The chain holds my little robot like a prisoner, but it still has a mind of its own. Like a small child, it can be capricious. Sometimes it does what I want it to do, but other times it does what it wants to do. Its brain shows that it's working by blinking a red light on its forehead. And even though my little robot looks old and tired, it usually works when I need it the most.

You may have noticed that many of the examples in this section use both narration and description. In fact, most effective writing—even a good résumé or biology lab report—calls for clear storytelling and vivid word pictures to engage the reader.

Writing Exercises

The following two exercises will help you develop your voice as a writer. For now, don't worry about topic sentences or thesis statements or any of the skills we'll teach you in the sections to come. Narration and description have their own logical structures. A narrated experience is a story with a beginning, a middle, and an end. And we describe things from top to bottom, side to side, and so on. You will find more Writing Exercises throughout this section.

Writing Exercise 1

NARRATE AN EXPERIENCE TO ILLUSTRATE A FAMOUS SAYING

The following is a list of well-known expressions. No doubt you have had an experience that proves at least one of these to be true. To *illustrate* means to prove with an example. Write a short essay that narrates a story from your own life to illustrate one of these sayings. See if you can tell which of the sayings "Wandering Home" on page 212 and "Missing Home" on page 216 illustrate. You might want to identify the expression you have chosen in your introductory paragraph. Then use vivid details to bring the beginning, middle, and end of the story to life. Finish with a brief concluding paragraph to share your final thoughts on the experience.

Experience is the best teacher.

We never know what we have until it's gone.

No two people are alike.

If at first you don't succeed, try, try again.

Money can't buy happiness.

Writing Exercise 2

DESCRIBE A PICTURE WORTH 250 WORDS

Describe a picture that you respond to in a powerful way—one that you are drawn to, one that you *like*. It could be an advertisement, a well-known historical image, a famous drawing or painting, or a moment from a popular movie. Print a copy of the picture and observe it carefully. Your goal is to help the reader *visualize* the picture and convey the impression it makes. Try to use details and comparisons that appeal to the reader's senses in some way. Look back at the examples for inspiration. Be sure to attach the copy of your picture to your description so that the reader can see exactly what you're describing.

IV. FINDING A TOPIC

You will most often be given a topic to write about; however, when the assignment asks you to choose your own topic without any further assistance, try to go immediately to your interests.

Look to Your Interests

If the topic of your paper is something you know about and—more important— something you *care* about, then the whole process of writing will be smoother and more enjoyable for you. If you collect coins, if you can draw, or even if you just enjoy going to the movies, bring that knowledge and enthusiasm into your papers.

Take a moment to think about and jot down a few of your interests now (no matter how unrelated to school they may seem), and then save the list for use later when deciding what to write about. One student's list of interests might look like this:

buying and selling on eBay

playing poker on weekends

skiing in the mountains in winter

shopping at flea markets

Another student's list might be very different:

playing the piano

going to concerts

watching "Bollywood" movies

drawing pictures of my friends

Still another student might list the following interests:

bowling in a league

participating in my book club

traveling in the summer

buying lottery tickets

These students have listed several worthy topics for papers. And because they are personal interests, the students have the details needed to support them. With a general topic to start with, you can use several ways to gather the details you will need to support it in a paragraph or an essay.

Focused Free Writing (or Brainstorming)

Free writing is a good way to begin. When you are assigned a paper, try writing for ten minutes, putting down all your thoughts on one subject—"traveling in the summer," for example. Don't stop to think about organization, sentence structures, capitalization, or spelling—just let details flow onto the page. Free writing will help you see what material you have and will help you figure out what aspects of the subject to write about.

Here is an example:

I like to draw pictures of my friends but sometimes they don't like it when I draw them. The nose is to big they think or the hair isn't just right. Once in awhile I get it perfect, but not that often. I like to style my drawings like cartoons kind of. Its almost like you'll see little baloons like in a cartoon strip with little sayings in them. I'm not a big talker myself, so I can express myself with my friends thru my drawings of them. Again, some of them like it and some of them don't.

Now the result of this free writing session is certainly not ready to be typed and turned in as a paragraph. But what did become clear in it was that the student could probably compare the two types of friends—those who like to be drawn and those who don't.

Clustering

Clustering is another way of putting ideas on paper before you begin to write an actual draft. A cluster is more visual than free writing. You could cluster the topic of "book clubs," for instance, by putting it in a circle in the center of a piece of paper and then drawing lines to new circles as ideas or details occur to you. The idea is to free your mind from the limits of sentences and paragraphs to generate pure details and ideas. When you are finished clustering, you can see where you want to go with a topic.

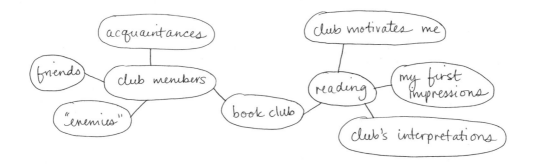

Talking with Other Students

It may help to talk to others when deciding on a topic. Many teachers divide their students into groups at the beginning of an assignment. Talking with other students helps you realize that you see things just a little differently. *Value* the difference—it will help your written voice that we discussed earlier, emerge.

Writing Exercise 3

LIST YOUR INTERESTS

Make a list of four or five of your own interests. Be sure that they are as specific as the examples listed on page 219. Keep the list for later assignments.

Writing Exercise 4

DO SOME FREE WRITING

Choose one of your interests, and do some focused free writing about it. Write for ten minutes with that topic in mind but without stopping. Don't worry about anything such as spelling or sentence structures while you are free writing. The results are meant to help you find out what you have to say about the topic *before* you start to write a paper about it. Save the results for a later assignment.

Writing Exercise 5

PRACTICE CLUSTERING IDEAS

Choose another of your interests. Put it in the center of a piece of paper, and draw a cluster of details and ideas relating to it following the sample on page 221. Take the cluster as far as it will go. Then choose one aspect to cluster again on its own. This way you will arrive at specific, interesting details and ideas—not just the first ones that come to mind. Save the results of all your efforts.

V. Organizing Ideas

Most important to keep in mind, no matter what you are writing, is the idea you want to get across to the reader. Whether you are writing a paragraph or an essay, you must have in mind a single idea that you want to express. In a paragraph, such an idea is called a *topic sentence;* in an essay it's called a *thesis statement,* but they mean the same thing—an idea you want to get across. We will begin with a discussion of thesis statements.

Thesis Statements

Let's choose one of the student interests listed on page 219. "Buying and selling on eBay" is just a general topic; it doesn't make a point. What about eBay? Why do you like it? What does it do for you or for others? What point about eBay would you like to present to your reader? You might write a sentence like this:

> Buying and selling on eBay is fun and educational.

This sentence is a start, but it's not focused enough to develop. You might move into more specific territory and write one of the following sentences:

> I've learned a lot about business and geography by buying and selling on eBay.
>
> or
>
> Buyers and sellers learn a lot about business and geography through their transactions on eBay.

Now you have said something specific in two different ways. The first sentence uses the first-person pronoun *I.* The second sentence discusses "buyers" and "sellers" in general and uses *their,* a third-person pronoun, to refer to them. Some writing instructors may ask you to avoid writing in the first person, and others may encourage you to use it. (See page 206 for more discussion of these approaches.) Whichever approach you use, when you write in one sentence the point you want to present to your reader, you have begun writing a thesis statement.

You may have a general idea in mind when you begin to write, but the support for it will evolve as you write. You can develop your thesis in various ways, but behind whatever you write will be your ruling thought, your reason for writing a particular essay, your thesis.

For any writing assignment, after you have done some free writing or clustering to explore your topic, the next step is to write a thesis statement. As you write your thesis statement, keep two rules in mind:

1. A thesis statement must be *a sentence with a subject and a verb* (not merely a topic).

2. A thesis statement must be *an idea that you can explain or defend* (not simply a statement of fact).

Writing Exercise 6

IDENTIFY A TOPIC, FACT, OR THESIS

Which of the following are merely topics or facts, and which are statements that you could explain or defend in an essay? In front of each one that is just a topic or a fact, write TOPIC or FACT. In front of each one that could be a thesis statement, write THESIS. Check your answers.

1. _____ Gasoline prices are rising again.

2. _____ Animals that seem to be able to predict earthquakes.

3. _____ On July 20, 1969, Neil Armstrong planted an American flag on the moon.

4. _____ Plagiarism is a misunderstood "crime."

5. _____ Computer-generated movie characters can affect us in the same ways as "real-life" characters.

6. _____ Voice-recognition technology may eventually weaken people's reading and writing skills.

7. _____ Home schooling advantages and disadvantages.

8. _____ Tiger Woods and his amazing career in golf.

9. _____ Traveling to different countries makes people more open-minded.

10. _____ Vegetarians can suffer from health problems related to their diets.

Writing Exercise 7

WRITE A THESIS STATEMENT

Use your free-writing or clustering results from Writing Exercises 4 and 5 (page 221) and write at least one thesis statement based on your interests. Be sure that the thesis you write is phrased as a complete thought that can be defended or explained in an essay.

Organizing an Essay

Once you have written a good thesis and explored your topic through discussion with others or by free writing and clustering, you are ready to organize your essay.

First, you need an introductory paragraph. It should catch the reader's interest, provide necessary background information, and either include or suggest your thesis statement. (See page 208 and page 215 for two examples of student writers' introductory paragraphs.) In your introductory paragraph, you may also list supporting points, but a more effective way is to let them unfold paragraph by paragraph rather than to give them all away in the beginning of the essay. Even if your supporting points don't appear in your introduction, your reader will easily spot them later if your paper is clearly organized.

Your second paragraph will present your *first* supporting point—everything about it and nothing more.

Your next paragraph will be about your *second* supporting point—all about it and nothing more.

Each additional paragraph will develop *another* supporting point.

Finally, you'll need a concluding paragraph. In a short paper, it isn't necessary to restate your points. Your conclusion may be brief; even a single sentence to round out the paper may do the job. Remember that the main purpose of a concluding paragraph is to bring the paper to a close by sharing your final thoughts on the subject. (See page 209 and page 217 for two examples of successful concluding paragraphs.)

Learning to write a brief organized essay of this kind will help you distinguish between the parts of an essay. Then when you're ready to write a longer paper, you'll be able to organize it clearly and be more creative in its design and content.

Topic Sentences

A topic sentence does for a paragraph what a thesis statement does for an essay—it states the main idea. Like thesis statements, topic sentences must be phrased as complete thoughts to be proven or developed through the presentation of details. But the topic sentence introduces an idea or subtopic that is the right size to cover in a paragraph. The topic sentence doesn't have to be the first sentence in a paragraph. It may come at the end or even in the middle, but putting it first is most common.

Each body paragraph should contain only one main idea, and no detail or example should be in a paragraph if it doesn't support the topic sentence or help to transition from one paragraph to another. (See page 208 and pages 216–217 for more examples of effective body paragraphs within essays and of paragraphs alone.)

Organizing Body Paragraphs (or Single Paragraphs)

A single paragraph or a body paragraph within an essay is organized in the same way as an entire essay, only on a smaller scale. Here's the way you learned to organize an essay:

Thesis: stated or suggested in introductory paragraph

First supporting paragraph

Second supporting paragraph

Additional supporting paragraphs

Concluding paragraph

And here's the way to organize a paragraph:

Topic sentence

First supporting detail or example

Second supporting detail or example

Additional supporting details or examples

Concluding or transitional sentence

You should have several details to support each topic sentence. If you find that you have little to say after writing the topic sentence, ask yourself what details or examples will make your reader believe that the topic sentence is true for you.

Transitional Expressions

Transitional expressions within a paragraph and between paragraphs help the reader move from one detail or supporting point in an essay to the next. When first learning to organize an essay, beginning writers may start each body paragraph and every new example with a transitional expression (*first, for example, next*). These common transitions are useful and clear, but they can sound mechanical. To improve the flow of your ideas and the strength of your written voice, try to replace some of these transitions with specific phrases (*at the start of the meeting* or *in many people's minds*) or with dependent clauses (*when drivers use cell phones* or *as I approached the intersection*).

Here are some transitions that show sequence:

Previously	Next	One (example, point . . .)
Later	Then	Another (example, point . . .)
Eventually	Finally	

Here are a few to show addition:

Also	First
Furthermore	Second
In addition	Third . . .

Here are several that show comparison or contrast:

Similarly	In the same way	In comparison
However	On the other hand	In contrast

Here are those that show consequence:

Therefore	Consequently	In conclusion
As a result	In other words	

Writing Exercise 8

ADD TRANSITIONAL EXPRESSIONS

Place appropriate expressions from the lists above into the blanks in the following paragraph to make the transitions clear. Then try to replace one or two with specific transitional phrases or clauses to improve the flow of ideas and to add interest. Compare your choices with the ones suggested in the answers.

_____, I used to plan my long road trips by going through the following routine. _____, I made sure that I had a map of the highways so that if I got lost along the way, I wouldn't panic. _____, even if I did have a map to the city of my destination, I would call the hotel for specific driving directions from the highway. _____ way that I planned ahead was to check my car's tires and have its engine serviced, if necessary. _____, I never forgot to bring my cell phone because I had learned how important they are on long drives. _____, before I left my house on the day of the trip, I checked the Highway Patrol updates to see if there were any road closures on my route. This routine always worked for me; _____, I can give it up now that I have a car with its own navigation system. I just need to figure out how it works!

Writing Exercise 9

WRITE A PARAGRAPH THAT INCLUDES TRANSITIONS

To practice using transitions, write a paragraph about the steps you take to get ready to sit down and write a paper. Feel free to use the paragraph in Writing Exercise 8 as a model. Where do you go? What materials do you gather? How do you get in the right frame of mind to write? Report the steps in order, one by one, using transitional expressions from the list on page 225 wherever you see fit. Sometimes it's helpful to add humor to a process-based paragraph or essay to liven up the steps involved in an ordinary process and connect with the reader.

VI. Supporting with Details

Now you're ready to support your main idea with subtopics and specific details. That is, you'll think of ways to prove that your thesis is true. How could you convince your reader that buying and selling on eBay can teach valuable lessons about business and geography? Try adding the word "because" to the end of your thesis to generate at least three more specific statements. You might come up with something like the following:

> I've learned a lot about business and geography by buying and selling on eBay. (because)
>
> **or**
>
> Buyers and sellers learn a lot about business and geography through their transactions on eBay. (because)

1. Honesty and fairness are very important when dealing with others on eBay.

2. Active eBay members must keep accurate records and be very organized.

3. Buyers and sellers learn about shipping methods and policies around the world.

NOTE—Imagining the word *because* at the end of your thesis will help you find subtopics that are clear and parallel in their level and presentation of ideas.

Types of Support

The subtopics developing a thesis and the details presented in a paragraph are not always *reasons* (like the ones outlined in the **analysis** of buying and selling on eBay, for instance). Supporting points may take many forms based on the purpose of the essay or paragraph. Other kinds of support include the following:

> *examples* (in an **illustration**)
>
> *meanings* (in a **definition**)
>
> *steps* or *stages* (in a "how-to" paper or **process analysis**)
>
> *types* or *kinds* (in a **classification**)
>
> *personal experiences* (in any kind of writing)
>
> *facts, statistics,* and *expert opinions* (in an **argument**)
>
> *causes* and/or *effects* (in a **causal analysis**)
>
> *similarities* and/or *differences* (in a **comparison-contrast**)

Whatever form they take, supporting points should develop the main idea expressed in the thesis statement of the essay or the topic sentence of the paragraph and help prove it to be true.

A Sample Final Draft

Here is the final draft of a first-person student essay about a challenging assignment for college students. Notice how the body paragraphs map out the writer's personal experience (using *I, me, my, we*) as she struggles through the process of learning to draw a self-portrait. This essay could also have presented the same stages from a third-person point of view, using *they* or *them*. The result would be more of an observation of the process that all art students go through when drawing self-portraits.

Drawing a Blank

On the day my drawing class started to learn about self-portraits last year, each of us had to bring a mirror to class. In backpacks and purses were make-up mirrors, dressing table mirrors—large and small mirrors of every shape and kind. I was nervous about drawing a self-portrait, so I brought only a tiny plastic pocket mirror. That way if I didn't do a good job, it would be my mirror's fault. I discovered that drawing a self-portrait involves observing myself from the outside and the inside.

I had never done well on human figure drawing. First our teacher, Ms. Newman, demonstrated the proportion of a human figure; she explained that a human body measures about seven times a human head. She used a tiny piece of chalk to draw on the board while she was talking. Then she showed how to sketch the face, from eyebrows to eyes, nose, mouth, and ears. After her lecture, she told us to begin drawing our self-portraits.

We all set up our mirrors. The ceiling danced with the reflections they made as we got to work. I looked down at my little square of scratched-up plastic and started to draw gingerly on my paper. I tried to put the eyes, nose, and mouth I had seen on the paper. When I finished, I wondered, "Who the heck is this?" The drawing didn't look anything like me. I was frustrated and sank down in my chair. After a minute, I told myself, "Try again." I drew another one, and it was a little better. But I could not really call it a self-portrait because it didn't look exactly like me.

I asked Ms. Newman for help. She glanced at my previous attempts and said, "A good self-portrait doesn't just look like you, it also shows your personality and your feeling." She did not see either of these in my other drawings. So I tried again. I borrowed my friend's big glass mirror and stared into it; I was not only looking at my face, but also deep inside my face. This time, I freely sketched the shape of my face. Then I roughly placed my eyebrows, eyes, nose, mouth, and ears. I looked into the mirror again and drew the expression I saw there.

When my portrait was finished, I wondered at the amazing work I had done. Even though it did not perfectly look like me, it really showed my personality and emotions through the contrast of light and dark. When Ms. Newman saw it, she applauded. Not only did I get an A on this project; it also became one of the strongest pieces in my portfolio. I realized that few things can be done successfully the first time. If I had given up after my first try, I would never have captured the real me.

(Note: See page 247 for a rough draft of this essay, before its final revisions.)

Learning to support your main ideas with vivid details is perhaps the most important goal you can accomplish in this course. Many writing problems are not really writing problems but *thinking* problems. Whether you're writing a research paper or merely an answer to a test question, if you take enough time to think, you'll be able to discover a clear thesis statement and support it with paragraphs full of meaningful details.

Writing Exercise 10

WRITE AN ESSAY ON ONE OF YOUR INTERESTS

Return to the thesis statement you wrote about one of your interests for Writing Exercise 6 on page 223. Now write a short but thoughtful essay about it (using either the first-person or third-person approach, see page 206). You can explain the allure of your interest, its drawbacks or its benefits. Don't forget to include details from the free writing or clustering you may have done on the topic beforehand and to use meaningful transitional expressions.

VII. Choosing and Using Quotations

Including quotations from another writer can add dimension and depth to your paragraphs and essays. Try to think of a reading as a friendly resource, inviting you to quote from it in order to present ideas beyond your own. Remember, you're in control of what any other writer "says" in your writing by choosing what to quote and where to include quotations in your paper.

Choosing Quotations

Imagine you've been asked to read a short selection and write a response that answers the following question: "Which is more important for success, talent or hard work?" You should have no trouble using the previously discussed methods to organize your ideas about talent vs. hard work and support them with details and observations of your own. But the assignment also requires that you include quotations from the reading prompt in your response.

Let's look at the sample reading below. It's about how hard work may have contributed as much to Mozart's music as his legendary talent did. As you read this brief excerpt from Geoff Colvin's book *Talent Is Overrated*, try to spot phrases or statements that you think would be particularly quotable in a paper about talent vs. hard work. Also notice that Colvin includes a quotation to support his own ideas:

> Mozart is the ultimate example of the divine-spark theory of greatness. Composing music at age five, giving public performances as a pianist and violinist at age eight, going on to produce hundreds of works, some of which are widely regarded as ethereally great and treasures of Western culture, all in the brief time before his death at age thirty-five—if that isn't talent, and on a mammoth scale, nothing is. . . .
>
> Mozart's method of composing was not quite the wonder it was long thought to be. For nearly two hundred years many people have believed that he had a miraculous ability to compose entire major pieces in his head, after which writing them down was mere clerical work. That view was based on a famous letter in which he says as much: "the whole, though it be long, stands almost finished and complete in my mind . . . the committing to paper is done quickly enough . . . and it rarely differs on paper from what it was in my imagination."
>
> That report certainly does portray a superhuman performer. The trouble is, this letter is a forgery, as many scholars later established. Mozart did not conceive whole works in his mind, perfect and complete. Surviving manuscripts show that Mozart was constantly revising, reworking, crossing out and rewriting whole sections, jotting down fragments and putting them aside for months or years. Though it makes the results no less magnificent, he wrote music the way ordinary humans do.

One way to begin quoting effectively is to highlight the details or phrasing that you respond to the most in a reading. Be choosy. Just as you would choose ring tones or clothes to reflect your personality, you can pick particular quotations from readings to enhance the effect of your writing. Remember that quotations must reproduce the original's exact wording, so transcribe them very carefully and place them within quotation marks. (See page 191.)

Let's say you've chosen these four sentences to quote from in your essay:

"Mozart is the ultimate example of the divine-spark theory of greatness."

"For nearly two hundred years many people have believed that he had a miraculous ability to compose entire major pieces in his head, after which writing them down was mere clerical work."

"Surviving manuscripts show that Mozart was constantly revising, reworking, crossing out and rewriting whole sections, jotting down fragments and putting them aside for months or years."

"Though it makes the results no less magnificent, he wrote music the way ordinary humans do."

Using Quotations

The next step is to cut the quotations down to a manageable size so they won't overpower your ideas.

"Mozart is the ultimate example ~~of the divine-spark theory~~ of greatness."

"For nearly two hundred years many people have believed that he had a miraculous ability to compose entire major pieces in his head~~, after which writing them down was mere clerical work~~."

"~~Surviving manuscripts show that Mozart was~~ constantly revising, reworking, crossing out and rewriting whole sections, jotting down fragments and putting them aside for months or years."

"~~Though~~ it makes the results no less magnificent, ~~he~~ wrote music the way ordinary humans do."

Read on to see how these shortened quotations can be included in the paper using signal phrases and proper punctuation to let the reader know where you've left out or changed wording from the original.

Signal Phrases and Punctuation

A quotation by itself—even if it's a complete statement such as "I have a dream"—cannot function as a sentence in your paper without a signal phrase. The job of a signal phrase is to identify the writer or source of the quotation and provide a subject and a verb to anchor the quotation within your paper. The italicized subject and verb in the following sentence make up its signal phrase:

In his famous speech, *Martin Luther King, Jr. declares*, "I have a dream."

A **signal phrase** should include the writer's name or other identification and a strong verb like the ones listed below. Avoid relying on the verb *says* or *writes* when so many more interesting verbs like the following are available:

explains	suggests	argues	feels
points out	asserts	illustrates	adds
believes	thinks	notes	insists
claims	observes	declares	reports
acknowledges	admits	states	concludes

A signal phrase can be placed *at the beginning, in the middle,* or *at the end* of the quotation to add variety to your sentences. Use commas to set off signal phrases and an **ellipsis** (. . .) to show where you have cut words from full-length quoted sentences. No ellipsis is necessary when quoting only phrases from the original. If an ellipsis ends the sentence, the period makes a total of four dots:

Signal phrase at the beginning of the quotation (a comma follows the signal phrase):

Geoff Colvin believes, "Mozart is the ultimate example of . . . greatness."

Signal phrase in the middle of the quotation (commas surround the signal phrase):

"For nearly two hundred years," **Colvin explains**, "many people have believed that he had a miraculous ability to compose entire major pieces in his head. . . ."

Signal phrase at the end of the quotation (a comma comes before the signal phrase):

Mozart worked very hard, "constantly revising, reworking, crossing out and rewriting whole sections, jotting down fragments and putting them aside for months or years," **Colvin adds**.

You may have noticed that the previous examples use an ellipsis when words have been left out of the *middle* or the *end* of a shortened quote, but not the *beginning* of one. When leaving off the first words of a quotation, maintain the small letter that the quoted part begins with to show that the opening words have been cut.

When a quotation is introduced by "that," the signal phrase does *not* require a comma. Note that any change made to a quote should placed within **brackets** [ ]:

> **Colvin feels *that*** "it makes [Mozart's] results no less magnificent. . . ."

Once you've identified the single source writer's name in previous sentences, you can include *brief* quotations without a signal phrase:

> As a music major myself, I'm glad to know that Mozart "wrote music the way ordinary humans do."

To read a sample paragraph that includes all of the quotations from Colvin's excerpt, see page 234.

GUIDELINES FOR INCLUDING QUOTATIONS

1. Choose a sentence that you would like to quote from a reading.
2. Consider shortening the phrasing of the original sentence for clarity.
3. Put quotation marks around the other writer's words.
4. Write a signal phrase to identify the writer or source of the quotation.
5. Use a comma (or commas) to set off the signal phrase in your sentence.
6. No comma is necessary if the word "that" introduces the quotation.
7. Use brackets [ ] to identify a change made within a quotation.
8. Use an ellipsis . . . in place of words cut from the middle or end of a quoted sentence (but not when quoting just a phrase).

These methods for including quotations are not difficult to learn; with practice, they will become second nature. Understanding how to include quotations from a single source effectively will help when you need to quote from multiple readings and to document them using the Modern Language Association (MLA) format.

Writing Exercise 11

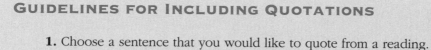

WRITE SENTENCES USING SIGNAL PHRASES AND QUOTATIONS

Return to Dominique Browning's essay "Wandering Home" on page 212, and choose five sentences that you like. Then practice quoting parts of them in sentences of your own using signal phrases, as explained on page 232. As you write your sentences, be sure to follow the "Guidelines for Including Quotations" on page 233.

VIII. Writing in Response to a Reading

Many of your future assignments will ask you to respond to one or more readings, just as the student writer of "Missing Home" on page 216 responds to Dominique Browning's essay "Wandering Home" on page 212. Think of reading-response assignments as opportunities to strengthen your position as a writer. Always participate fully with a reading by highlighting quotable sentences and noting similar observations or contrasting experiences of your own.

Read the following paragraph-length response to the reading about Mozart on page 230. Note how the writer includes quotations from Colvin's excerpt, using well-punctuated signal phrases, to enhance her own ideas and experiences.

A Sample Paragraph Response Using Quotations

I always thought that talent was more important than hard work. I never tried anything for too long if I didn't have the ability to do it easily. For instance, I started learning the violin but gave it up within two weeks because it didn't feel natural to me. After reading Geoff Colvin's information about Mozart, I wish I had tried harder. Many people think of Mozart when the word *talent* comes up. Colvin believes, "Mozart is the ultimate example of . . . greatness." Without even studying Mozart's life, everyone seems to know about his gifts. "For nearly two hundred years," Colvin explains, "many people have believed that he had a miraculous ability to compose entire major pieces in his head. . . ." However, Mozart worked very hard, "constantly revising, reworking, crossing out and rewriting whole sections, jotting down fragments and putting them aside for months or years," Colvin adds. I never pictured Mozart doing so much hard work. Colvin feels that "it makes [Mozart's] results no less magnificent. . . ." I agree with him. As a music major myself, I'm glad to know that Mozart "wrote music the way ordinary humans do." Next semester, I might give the violin one more try.

In-class (or timed) writing assignments often include *prompts*, thought-provoking readings that "prompt" writers to generate their own ideas while providing quotable content to use as support. Here's an example of an assignment that asked students to read the following prompt, an excerpt from the book *Manwatching*, and respond to Desmond Morris's observations about "Personal Space."

Sample Reading Prompt 1

If a man enters a waiting room and sits at one end of a long row of empty chairs, it is possible to predict where the next man to enter will seat himself. He will not sit next to the first man, nor will he sit at the far end, right away from him. He will choose a position about halfway between these two points. The next man to enter will take the largest gap left, and sit roughly in the middle of that, and so on, until eventually that latest newcomer will be forced to select a seat that places him right next to one of the already seated men. . . . This is a reflection of the fact that we all carry with us, everywhere we go, a portable territory called a Personal Space. If people move inside this space, we feel threatened. If they keep too far outside it, we feel rejected.

After reading this prompt, one student wrote the following in-class essay. The directions asked her to summarize Morris's concept of "Personal Space," quote from the excerpt to include Morris's voice, and respond to his ideas with insights and examples of her own.

A Sample Essay Response Using Quotations

Space Games

The idea of "Personal Space" suggested by Desmond Morris is that everyone likes to have choices. They like to be able to select the amount of space they want or in some cases need. Morris shares his perception that people pick their places in a waiting room based on their comfort zones, so to speak. The example he gives is much like anything else in life where people have to share space. The thought that choices about personal space are "possible to predict," but usually unnoticed, is interesting and a little peculiar.

Riding in someone else's car, standing in line at the bank, even putting food on our plates—all of these say the same thing about us. We want choices. If someone sits in the wrong spot or stands too close, we can feel claustrophobic or "threatened," as Morris points out. If another person is distant or sits "too far" away, we might "feel rejected." People lead their lives on choice to mold their lives into what they dream. With personal space, it's a choice of how close and how far.

My personal space is definitely variable. I have found that there are some days when my personal space doesn't matter. Other people can get as close as they want, or stay as far as the eye can see, and it wouldn't make me feel any different. Then there are days when I need two empty seats worth of space on both sides. When I get a ride to school, I hold my belongings close to me. With people who, on a scale of 1 to 10 (1 being stranger and 10 being relative), range from 1 to 3, my belongings don't leave my lap. With people who range from 4 to 7, I may place my stuff on the seat next to me. And with those from 8 to 10, I just throw my stuff on the floor.

I never gave personal space much thought before reading Morris's paragraph, but I pay close attention to everything around me, especially the reactions and expressions on people's faces. Life makes more sense when I see the examples of everyone else's. I definitely recognize the look of someone whose personal space has been invaded. I remember one moment on the train the other day when a little boy got tired and dozed off with his head against the woman next to him, not his mother. The woman kept looking down at the child until it was clear that he meant no harm. She had no choice but to readjust her space to include the sleepy little boy until his stop came.

My feelings and other people's reactions support Morris's idea that "we all carry with us, everywhere we go, a portable territory called a Personal Space." We protect this territory whenever we have a choice, but it is adjustable, so the more conscious of it we are, the better.

Clearly, even though it was written under the pressure of time, the student participated fully with Morris's reading, which prompted her to think about the unconscious habits that we all have when negotiating for our "Personal Space." The result is a successful in-class essay.

TIPS FOR IN-CLASS WRITING

In-class (or timed) writing is a special skill that reveals how you think and write under pressure. Keep the following five areas in mind when writing an in-class essay or a timed essay online:

1. **Topic or Prompt Analysis:** *Really think* about the topic or prompt before starting to write; highlight key (or quotable) parts and briefly map out your own ideas and details in response. Then start your paper with a direct response to the topic (or reading prompt) and an idea/thesis of your own that relates to it.

2. **Organization:** In-class essays don't need long introductions because they are prompted by a reading or question that both the writer and reader already know. Begin your response immediately and follow the order of tasks shown by key verbs in the question (summarize, explain, describe . . .). If no question accompanies the prompt, start a new paragraph at each natural break in your ideas or support. Conclude with your *final* insights about the topic or prompt, not just a review of your points. Finally, choose a unique phrase that fits your paper, and use it as a title.

3. **Detail:** To find real details, tell yourself to "Mine what is mine." In other words, think of your experiences and observations (as well as the best parts of the prompt) as diamonds in a mine. All you need to do is gather the ones *you* want to present to your reader. Don't forget to choose the best "diamonds" (your *own* real-life details, supported by quotations if there's a prompt) and to cut and polish them into strong sentences with meaningful punctuation.

4. **Word Use, Sentence Structure, and Punctuation:** Use Standard English spelling, sentence structure, punctuation, and capitalization. Avoid slang expressions ("guy," for example) and short-cuts like "&," "u," "w/," "etc." Remember, proofreading is more important than finishing every point you planned to make.

5. **Presentation:** *Relax* as much as possible so that your handwriting and written "voice" are clear and confident. If you make a mistake, don't scratch it out or frantically apply correction tape to it. Cross it out with *one* line; then include your correction above it. Self-editing is the sign of a strong writer, so let the reader see any changes you've made.

To see these tips at work, review the sample in-class essays on pages 216, 235, and 239.

Sample Reading Prompt 2

Essentially, the family is a breeding unit and the family territory is a breeding ground. At the center of this space, there is the nest—the bedroom—where, tucked up in bed, we feel at our most territorially secure. In the typical house, the bedroom is upstairs, where a safe nest should be. This puts it farther away from the entrance hall, the area where contact is made, intermittently, with the outside world. The less private reception rooms, where intruders are allowed access, are the next line of defense. Beyond them, outside the walls of the building, there is often a symbolic remnant of the ancient feeding grounds—a garden. Its symbolism often extends to the plants and animals it contains, which cease to be nutritional and become merely decorative— flowers and pets.

Writing Exercise 12

WRITE A PARAGRAPH OR ESSAY IN RESPONSE TO A READING

Using the sample paragraph and essay responses in this section as models, write a paragraph or essay response to Reading Prompt 2, Desmond Morris's excerpt about "Family Territory." First, summarize Morris's concept of "Family Territory," quote from the excerpt to include Morris's voice, and respond to his ideas with insights and examples of your own. Refer to the "Guidelines for Including Quotations" on page 233 whenever necessary.

IX. WRITING AN ARGUMENT

Writing assignments often ask you to take a stand on an issue or to share an opinion and prove that it is valid. Such writing is called *argumentation,* but it doesn't involve "fighting" or "arguing" in the sense that these words might be used in everyday life. In fact, intense emotions can weaken an argument if they are not balanced by logic and fairness. The purpose of a written argument is to convince the reader to value your opinion and possibly to agree with it.

Taking a Stand and Proving Your Point

A strong written argument fulfills three basic requirements. First, it takes a clear stand on an issue or a controversial topic. Second, it provides logical and relevant support for the writer's position. And third, it discusses the issue or topic in a fair-minded way, taking other points of view into account. Let's look at some examples by both professional and student writers.

As an in-class assignment, students were asked to write a short essay in response to the following excerpts from Leon Botstein's book *Jefferson's Children: Education and the Promise of American Culture.* In Chapter III, "Replacing the

American High School," Botstein argues that young people in America should enter the "real world" two years earlier than they do now. Here are the excerpts that the students read from Botstein's book:

> The American high school is obsolete. It can no longer fulfill the expectations we legitimately place on it. It offers an inadequate solution to the problem of how best to motivate and educate American adolescents. . . .
>
> The key reason for reducing the total number of years in school before college is educational. Children and young adults can begin learning sooner and more quickly. Since they mature earlier, they need to be released from the obligations of compulsory education at an earlier age. The high school diploma as we define it, which is now given to Americans at age eighteen, could be awarded at age sixteen. . . .
>
> Those interested in going to college will be able to exercise greater choice in the new system. For those who stay at home, the community college system is the most likely option. Already these institutions are dedicated to repairing the damage done in high school or doing what ought to have been done. The basic organization of the community college is more respectful of the incipient adult. Classes are selected and scheduled by the individual. There is a campus. The day is divided so that night classes are an option. The classes are run by faculty with better training in the subject matter. The presumption of the classroom is not rote fulfillment of state requirements, but rather teaching in response to the ambitions of students to learn and get ahead. Community colleges have large numbers of older students, well beyond the so-called traditional college age. As teachers know, nothing better serves the swaggering sixteen- and seventeen-year-old more obsessed with style and the peer group than being in classes with students in their late twenties and early thirties, for whom school has become truly voluntary and serious.

A Sample Argument

As you might imagine, Botstein's idea to shorten high school and send sixteen-year-olds directly to college drew mixed reactions from student writers. In the short essay that follows, one student argues that the last two years of high school are extremely important based on her own high school experiences:

College at 16? I Think Not!

    I strongly disagree with Leon Botstein's idea to eliminate the American high school. I don't believe that all teenagers mature early enough to attend college at sixteen. Yes, there is a small percentage (that could be counted on the fingers of my left hand) who could indeed go off to college and do very well at sixteen years of age, but is it really worth letting the other ninety-five percent go, too?

When I think of my high school experience and the kids who attended with me, I think of just that—kids. Most of the students at my high school sought pleasure in spitting over the third floor balcony onto the lunch crowd below. Half of the population of my school had not learned how to throw their trash into the trashcan five feet away from them. Most weren't mature enough to leave high school at eighteen, let alone sixteen.

How would my life have been without high school? Well, that would have been interesting, and Botstein's ideas do make me wonder if I might have accomplished more sooner. But I believe that if I had gone off to college at sixteen, I would have lost more than I gained. I learned a lot from my high school experience, not from the mandatory classes that were required for graduation, but from the classes that I chose to take and that I participated in with my teenage peers.

It may sound strange to say so, but my dance and drama classes taught me a lot of very important life skills. I learned responsibility by multitasking to be able to fit weekend rehearsals and practices into my full load of regular classes, homework, and after-school activities. I learned that it is possible to get out of bed before ten o'clock on Saturday because 3 a.m. roll calls, teamwork, dedication, and competition can take you anywhere you want to go.

Without my valuable high school experiences, I know I wouldn't be the well-rounded person I am today. If I had to compete with Botstein's thirty-year-old community college students and meet them at 3 a.m. on Saturdays for dance rehearsals as my introduction to responsibility, the effects would not have been the same. In high school, we matured together, and that was important.

This student's in-class essay fulfills the three requirements of a strong written argument by clearly stating her position in her opening sentences, by describing her own vivid high school experiences to support her position, and by fairly acknowledging that some people in high school would be better off in college and even wondering what would have happened if she had graduated earlier.

Obviously, the student's paper would have been longer and more developed if it had been an out-of-class essay with a two- or three-week deadline. Then this student could have responded to Botstein's whole book and included factual support with her personal experiences. She could have interviewed fellow students and included their comments. She might have found an expert who shares her opinion about high school and written her essay as a comparison-contrast of Botstein's and the other expert's opinions.

THREE REQUIREMENTS OF A STRONG WRITTEN ARGUMENT

1. Takes a clear stand on an issue or a controversial topic.
2. Provides logical and relevant support (personal experience, opinions of experts, facts and statistics, results of interviews).
3. Discusses the issue or topic in a fair-minded way, allowing for other points of view.

Writing Exercise 13

WRITE AN ARGUMENT ABOUT GRADES

Read and carefully consider the following paragraph proposing a few changes in education:

> Education at all levels should be changed so that it is completely grade-free and noncompetitive. All letter grades should be eliminated and replaced by a pass/fail system, and scores of any kind should be provided as information only, not for the purpose of ranking. Students should also receive credit for self-study and Internet-gained knowledge and skills. Attendance and completion of assignments should be the only requirements for moving ahead in a course of study. In addition, students should be allowed to repeat courses, even after successfully completing all of the assignments, if they so choose. Students should take charge of their own educations and learn at their own pace.

Do you agree or disagree with this hypothetical proposal to eliminate grades and give students total flexibility in their studies? Take care to consider the issue from all angles. How would such profound changes affect students, teachers, parents, school officials, and the public? Then use what you've learned about argumentation to write a brief essay in which you take a stand on one side of this issue or the other. Refer to the student sample "College at Sixteen? I Think Not!" as a model for using relevant experiences and observations to prove your point, and remember to be fair-minded in your presentation.

X. WRITING SUMMARIES

One of the best ways to learn to read carefully and write concisely is to write summaries. A summary is a brief piece of writing (a paragraph, usually) that presents the main ideas of a reading—a book chapter, an article, a speech, or a long essay—in your own words. It does not call for any reactions, opinions, or experiences of your own for support. Summaries contain only the most important points of the original and leave everything else out. Writing summaries strengthens your reading and writing skills. You have to understand the essence of a reading, gather its supporting points, and rephrase them in your *own* words (without including quotations from the original). Here's a tip: put the original away while you make a list of its four or five "big ideas." Then you can write sentences that express those ideas and combine them in paragraph form.

A summary, by definition, should always be shorter than the original. Writing something *short* sounds easy, but actually it isn't. Rephrasing the main ideas of a reading in a short paragraph is a time-consuming task—not to be undertaken in the last hour before class. However, if you practice writing summaries conscientiously, you will improve as a reader and will be able to write concise, clear, smooth paragraphs. These skills will then carry over into your reading and writing for other courses.

A Sample Reading

Read the following excerpt from the book *Bollywood Crafts—20 Projects Inspired by Popular Indian Cinema*. It will be followed by a sample summary.

Bollywood Film Facts

Bollywood is the biggest film industry in the world. Approximately one thousand films are made in India under the "Bollywood" umbrella each year (that is double the amount of Hollywood films) and over 12 million Indians watch a Bollywood film every day. The films are also popular throughout the Middle East, Russia and Africa, and, increasingly, Western audiences are surrendering to the charms of Indian cinema.

Bollywood is also referred to as Hindi cinema—there are 22 official languages spoken in India; however, the major movies are made in Hindi as it is the country's dominant language, though films in other languages, such as Tamil and Urdu, are also made. Although the main hub of production companies are based in Mumbai (Bombay), films are shot in locations all over the country and recent films have even been set abroad [in England, Europe, Australia, and America].

Like mainstream Hollywood movies, Bollywood films also fall into specific genres, such as action or romance, but most are multi-genre, family movies. In India, going to the movies is a family event, and often several generations watch a film together. This means the content has to appeal to all. It also means filmmakers have to be creative in their approach to telling narratives. How they express emotions is a key element. Emotions are represented not just through acting, but also through the use of spectacle—songs and dance.

The key to a successful [Bollywood] movie is to have a popular soundtrack, and for the choreography that accompanies it to be equally impressive. Song sequences usually start in the middle of a dialogue and are a break from the reality of the storyline. Characters are transported to different locations and their costumes become very significant; a leading lady can go through several costume changes per dance scene, which makes for compelling viewing! When you're watching a song from a film, it's best to ignore the subtitles and instead let yourself be entertained by the visuals. The choreography is a mixture of Indian dancing styles with global influences such as MTV. Extras play a key role in bringing the dances to life, and as a viewer, I often want to get up and join in!

Some Bollywood films are inspired by Hollywood tales, but most are original ideas, often based on moral or family dilemmas. Like Hollywood, the star system is an important part of Bollywood and the biggest actors and actresses are celebrities in their own right. Unlike Hollywood, however, Indian actors often work on several films at one time, even switching between movie sets in the same day. And while Hollywood left behind its musicals in the 1950s, Bollywood films always contain a performance element. Actors have to demonstrate impeccable dancing skills as well as acting ability.

If you have yet to watch a Bollywood movie, don't worry! They are far more accessible than you may think, with cinemas and rental stores responding to audience demands by showing and stocking new movies. Don't be alarmed by the length; Bollywood movies are longer than other films to allow for the songs, but there is always an interval [intermission].

Bollywood films are an exciting and original contribution to the filmmaking world and, as the popularity of Bollywood continues to spread around the globe, Indian filmmakers are getting more progressive with their plots, special effects and visuals. This means that films will develop stylistically even further and continue to get better—something I'm really looking forward to!

Source: From *Bollywood Crafts—20 Projects Inspired by Popular Indian Cinema,* by Momtaz Begum-Hossain, a freelance crafts maker and customized clothing designer (*www. momtazbh.co.uk*). Reprinted by permission of the author.

A good summary begins with a statement of the reading's "biggest" idea, written in your own words. An effective summary does not just translate or re-order the words of the original. Some single words from the original—"India," "Hollywood," and "Bollywood," in this case—may be used in a summary when they lack a substitute. However, as the writer of an effective summary, you must find new ways to phrase the original reading's ideas, present them in a condensed form, and reveal your understanding of the original in the process.

A Sample Summary

> In "Bollywood Film Facts," Momtaz Begum-Hossain explains that India has its own version of Hollywood—called Bollywood—that produces movies that are growing in popularity worldwide. Bollywood releases twice as many movies a year as Hollywood does. Unlike Hollywood movies, Bollywood movies can include different languages besides their main language, Hindi. These films also include more music and dancing than Hollywood movies do. Elaborate, well-performed songs are essential and unique to Bollywood films. Therefore, movie stars in India have to act well and dance well, too. Indian movies are longer than Hollywood movies and might require subtitles, but they continue to attract new audiences because of their high entertainment value and universal appeal.

Writing Exercise 14

WRITE A SUMMARY OF A READING

Return to Judy Jones and William Wilson's excerpt about the artists Christo and Jeanne-Claude on page 130, and read it carefully. Then follow the instructions below to write a practice summary:

A good way to begin the summary of a reading is to identify the most general idea that the author—in this case, two authors—want to get across to the reader. Write your own sentence expressing the main idea of the excerpt now.

You may have written a sentence like this:

> Christo and Jeanne-Claude are two married artists who work as a team to make their mark on the world.

Next, it's important to add the authors' names and the reading's title to identify what you are summarizing. Note that you may have to adapt your phrasing to avoid repeating the artists' names since they are included in the reading's title:

> In "Christo and Jeanne-Claude (1935-, 1935-)," Judy Jones and William Wilson explain how these two married artists work as a team to make their mark on the world.

Now that you have your first sentence, summarize the rest of the reading by rephrasing only its "big ideas." Be sure to use your *own* words. Since the excerpt is already short, you may be able to summarize it in as few as four or five sentences. It's not difficult if you remember to put the reading aside and write as if you're telling a friend the essay's main ideas in your own way. The first draft of your summary may be too long. Cut it down by including only the essential points and omitting any of its details or examples. Stay within a limit of 100–120 words.

When you have written the best summary you can, compare it with the sample summary on the last page of the Answers section. If you look at the sample sooner, you'll cheat yourself of the opportunity to learn the valuable skill of writing summaries. If you read the sample summary before writing your own, it will be impossible not to be influenced by it. So do your own thinking and writing, and then compare.

SUMMARY CHECKLIST

Even though your summary is different from the sample, it may be just as good. If you're not sure how yours compares, consider these questions:

1. Have you included all of the writer's main ideas *without* adding your own reactions or opinions?
2. Have you written the summary in your own words *without* using any quotations?
3. Have you left out all of the writer's examples and supporting details?
4. Does your summary read smoothly?
5. Would someone who had not read the original get a clear overview of it from your summary?

XI. REVISING, PROOFREADING, AND PRESENTING YOUR WORK

Great writers don't just sit down and write a final draft. They write and revise. You may have heard the expression, "Easy writing makes hard reading." True, it is *easier* to turn in a piece of writing as soon as you finish the first draft. But your reader (and eventually you) will probably be disappointed by the results. Try to think of revision as an opportunity instead of a chore, as a necessity instead of a choice.

Whenever possible, you should write a paper several days before it is due. Let it sit for a while. When you reread it, you'll see many ways to improve the organization, add more details, and clarify phrasing. After revising the paper, put it away for another day, and try again to improve it. Save all of your drafts along the way to see the progress you've made or possibly to find text deleted in an early draft that fits in again after revision.

Don't call any paper finished until you have worked through it several times. Revising is one of the best ways to improve your writing.

A Sample Rough Draft

Take a look at an early draft of the student essay you read on page 228 about learning to draw a self-portrait. Notice that the student has revised her rough draft by crossing out weak parts, correcting word forms, and adding new phrasing or reminders for later improvement.

Drawing a Blank

~~If at First You Don't Succeed . . . Try, Try Again~~

On the day ~~that~~ my drawing class started to learn

about self‑portraits last year, each of us had to bring a

mirror to class. ~~There~~ *In backpacks and purses* were make-up mirrors, dressing

table mirrors—large and small mirrors of every shape and

kind. I was nervous about drawing a self‑portrait, so I

brought *only* a tiny plastic pocket mirror. That way if I   *Add a thesis*

didn't do a good job, it would be my mirror's fault.

I had never done well on human figure drawing. ~~Anyway,~~ *First,*

our teacher *, Ms. Newman, demonstrated* ~~showed us how to do~~ the proportion of a human

figure; ~~something like~~ *she explained that* a human body measures about seven

times a human head. She used a tiny piece of chalk to

draw on the board while she was talking. Then she ~~also~~

showed how to sketch ~~out~~ the face, from eyebrows to eyes,

nose, mouth and ears. After ~~all that~~ *her lecture*, she ~~led~~ *told* us to ~~start~~ *begin*

~~our~~ drawing *our self-portraits.*

~~Everyone in the class~~ *We all* set up ~~their~~ *our* mirrors, and ~~the~~ The

ceiling danced with ~~all of~~ the reflections they made. *as we got to work.*

~~Then we started to draw.~~ I looked down at my little

square, *of* scratched-up *plastic* ~~mirror~~ and started to draw gingerly

on my ~~drawing~~ paper. ~~I looked at my face, eyebrows, eyes,~~

~~nose, mouth, and ears.~~ I tried to put ~~what~~ *the eyes, nose, and mouth* I had seen on

the paper. ~~Then~~ *When* I finished, I ~~was like~~ *wondered,* "Who the heck is

this?" The drawing ~~was totally bad. Nothing looked~~ *didn't look anything* like

me. I was ~~so~~ frustrated and sank down in my chair. After a minute, I told myself, "Try again~~,~~" ~~the next one will be better~~" I drew another one, and it was a little better. ~~It looked a little like me. Nevertheless,~~ But I could not really ~~say that~~ call it ~~was~~ a self-portrait because it did not look exactly like me.

I asked ~~my teacher to come over and help me out.~~ Ms. Newman for help. She glanced at ~~saw~~ my previous ~~drawings~~ attempts and said, "A good self-portrait doesn't just look like you, it also shows your personality and ~~characteristics.~~ your feelings." ~~From my drawing~~ she did not see in my ~~other~~ drawings. any of these. So I tried again. I borrowed my friend's big glass mirror and stared into it; I was not only looking at my face, but also deep inside my face. This time, I freely sketched ~~out~~ the shape of my face ~~shape first.~~ Then, I roughly placed my eyebrows, eyes, nose, mouth, and ears. ~~And~~ I looked into ~~at~~ the mirror~~, seeing my reflection closely. I~~ again and drew ~~what I felt to be like in the mirror.~~ the expression I saw there.

When my ~~drawing~~ Portrait was finished, I wondered at ~~what an~~ the amazing work I had done. Even though it did not perfectly look like me, it really showed my personality and emotions ~~characteristics~~ through the contrast of ~~the~~ light and dark. When ~~my teacher~~ Ms. Newman saw it, she applauded. ~~my drawing and she really liked it.~~ Not only did I get an A ~~in~~ on this project; it also became one of the strongest pieces in my portfolio. I ~~recognized~~ realized that ~~nothing could~~ few things can be done successfully the first time. If I ~~gave~~ had given up after my first try, I would never have ~~known I could have done~~ captured the real me. ~~such a great job. Now I know I will succeed no matter how many times I must try.~~

Can you see why each change was made? Analyzing the reasons for the changes will help you improve your own revision skills.

Writing Exercise 15

REVISE A NEW PIECE OF WRITING

The old test of optimism and pessimism is to look at a glass filled to the midpoint. An optimist, or positive thinker, sees it as "half *full*." But a pessimist, or negative thinker, considers it "half *empty*." Is it better to be an optimist or a pessimist? What are the consequences of focusing on the bright side or on the dark side? Do you think Alain de Botton focuses on the light or the dark side in his excerpt about friendship on page 76? Think about these questions, do some free writing or clustering about them, come up with a thesis statement, and organize your results into the structure of a brief essay.

Write a rough draft of the paper and set it aside. A day or two later, revisit your paper to see what improvements you can make to your rough draft. Use the following checklist to help guide you through this or any other revision.

REVISION CHECKLIST

Here's a checklist of revision questions. If the answer to any of these questions is no, revise that part of your paper until you're satisfied that the answer is yes.

1. Does the introductory paragraph identify the topic and any readings clearly and include a main idea (thesis statement) that the paper will explain or defend?
2. Do all of the body paragraphs develop and support the thesis statement?
3. Does each body paragraph begin with a topic sentence to identify its focus on one part or point relating to the thesis?
4. Do the body paragraphs contain relevant details, smooth transitions, and correct quotations (if the paper responds to a reading)?
5. Does the concluding paragraph bring your (the writer's) thoughts or argument to a smooth, convincing close?
6. Does your (the writer's) voice come through, and are other points of view included for fairness?
7. Do the sentences read smoothly and appear to be correct?
8. Are words well chosen and are spelling and punctuation consistent and correct?

Exchanging Papers (Peer Evaluations)

The preceding checklist can also be used if you exchange papers with another student. Since you both have written a response to the same assignment, you will understand what the other writer has been going through and learn from the differences between the two papers.

Proofreading Aloud

Finally, you should read your finished paper *aloud*. If you read it silently, your eyes will see what you *think* is there, but you are sure to miss some errors. Read your paper aloud slowly, pointing to—and listening carefully to—each word as you read it. When you *hear* your sentences, you will notice missing words and find errors in spelling and punctuation. Reading a paper to yourself this way may take fifteen minutes to half an hour, but it will be time well spent. You can also ask a friend or relative to read your paper to you. This method can be fun as well as helpful. If you don't like the way something sounds, don't be afraid to change it! Make it a rule to read each of your papers *aloud* before handing it in.

PRESENTING YOUR WORK

Part of the success of a paper could depend on how it looks. The same paper written sloppily or typed neatly might even receive a completely different grade. It is human nature to respond positively to an object created and presented with care. Here are some general guidelines to follow.

Paper Formats

Following instructions and standard formats is essential. Your paper should be typed, double-spaced, or written neatly in ink on 8 1/2-by-11-inch paper. A 1-inch margin should be left around the text on all sides for your instructor's comments. The beginning of each paragraph should be indented.

Most instructors specify a particular format for presenting your name and the course material on your papers. Always follow such instructions and other formats carefully in preparation for following more complicated formats in the future.

Titles

A strong title makes an important first impression. Look at the following pairs—each with a generic title on the left and a unique title on the right. In just a few well-chosen words, each title on the right prepares the reader for the topic *and* tone of the essay.

Immigration in America	American Beauty: Diversity
An Embarrassing Experience	Gone in a Flush!
Process Analysis Essay	Got Silk?

Just as you're more likely to pick up a book or see a movie with a special title, so your readers will want to read your paper if its title distinguishes it as something special. To present your own titles correctly, use the following guidelines:

1. Capitalize only the first, the last, and the important words within a title. Don't capitalize articles (*a*, *an*, or *the*), prepositions (*to*, *at*, *in*, *around* . . .), or the connecting words (*and*, *or*, *but* . . .) in the middle of a title. (See page 197.)

    A Night on Eagle Rock   To the Limit of Endurance and Beyond

2. Don't use quotation marks unless your title includes a quotation or the title of an article, a poem, a song, or other short work. (See page 192.)

    Mozart's "Divine" Talent   The Call of "The Raven"

3. Don't underline or use italics in your title unless it includes the title of a book, movie, magazine, or other long work. (See page 192.)

    Promises in The Pact   *Avatar* Sinks *Titanic*

Remember that "Haste is the assassin of elegance." Instead of rushing to finish a paper and turn it in, take the time to give your writing the polish that it deserves.

Answers

GUIDELINES FOR DOUBLING A FINAL LETTER (PP. 4–7)

EXERCISE 1
1. masking
2. deferring
3. pushing
4. waxing
5. fitting
6. offering
7. rowing
8. clicking
9. feeding
10. reviewing

EXERCISE 2
1. towing
2. ripping
3. peeling
4. referring
5. investing
6. ordering
7. profiting
8. screaming
9. slipping
10. predicting

EXERCISE 3
1. tripping
2. munching
3. rolling
4. mopping
5. flavoring
6. cashing
7. beeping
8. talking
9. traveling
10. planning

EXERCISE 4
1. patting
2. sawing
3. feeding
4. playing
5. occurring
6. brushing
7. gathering
8. knotting
9. offering
10. boxing

EXERCISE 5
1. helping
2. flexing
3. assisting
4. needing
5. selecting
6. wishing
7. trying
7. trying
9. polishing
10. leading

WORDS OFTEN CONFUSED, SET 1 (PP. 8–17)

EXERCISE 1

1. an, new

2. It's, due

3. choose, an

4. a, its

5. already

6. complement

7. choose

8. It's, know, accept

9. hear, do

10. an, it's

EXERCISE 2

1. advice, a

2. a

3. accept

4. break

5. choose

6. already, course

7. are, due

8. know, do

9. have, chose

10. feel, it's

EXERCISE 3

1. It's, new

2. have, accepted

3. feel, an

4. chose

5. already, fourth

6. fill, except, have

7. hear, an, advice

8. are

9. course, effects

10. complemented

EXERCISE 4

1. clothes, an

2. Due, a

3. accept

4. course, are, all ready

5. coarse, new

6. conscious

7. an

8. break, feel

9. have, already

10. It's, no

EXERCISE 5

1. are

2. our

3. accept

4. It's

5. New, forth

6. effects

7. know, fill

8. It's, feel

9. effect

10. fill, an

PROOFREADING EXERCISE

In the middle of a debate in my speech class last week, I suddenly became very self-~~conscience~~ *conscious*. My heart started beating faster, and I didn't ~~no~~ *know* what to ~~due~~ *do*. I looked around to see if my show of nerves was having ~~a~~ *an* ~~affect~~ *effect* on the audience. Of ~~coarse~~ *course*, they could ~~here~~ *hear* my voice trembling. The topic that we were debating involved whether it would be best to eliminate letter grades in college, and everyone else was doing so well. But for some reason, my face turned red, and I would ~~of~~ *have* left the room if the door had been closer. After the debate, my classmates tried to give me ~~complements~~ *compliments,* but I ~~new~~ *knew* that they were just trying to make me feel better.

WORDS OFTEN CONFUSED, SET 2 (PP. 18–26)

EXERCISE 1

1. There
2. through
3. to
4. They're

5. personnel
6. past, lose
7. there

8. led, through, were
9. than
10. whether

EXERCISE 2

1. whose
2. quite
3. than, personnel
4. whether

5. their, principle
6. led, to
7. were

8. to
9. passed
10. than

EXERCISE 3

1. through
1. You're
3. whose, too, to
4. past, there

5. peace, quiet, their
6. through, they're
7. there, lose, their, right, personal

8. where
9. Then, to, than
10. Whether, you're, quite

EXERCISE 4

1. were
2. weather
3. led
4. past, whether

5. passed
6. past, there
7. quiet

8. lose, two, right
9. through, past
10. piece, weather

EXERCISE 5

1. your
2. you're, than
3. whether
4. piece, women

5. They're, their
6. principle
7. to, than

8. principal, their
9. to, then
10. they're, through

PROOFREADING EXERCISE

Yesterday, we watched and discussed a short animated video in my philosophy class. The film shows office workers in a high-rise building looking down from ~~there~~ *their* windows and watching pedestrians walk ~~passed~~ *past* a small construction site on the street below, ~~wear~~ *where* a jack hammer has broken a ~~peace~~ *piece* of the sidewalk. As pedestrians walk over the ~~lose~~ *loose* brick, several of them trip and fall but are not injured. The office personnel who are watching from above find each accident funnier ~~then~~ *than* the one before until an old man with a cane approaches the dangerous site. His weak condition makes the office workers remember their ~~principals~~ *principles* of ~~write~~ *right* and wrong, and they all try ~~too~~ *to* warn the old man before he falls too. The film ends in a way that is ~~quiet~~ *quite* a surprise.

THE EIGHT PARTS OF SPEECH (PP. 27–33)

EXERCISE 1

(Notice that this *exercise* includes several proper nouns that are made of two or more capitalized words acting as one noun.)

                n   v   adj   n prep   n
1. Bette Nesmith Graham invented correction fluid in the 1950s.

   pro   adv   v   adj   n   n
2. She originally called her invention Mistake Out.

   adv pro   v   adj n prep   n
3. Later, she changed its name to Liquid Paper.

    adv   n   v   prep   n   conj pro adv   v   n
4. Originally, Graham worked as a typist, and she often made mistakes.

   pro   v   adj   n prep n   conj   v   adj   n prep pro
5. She brought white paint to work and covered her typos with it.

   adv   pro   v   n prep adj   adj   n
6. Soon everyone wanted a bottle of Graham's correction paint.

   pro   v   n prep adj   n   conj   v pro prep   adj   n
7. She mixed the product in her kitchen and bottled it like fingernail polish.

      adv   n   v   n   pro v   n prep n
8. Single-handedly, Graham developed a product that made millions of dollars.

   adj n   n   adv   v   prep adj   n
9. Her son, Michael Nesmith, also benefited from her success.

   pro   v   n   prep   n   adj   adj   n prep   n
10. He was a member of The Monkees, a popular boy band in the 1960s.

EXERCISE 2

      n   v   adj   n   n prep n
1. Clyde Tombaugh discovered the ninth "planet," Pluto, in 1930.

     n   v prep n prep   n prep n
2. Tombaugh died in 1997 at the age of 90.

    n   v   adj   n prep   n   adj   n   pro
3. Scientists loaded Tombaugh's ashes onto New Horizons, a space probe that

   v   v   prep   n   prep n
was launched in January of 2006. (Note: *That* is a relative pronoun standing for "probe.")

       n   v   v   prep   n prep n

4. New Horizons will arrive near Pluto in 2015.

prep   n   prep   n   n   v   n   prep   n prep

5. After the launch of New Horizons, astronomers deleted Pluto from the list of

adj   n

real planets.

    pro   v   conj adj   n   v   v   adj   adj   n

6. They determined that real planets must control their own orbits.
   (Note: In this sentence, *that* acts as a conjunction joining two clauses.)

     n   v   adj n   prep   n   prep   adj   n

7. Pluto is an icy ball under the influence of Neptune's orbit.

        n   v   n   prep adj   n

8. Astronomers put Pluto into a new category.

     adv   adj   n   prep n   v   v   prep n

9. Therefore, the official number of planets has changed to eight.

   interj   pro v   adj   n

10. Wow! That is an amazing development.

EXERCISE 3

  prep   n prep n   n   v   adj   n

1. In the summer of 2005, London Zoo opened a temporary exhibit.

     n prep   n   v   adj   n

2. The title of the exhibit was "The Human Zoo."

    adj   n   v   adj   adj   n

3. Zoo officials selected eight human volunteers.

    adv   pro   v   n   prep   n   prep adj   n

4. Then they put the humans on display for several days.

      n   prep n   v   v   adv   prep   n

5. Dozens of people had applied online for the project.

        n   v   adj   n   conj adj   n

6. The exhibit showcased three males and five females.

   pro   v prep adj adj   n   pro   v   adj   n   conj   adj   n

7. They dressed in fake fig leaves that covered their shorts and bikini tops.

    prep adj adj   n   conj   adj   n   n   v   adv

8. With its rocky ledges and cave-like structures, the enclosure had previously

    v   n

housed bears.

    adj   n   v   v   n   conj   v   n prep   n

9. The eight humans talked, played games, and received a lot of attention.

    prep   n   n   v   n   prep   adj   n   n   conj

10. Outside the exhibit, the zoo posted signs about human diet, habitat, and

    n

behavior.

EXERCISE 4

    interj   n   v   adj   n   prep adj   n

1. Wow, pigeons have a built-in compass in their brains!

    adj   n   v   pro prep   adj   n   conj pro   v

2. This compass points them in the right direction as they fly.

    adv   adj   n prep   n   v   n prep adj   n

3. Recently, pigeon experts in England conducted a study of these birds.

    n   v   n prep adj   n prep adj   n

4. The study tracked the flights of certain pigeons for two years.

    n   v   adv   adj

5. The results were very surprising.

    adj   n   adv   v   adj adj   n

6. Modern pigeons usually ignored their inner compasses.

    pro   v   prep adj   n   adv

7. They navigated by other methods instead.

    n   adv   v   adv conj   v   adj   n

8. The pigeons simply looked down and followed human highways.

    pro   v   n prep   adj   n conj v   adj   n   adv

9. They remembered roads from previous flights and took the same roads home

    adv

again.

    n   adv   v   adj   n   n   conj   n   conj pro   v

10. The pigeons even traced the roads' turns, curves, and roundabouts as they flew.

EXERCISE 5

    adj   n   v   adj   n conj adj   n
1. Some people collect rare coins and paper money.

        adj   adj   n v adv adj
2. The Del Monte twenty-dollar bill is very famous.

      n   v   n   conj pro   v   adj n
3. The mint made a mistake when it printed this bill.

     n prep   n   adv   v   pro prep   n   prep
4. A sticker from a banana accidentally attached itself to the paper during the

     adj   n
printing process.

      adj   adj conj adj   n   v   n prep   n
5. The round green and red sticker became a part of the bill.

    adj   n   adv   v prep adj   n
6. Such mistakes usually lead to a bill's destruction.

    adj   adj   n   adv   v   n prep   adj   n
7. This flawed note, however, left the mint with the normal twenties.

     n   adv   v   adj adj   n
8. Experts immediately authenticated its rare status.

     n adv   v prep n prep   n
9. The bill first sold on eBay for $10,000.

    adv   n   prep   n   v   n prep adj   adj   n
10. Eventually, a couple from Texas paid $25,000 for this one-of-a-kind note.

PARAGRAPH EXERCISE

    conj pro v   adv prep adj n conj   n prep adj   n   pro adv   v conj
When I look back over my life and the lives of my friends, I also see that
   n   prep adj conj   adj   n   v   pro conj pro v
involvement in school and community activities helped us [when we felt] the
   adj   n prep adj   n   pro v   n   prep   adj   n
negative pull of our peers. I joined the Shakespeare Club in elementary school
conj   n   prep adv adj   n   conj pro v   n
and the Police Athletic League in junior high school, and I played baseball
prep adj   n   n   v   adj   n   prep   adj   n   prep   adj adj   n
in high school. Sam took karate lessons from grade school through his early years
prep adj   n   conj adv   v prep adj   adj   adj   n   conj   n   v
in high school and also played on our high-school baseball team. And Rameck took
  adj   n   prep adv   adj   n   conj prep adj   n   pro v   adj   n
drama lessons in junior high school, and in high school he joined the drama club.

ADJECTIVES AND ADVERBS (PP. 34–40)

EXERCISE 1

1. adverb adding to the verb *attract*

2. adjective adding to the noun *entrance*

3. adjective adding to the noun *paperbacks*

4. adjective adding to the noun *topics*

5. adverb adding to the verb *discovered*

6. adverb adding to the adjective *straightforward*

7. adjective adding to the noun *subtitle*

8. adverb adding to the adjective *pink*

9. adverb adding to the verb *considered*

10. adverb adding to the verb *took*

EXERCISE 2

1. adjective adding to the noun *coupon*

2. adverb adding to the adjective *one*

3. adjective adding to the pronoun *I*

4. adverb adding to the verb *sells*

5. adjective adding to the noun *software*

6. adjective adding to the noun *hardware*

7. adjective adding to the noun *Spanish*

8. adjective adding to the noun *students*

9. adjective adding to the noun *child*

10. adjective adding to the pronoun *she*

EXERCISE 3

1. close

2. closely

3. close

4. badly

5. bad

6. badly

7. very happily

8. very happy

9. good

10. well

EXERCISE 4

1. the smallest

2. a small

3. smaller

4. the newest

5. newer

6. newer

7. better

8. the best

9. better

10. more important

EXERCISE 5

(Notice that *online* is used as both an adjective and an adverb in this exercise.)

        adj   adv
1. I took a helpful class online in the spring.

        adj   adj
2. An Internet specialist taught me research skills.

        adv adj   adj
3. I discovered very useful tools for Web research.

        adv   adj   adj
4. The instructor clearly explained various kinds of online resources.

        adj   adj   adj
5. She gave me several optional topics for each assignment.

        adv   adj   adj
6. I especially enjoyed the articles from my two projects about world music.

        adv adv   adj
7. Now I fully understand the benefits of online classes.

        adj   adj   adj adj
8. They are fun and rewarding because students work at their own pace.

        adv adv adj   adj
9. I am definitely less confused about online sources.

        adv   adv
10. I can do research online and enjoy the process completely.

PROOFREADING EXERCISE

    I didn't do very ~~good~~ *well* during my first semester at community college. I feel ~~badly~~ *bad* whenever I think of it. I skipped classes and turned in sloppy work. My counselor warned me about my negative attitude, but I was ~~real~~ *really* stubborn. I dropped out for a year and a half. Now that I have come back to college, I am even ~~stubborner~~ *more stubborn* than before. I go to every class and do my best. Now, a college degree is ~~only~~ my *only* goal.

CONTRACTIONS (PP. 41–46)

EXERCISE 1

1. aren't
2. no contractions
3. weren't
4. no contractions
5. there's
6. no contractions
7. They've
8. it's
9. no contractions
10. It's

EXERCISE 2

1. What's
2. You're, you're
3. no contractions (The word *its* is possessive; it does not mean *it is* or *it has.*)
4. it's, it's, it's (The third *its* is possessive; it does not mean *it is* or *it has.*)
5. there's
6. don't, they're
7. There's
8. doesn't, won't
9. It's, isn't
10. They'll, won't

EXERCISE 3

1. There's
2. it's
3. someone's
4. person's
5. no contractions
6. there's, we'll, we're
7. We'll
8. there's
9. they're
10. That's

EXERCISE 4

1. wasn't
2. I'll
3. isn't
4. It's, It's, I'm
5. you've
6. don't, don't
7. there's
8. you'll
9. haven't
10. we'd

EXERCISE 5

1. I'm, she's
2. We've, we've
3. aren't
4. they're
5. they're
6. that's
7. We've, can't, doesn't
8. we'd
9. that's, it's, they're
10. isn't

PARAGRAPH EXERCISE

~~I have~~ *I've* had the same group of friends since I was in junior high school. Now that ~~we are~~ *we're* all in college, my friends ~~do not~~ *don't* spend as much time on schoolwork as I do. Whenever ~~I am~~ *I'm* studying for an exam or working on a project, they call and ask if ~~I would~~ *I'd* like to see a movie or go to a game. ~~It is~~ *It's* the worst in the summer. ~~I have~~ *I've* been enrolling in summer school classes for the past two years so that ~~I will~~ *I'll* be ready to transfer soon. However, none of my friends has taken a class during the summer. At the rate ~~they are~~ *they're* going, my friends ~~will not~~ *won't* ever transfer.

POSSESSIVES (PP. 47–52)

EXERCISE 4

1. Claude Monet's
2. London's
3. fog's
4. weather's
5. no possessive nouns

6. no possessive nouns
7. People's (Note: No apostrophe is needed for the possessive pronoun *its*.)

8. no possessive nouns
9. artist's
10. "Monet's London."

EXERCISE 5

1. Manning's
2. critic's, Columbia Pictures'
3. Manning's, *Knight's*

4. writer's
5. Manning's
6. studio's
7. Manning's

8. public's
9. no possessives
10. films'

PROOFREADING EXERCISE

I'm not satisfied with my ~~cars~~ car's ride; it's too rough. For instance, when a ~~roads~~ road's surface has grooves in it, the wheels get pulled in every direction. My ~~tires~~ tires' treads seem too deep for ordinary city driving. Bumps and potholes usually send my ~~passenger's~~ passengers' heads straight into the roof. When I bought my car, I asked about ~~it's~~ its stiff suspension and heavy-duty tires. The salesperson told me that the suspension's elements would eventually soften for a smoother ride, but they haven't. I should have known not to trust ~~anyones~~ anyone's words more than my own instincts.

REVIEW OF CONTRACTIONS AND POSSESSIVES (P. 53)

1. isn't
2. cloud's, it's
3. aren't
4. They're

5. Sloane's, clouds'
6. shouldn't
7. They're, they're

8. artist's
9. mustn't
10. It's, cloudscape's

I consider my friend Alexis to be one of the smartest people I know. Alexis is a twenty-five-year-old film student at a nearby university. ~~Shes~~ She's presently in her senior year, but ~~thats~~ that's just the beginning for Alexis. She plans to take full advantage of her ~~universitys~~ university's resources to learn what she needs before starting her own filmmaking career. She has access to her fellow ~~students~~ students' talent, her different ~~teachers~~ teachers' equipment and experience, and the film ~~schools~~ school's many contacts. Alexis ~~doesnt~~ doesn't agree with a lot of the advice she gets from people in the film industry. They try to discourage her sometimes, but she ~~wont~~ won't let anything distract her from her goal of making great movies. ~~Ive~~ I've always been impressed by ~~Alexis~~ Alexis' (or *Alexis's*) self-confidence, and ~~its~~ it's inspired me to believe in myself more than I ever have before.

PROGRESS TEST (P. 54)

1. B. They should *have* practiced more.

2. A. Kyle bought a *new* phone with his first paycheck.

3. A. My teacher *complimented* me on my writing style.

4. B. I feel *bad* whenever I hurt someone's feelings.

5. A. The tutors didn't know *where* the extra handouts were.

6. B. *It's* fun to shift gears.

7. A. Our new computer has *already* frozen several times.

8. B. I'm learning more from one of them *than* the other.

9. A. Eating a snack before an exam can have positive *effects*.

10. A. I always *accept* my best friend's advice.

SENTENCE STRUCTURE

FINDING SUBJECTS AND VERBS (PP. 57–63)

EXERCISE 1

1. Many people know the name of Uggie, the dog actor.

2. Uggie became famous in the Oscar-winning silent movie *The Artist*.

3. His big break came after ten years of work in other films and projects.

4. With his role in *The Artist*, Uggie showcased the skills and expressions of Jack Russell terriers and made them very popular.

5. Originally, Uggie's trainer rescued him from an animal shelter.

6. In June 2012, Uggie retired from his long acting career due to a physical setback.

7. Before his retirement, this famous little dog left his mark on Hollywood—literally.

8. On June 25, 2012, Uggie put his paw prints in cement at Grauman's Chinese Theater.

9. Crowds of fans gathered on Hollywood Blvd. in honor of Uggie's work in films.

10. They were the first canine footprints in the history of this famous landmark.

EXERCISE 2

1. In 1940, four <u>teenagers</u> <u>took</u> a walk and <u>discovered</u> something marvelous.

2. <u>They</u> <u>entered</u> an underground cavern in Lascaux, France, and <u>found</u> vivid images of animals on its walls.

3. There <u>were</u> horses, deer, bulls, cats, and <u>oxen</u>.

4. The prehistoric <u>artists</u> also <u>left</u> tracings of their handprints on the walls.

5. <u>Scientists</u> <u>dated</u> the paintings and engravings at approximately 17,000 years old.

6. After its discovery, the Lascaux <u>cave</u> <u>became</u> a popular tourist attraction.

7. Twelve hundred <u>people</u> <u>visited</u> the site daily.

8. These <u>visitors</u> <u>had</u> a negative impact on the cave's prehistoric artwork.

9. <u>They</u> <u>breathed</u> carbon dioxide into the cave and <u>increased</u> its humidity.

10. French <u>officials</u> <u>closed</u> the Lascaux cave to the public in 1963.

EXERCISE 3

1. <u>Harold Lloyd</u> <u>became</u> a star of comic films during the silent era of Hollywood.

2. <u>Lloyd</u> <u>worked</u> in Hollywood at the same time as Charlie Chaplin and Buster Keaton.

3. The <u>name</u> of Harold Lloyd's character in many of his films <u>was</u> also Harold.

4. One <u>accessory</u> <u>distinguished</u> Harold from other silent-film characters—a pair of perfectly round eyeglasses.

5. The <u>glasses</u> <u>had</u> no lenses but <u>fit</u> his face and <u>gave</u> him a distinct personality.

6. A <u>suit</u> and a straw <u>hat</u> <u>completed</u> Harold's simple yet memorable costume.

7. Unlike Chaplin and Keaton's clownish characters, <u>Harold</u> <u>looked</u> like a normal young man out for adventure—anything from good fun to a great fight.

8. As Harold, <u>Lloyd</u> <u>performed</u> incredible stunts in spite of an injury from an accident with a prop bomb early in his career.

9. <u>He</u> <u>lost</u> part of his hand and <u>covered</u> it in his films with a special glove.

10. In his most famous film, *Safety Last!*, <u>Harold</u> <u>climbed</u> outside a tall building and <u>dangled</u> dangerously from the hands of its clock.

EXERCISE 4

1. There <u>are</u> a <u>number</u> of world-famous trees in California.

2. Among them <u>are</u> the oldest <u>trees</u> on the planet.

3. These <u>trees</u> <u>live</u> somewhere in Inyo National Forest.

4. <u>One</u> of these ancient trees <u>is</u> a bristlecone pine.

5. <u>Scientists</u> <u>call</u> it the Methuselah Tree.

6. <u>They</u> <u>place</u> its age at five thousand years.

7. The <u>soil</u> and <u>temperatures</u> around it <u>seem</u> too poor for a tree's health.

8. But the <u>Methuselah Tree</u> and its <u>neighbors</u> obviously <u>thrive</u> in such conditions.

9. Due to its importance, the Methuselah Tree's exact <u>location</u> <u>is</u> a secret.

10. Such important natural <u>specimens</u> <u>need</u> protection.

EXERCISE 5

1. Ancient <u>Egyptians</u> <u>worshipped</u> cats of all sizes.

2. <u>Archeologists</u> <u>find</u> many mummies of cats in Egyptian tombs.

3. <u>Carvings</u> in the tombs <u>reveal</u> a strong belief in the god-like powers of large cats.

4. <u>Scientists</u> always <u>look</u> for new evidence of ancient beliefs.

5. <u>Archaeologists</u> recently <u>discovered</u> the mummy of a lion in a tomb in Saqqara, Egypt.

6. <u>It</u> <u>is</u> the first discovery of a lion skeleton in an Egyptian tomb.

7. There <u>were</u> no <u>bandages</u> around the lion.

8. But there <u>were</u> other <u>signs</u> of mummification.

9. The <u>lion</u> <u>rested</u> in the tomb of King Tutankhamen's nurse.

10. <u>Archaeologists</u> now <u>have</u> real evidence of lion worship in Egypt.

PARAGRAPH EXERCISE

The 1960s and 1970s: Renewal through Independence

The golden <u>age</u> of cinema <u>was</u> over. A new <u>generation</u> of filmmakers . . . <u>emerged</u> on the scene during this period of crisis.

Worldwide Awakening

Everywhere there <u>was</u> a <u>renewal</u> of film and cinema. In Latin America, the Brazilian <u>Glauber Rocha</u> <u>provided</u> the impetus for *Cinema Novo* with his cinema as political allegories. In the U.S., a <u>group</u> of young directors, actresses, and actors <u>responded</u> to the creative standstill of the large studios—the <u>first</u> [<u>were</u>]

Dennis Hopper and Peter Fonda with their naively pessimistic interpretation of the American Dream in "Easy Rider" (1969). George Lucas ("THX 1138," 1970) and Steven Spielberg ("Duel," 1971) made their debut. Martin Scorsese ("Mean Streets," 1973; "Taxi Driver," 1976; "Raging Bull," 1980) and Francis Ford Coppola ("The Conversation," 1974; "The Godfather," 1972; "Apocalypse Now," 1979) directed their best films. The decade of "New Hollywood" was a stroke of luck for cinema and the film industry.

LOCATING PREPOSITIONAL PHRASES (PP. 64–69)

EXERCISE 1

1. Viganella is a tiny village (at the bottom) (of the Alps) (in Italy).

2. Due (to its physical position) (between the mountains), the town (of Viganella) suffered (from an unusual problem).

3. The sun's rays never reached the village (from the middle) (of November) (to the first week) (in February).

4. The mountains kept the little town (in shadow) (without any direct sunlight) (for several months) each year.

5. Then Giacomo Bonzani found a high-tech solution (to Viganella's dreary situation).

6. (In 2006), engineers installed a huge mirror thousands (of feet) (above Viganella) (on the side) (of one) (of the mountains) (around it).

7. A computer (at the mirror's location) keeps track (of the sun's movements).

8. The computer's software rotates the mirror (into the perfect position) to reflect sunlight (into the village square). [Note: "To reflect sunlight" is a verbal, not a prepositional phrase.]

9. The mirror began its work (in December) (of 2006).

10. Now the sun "shines" (on the town) (of Viganella) (during all months) (of the year).

EXERCISE 2

1. One fact (about William Shakespeare and his work) always surprises people.

2. There are no copies (of his original manuscripts).

3. No museum or library has even one page (from a Shakespeare play) (in Shakespeare's own handwriting).

4. Museums and libraries have copies (of the First Folio) instead.

5. (After Shakespeare's death) (in 1616), <u>actors</u> (from his company) <u>gathered</u> the texts (of his plays) and <u>published</u> them (as one book), the First Folio, (in 1623).

6. <u>They</u> <u>printed</u> approximately 750 copies (at the time).

7. Currently, there <u>are</u> 230 known <u>copies</u> (of the First Folio) (in the world).

8. Many <u>owners</u> (of the Folio) <u>remain</u> anonymous (by choice).

9. One <u>woman</u> <u>inherited</u> her copy (of the Folio) (from a distant relative).

10. Another <u>copy</u> (of the First Folio) recently <u>sold</u> (for five million dollars).

EXERCISE 3

1. <u>Most</u> (of us) <u>remember</u> playing (with Frisbees) (in our front yards) (in the early evenings) and (at parks or beaches) (on weekend afternoons).

2. <u>Fred Morrison</u> <u>invented</u> the original flat Frisbee (for the Wham-O toy company) (in the 1950s).

3. <u>Ed Headrick</u>, designer (of the professional Frisbee), <u>passed</u> away (at his home) (in California) (in August) (of 2002).

4. Working (at Wham-O) (in the 1960s), <u>Headrick</u> <u>improved</u> the performance (of the existing Frisbee) (with the addition) (of ridges) (in the surface) (of the disc).

5. Headrick's <u>improvements</u> <u>led</u> (to increased sales) (of his "professional model" Frisbee) and (to the popularity) (of Frisbee tournaments).

6. (After Headrick's redesign), <u>Wham-O</u> <u>sold</u> 100 million (of the flying discs).

7. <u>Headrick</u> also <u>invented</u> the game (of disc golf).

8. (Like regular golf) but (with discs), the <u>game</u> <u>takes</u> place (on special disc golf courses) (like the first one) (at Oak Grove Park) (in California).

9. (Before his death), <u>Headrick</u> <u>asked</u> (for his ashes) to be formed (into memorial flying discs) (for select family and friends). [*To be formed* is a verbal. See page 125.]

10. <u>Donations</u> (from sales) (of the remaining memorial discs) <u>went</u> (toward the establishment) (of a museum) (on the history) (of the Frisbee and disc golf).

EXERCISE 4

1. <u>Roald Dahl</u> <u>is</u> the author (of *Charlie and the Chocolate Factory*).

2. (In his youth), <u>Dahl</u> <u>had</u> two memorable experiences (with sweets).

3. <u>One</u> (of them) <u>involved</u> the owner (of a candy store).

4. <u>Dahl</u> and his young <u>friends</u> <u>had</u> a bad relationship (with this particular woman).

5. (On one visit) (to her store), <u>Dahl</u> <u>put</u> a dead mouse (into one) (of the candy jars) (behind her back).

6. The <u>woman</u> later <u>went</u> (to his school) and <u>demanded</u> his punishment.

7. <u>He</u> and his <u>friends</u> <u>received</u> several lashes (from a cane) (in her presence).

8. (During his later childhood years), <u>Dahl</u> <u>became</u> a taste-tester (for the Cadbury chocolate company).

9. Cadbury <u>sent</u> him and other schoolchildren boxes (of sweets) to evaluate. [*To evaluate* is a verbal, not a prepositional phrase. See page 125 for more.]

10. <u>Dahl</u> <u>tried</u> each candy and <u>made</u> a list (of his reactions and recommendations).

Exercise 5

1. (At 2 a.m.) (on the second Sunday) (in March), <u>something</u> <u>happens</u> (to nearly everyone) (in America): Daylight Saving Time.

2. But few <u>people</u> <u>are</u> awake (at two) (in the morning).

3. So <u>we</u> <u>set</u> the hands or digits (of our clocks) ahead one hour (on Saturday night) (in preparation) (for it).

4. And (before bed) (on the first Saturday) (in November), <u>we</u> <u>turn</u> them back again.

5. (For days) (after both events), <u>I</u> <u>have</u> trouble (with my sleep patterns and my mood).

6. (In spring), the <u>feeling</u> <u>is</u> one (of loss).

7. That Saturday-night <u>sleep</u> (into Sunday) <u>is</u> one hour shorter than usual.

8. But (in fall), <u>I</u> <u>gain</u> a false sense (of security) (about time).

9. That endless Sunday <u>morning</u> quickly <u>melts</u> (into the start) (of a hectic week) (like the other fifty-one) (in the year).

10. <u>All</u> (of this upheaval) <u>is</u> due (to the Uniform Time Act) (of 1966).

Paragraph Exercise

    <u>I</u> <u>put</u> the red paperclip (on the desk) and <u>took</u> a picture (of it). <u>I</u> <u>walked</u> (to the door) and <u>pulled</u> the handle. The <u>door</u> <u>swung</u> open. <u>I</u> <u>lifted</u> my right foot (into the air). As my right <u>foot</u> <u>came</u> forward (to the threshold) (of the doorframe), the <u>phone</u> <u>rang</u>. My <u>foot</u> <u>hung</u> (in the air), just short (of the outside hallway). The <u>phone</u> <u>rang</u> again. <u>I</u> <u>spun</u> around slowly, almost (in slow motion). <u>I</u> slowly <u>slunk</u> away (from the door) and <u>lifted</u> the phone (from the receiver). [Note that this writer also uses several single-word adverbs to show position— *open, forward, around,* and *away*.]

UNDERSTANDING DEPENDENT CLAUSES (PP. 70–77)

EXERCISE 1

1. Edgar and Nina Otto, who live in Florida, were the winning bidders in an unusual auction in 2008.

2. Whoever placed the highest bid won the opportunity of a lifetime: a chance to clone their dog. [Note: The dependent clause acts as the subject of the sentence.]

3. The company that held the auction and provided the service was BioArts International.

4. The Ottos wanted to clone Sir Lancelot, a yellow Labrador that died in 2008.

5. The price that they paid exceeded $150,000.

6. Once the auction ended, the scientists at BioArts went to work.

7. They used the DNA that the Ottos saved from Sir Lancelot to produce a genetic match.

8. The complex process, which took place in South Korea, yielded an adorable puppy.

9. The puppy looked so much like Sir Lancelot that the company named him Encore Lancelot, Lancey for short.

10. At the first meeting with their new dog in January of 2009, the Ottos were overjoyed that Lancey walked with crossed feet, just like Sir Lancelot.

EXERCISE 2

1. When I was on vacation in New York City, I loved the look of the Empire State Building at night.

2. I thought that the colored lights at the top of this landmark were just decorative.

3. I did not know that their patterns also have meaning.

4. While I waited at the airport, I read about the patterns.

5. Some of the light combinations reveal connections that are obvious.

6. For instance, if the occasion is St. Patrick's Day, the top of the building glows with green lights.

7. When the holiday involves a celebration of America, the three levels of lights shine red, white, and blue.

8. There are other combinations that are less well known.

9. Red-black-green is a pattern that signals Martin Luther King, Jr. Day.

10. Whenever I visit the city again, I'll know that the lights on the Empire State Building have meaning.

EXERCISE 3

1. When people visit Google's homepage on one evening in March each year, they are often surprised.

2. They notice immediately that the whole page is black instead of white.

3. After they look into it further, they discover the reason for the temporary color change.

4. The black page signifies that Google is a participant in Earth Hour.

5. In 2008, Google joined countless cities, companies, and individuals who turn their lights off for one hour in an international effort to encourage energy conservation.

6. People around the globe cut their electricity and live in the dark as soon as clocks strike 8 p.m. in their locations.

7. When the hour is up at 9 p.m., they turn the electricity back on.

8. Earth Hour is an idea that began in Australia.

9. In 2007, the first Earth Hour that the Australians celebrated occurred between 7:30 and 8:30 p.m. on March 31.

10. Even though some people dismiss Earth Hour as a minor event, others believe in its power as a symbol of environmental awareness.

EXERCISE 4

1. On June 8, 1924, George Mallory and Andrew Irvine disappeared as they climbed to the top of Mount Everest.

2. Earlier, when a reporter asked Mallory why he climbed Everest, his response became legendary.

3. "Because it is there," Mallory replied.

4. No living person knows whether the two British men reached the summit of Everest before they died.

5. Nine years after Mallory and Irvine disappeared, English climbers found Irvine's ice ax.

6. In 1975, a Chinese climber spotted a body that was frozen in deep snow on the side of the mountain.

7. He kept the news secret for several years but finally told a fellow climber on the day before he died himself in an avalanche on Everest.

8. In May 1999, a team of mountaineers searched the area that the Chinese man described and found George Mallory's frozen body still intact after seventy-five years.

9. After they took DNA samples for identification, the mountaineers buried the famous climber on the mountainside where he fell.

10. The question remains whether Mallory was on his way up or down when he met his fate.

EXERCISE 5

1. I just read an article with a list of "What Doctors Wish [that] You Knew."

2. One fact is that red and blue fruits are the healthiest.

3. Patients who have doctor's appointments after lunchtime spend less time in the waiting room.

4. Drivers who apply more sunscreen to their left sides get less skin cancer.

5. People who take ten deep breaths in the morning and evening feel less stress.

6. A clock that is visible from the bed makes insomnia worse.

7. People often suffer from weekend headaches because they get up too late.

8. They withdraw from caffeine by skipping the coffee that they usually drink on workdays.

9. Doctors suggest that people maintain weekday hours on weekends.

10. I am glad that I found this list.

PARAGRAPH EXERCISE

We have numbered the dependent clauses in the excerpt for clarity's sake.

We don't exist (1) unless there is someone (2) who can see us existing, (3) what we say has no meaning (4) until someone can understand, (5) while to be surrounded by friends is constantly to have our identity confirmed; their knowledge and care for us have the power to pull us from our numbness. In small comments, many of them teasing, they reveal (6) [that] they know our foibles and accept them and so, in turn, accept (7) that we have a place in the world. We can ask them "Isn't he frightening?" or "Do you ever feel that . . . ?" and be understood, rather than encounter the puzzled 'No, not particularly'— (8) which can make us feel, even when in company, as lonely as polar explorers.

True friends do not evaluate us according to worldly criteria; it is the core self (9) [that] they are interested in; like ideal parents, their love for us remains unaffected by our appearance or position in the social hierarchy, and so we have no qualms in dressing in old clothes and revealing (10) that we have made little money this year. The desire for riches should perhaps not always be understood as a simple hunger for a luxurious life; a more important motive might be the wish to be appreciated and treated nicely. We may seek a fortune for no greater reason than to secure the respect and attention of people (11) who would otherwise look straight through us. Epicurus, discerning our underlying need, recognized (12) that a handful of true friends could deliver the love and respect (13) that even a fortune may not.

CORRECTING FRAGMENTS (PP. 78–83)

EXERCISE 1
Possible revisions to make the fragments into sentences are *italicized*.

1. Correct
2. Improvements in fabric coatings *are* making it possible.
3. Clothes *are* treated with certain chemicals.
4. Correct
5. *They have already been tested* by the military for soldiers' uniforms.
6. Correct
7. Correct
8. *They* helped cure soldiers' skin problems, too.
9. Correct
10. *It could also* be used for hospital bedding, kitchen linens, and sport-related clothing.

Possible revisions to make the fragments into sentences are *italicized*.

1. Correct

2. *It is* good at holding objects together firmly.

3. Campers *use* it to patch holes in backpacks and tents.

4. Correct

5. Books *have been* written about the unique uses for it.

6. *The makers of Duck Brand duct tape hold a yearly contest.*

7. Correct

8. Strips of duct tape *form* tuxedos, cummerbunds, gowns, hats, and corsages.

9. A $5,000 prize *goes* to the couple with the best use of duct tape and another $5,000 *goes* to their high school.

10. Correct

EXERCISE 3

Answers may vary, but here are some possible revisions.

1. A worker at the Smithsonian discovered an important historical object on a shelf in one of the museum's storage rooms.

2. Made of cardboard and covered with short, smooth fur, it was a tall black top hat.

3. The hat didn't look like anything special—more like an old costume or prop.

4. It was special, however, having been worn by Abraham Lincoln on the night of his assassination.

5. Once found and identified, Lincoln's hat traveled with the 150th anniversary exhibition, called "America's Smithsonian."

6. For such a priceless object to be able to travel around the country safely, experts needed to build a unique display case for Lincoln's top hat.

7. The design allowed visitors to view the famous stovepipe hat without damaging it with their breath or hands.

8. The hat traveled in a sealed box that was designed against even earthquakes.

9. Keeping the hat earthquake-proof was an important concern because it would be on display in California for part of the time.

10. Among the millions of objects in the archives of the Smithsonian, President Lincoln's hat is one of the most impressive.

EXERCISE 4

Answers may vary, but here are some possible revisions.

1. When Nathan King turned twelve, he had a heart-stopping experience.

2. Nathan was tossing a football against his bedroom wall, which made the ball ricochet and land on his bed.

3. In a diving motion, Nathan fell on his bed to catch the ball as it landed.

4. After he caught the ball, Nathan felt a strange sensation in his chest.

5. To his surprise, he looked down and saw the eraser end of a no. 2 pencil that had pierced his chest and entered his heart.

6. Nathan immediately shouted for his mother, who luckily was in the house at the time.

7. Because Nathan's mom is a nurse, she knew not to remove the pencil.

8. If she had pulled the pencil out of her son's chest, he would have died.

9. After Nathan was taken to a hospital equipped for open-heart surgery, he had the pencil carefully removed.

10. Fate may be partly responsible for Nathan's happy birthday story since it turned out to be his heart surgeon's birthday too.

EXERCISE 5

Answers may vary, but here are some possible revisions. (Changes and additions are in *italics*.)

1. One of the people sitting next to me on the train *sneezed four times in a row.*

2. Taking good pictures with my cell phone camera *is easy.*

3. Before the paint was dry in the classrooms, *the new semester began.*

4. The judge's question and the answer it received *surprised everyone.*

5. Because there were fewer students in the program this year, *it ran smoothly.*

6. *His speech lasted* for over an hour.

7. Whenever the teacher reminds us about the midterm exam, *we get nervous.*

8. If we move to Kentucky and stay for two years, *we will save money.*

9. *Please notify us* as soon as the order form reaches the warehouse.

10. Buildings with odd shapes always interest me.

Answers may vary, but here is one revision to eliminate the seven fragments. Areas of revision are in *italics*.

On June 15, 2012, Nik Wallenda made *history by being* the first person to walk on a tightrope from the U.S. to Canada directly above the raging falls of Niagara Gorge. His trip on the high wire that misty evening took 30 minutes. *It was* a nail-biting half hour that one major network, ABC, televised live. To be on the safe side, the network made sure that Wallenda attached himself to a safety cable in case he fell off the wire on live TV. Nik Wallenda comes from a long line of daredevil *performers, the famous family* known as the Flying Wallendas. Nik represents the seventh generation of people willing to risk their lives in the name of entertainment. Before attempting his spectacular walk across Niagara Falls, Wallenda fought hard to get permission from both U.S. and Canadian *officials so that* he was not arrested—as previous stunt performers have been—when he reached the other side. Instead of handcuffs waiting for him on the Canadian bank of the *falls, Nik Wallenda* heard the cheers of 100,000 supporters welcoming him back to earth.

A year later, Wallenda also succeeded in crossing a gorge near the Grand *Canyon, this time without a safety cable.* His tightrope *was* 1,500 feet above the canyon floor. Winds were so strong that he had to stop twice in the middle of the crossing and crouch down to maintain his position on the wire.

CORRECTING RUN-ON SENTENCES (PP. 84–90)

EXERCISE 1

1. Mary Mallon is a famous name in American history, but she is not famous for something good.

2. Most people know Mary Mallon by another name, and that is "Typhoid Mary."

3. The sentence is correct.

4. The sentence is correct.

5. Mary Mallon was the first famous case of a healthy carrier of disease, but she never believed the accusations against her.

6. Mallon, an Irish immigrant, was a cook; she was also an infectious carrier of typhoid.

7. By the time the authorities discovered Mallon's problem, she had made many people ill. A few of her "victims" actually died from the disease.

8. A health specialist approached Mallon and asked her for a blood sample; she was outraged and attacked him with a long cooking fork.

9. Eventually, the authorities dragged Mallon into a hospital for testing, but she fought them hysterically the entire time.

10. The lab tests proved Mallon's infectious status, and health officials forced Mary Mallon to live on an island by herself for twenty-six years.

EXERCISE 2

Your answers may differ depending on how you chose to separate the two clauses.

1. I just read an article about prehistoric rodents, and I was surprised by their size.

2. Scientists recently discovered the remains of a rat-like creature called *Phoberomys;* it was as big as a buffalo.

3. *Phoberomys* sat back on its large rear feet and fed itself with its smaller front feet in just the way rats and mice do now.

4. This supersized rodent lived in South America, but luckily that was nearly ten million years ago.

5. At that time, South America was a separate continent; it had no cows or horses to graze on its open land.

6. South America and North America were separated by the sea, so there were also no large cats around to hunt and kill other large animals.

7. Scientists believe that *Phoberomys* thrived and grew large because of the lack of predators and competitors for food.

8. The *Phoberomys'* carefree lifestyle eventually disappeared, for the watery separation between North and South America slowly became a land route.

9. The big carnivores of North America could travel down the new land route, and the big rodents were defenseless against them.

10. The rodents who survived were the smaller ones who could escape underground, and that is the reason we have no buffalo-sized rats today.

EXERCISE 3

Your answers may differ since various words can be used to begin dependent clauses.

1. Pablo Wendel is a German student of art who feels a special connection with a particular group of ancient sculptures.

2. When Pablo acted on this feeling in September of 2006, he won his "fifteen minutes of fame."

3. The sentence is correct.

4. The sentence is correct.

5. He made a special clay-covered costume that was complete with armor and a helmet.

6. Pablo took this outfit and a pedestal with him to the museum, which is located in Xian, China.

7. The sentence is correct.

8. The sentence is correct.

9. Pablo, in disguise, stood among his fellow "soldiers" and didn't move until eventually someone saw him.

10. Although the museum guards took Pablo's clay costume, they let him go with just a warning.

EXERCISE 4
Your answers may differ since various words can be used to begin dependent clauses.

1. Since I've been reading about sleep in my psychology class, I know a lot more about it.

2. Sleep has four stages, which we usually go through many times during the night.

3. The first stage of sleep begins as our muscles relax and mental activity slows down.

4. The sentence is correct.

5. Stage two takes us deeper than stage one so that we are no longer aware of our surroundings.

6. The sentence is correct.

7. Next is stage three, in which we become more and more relaxed and are very hard to awaken.

8. Stage four is so deep that we don't even hear loud noises.

9. The most active type of sleep is called REM (rapid eye movement) sleep because our eyes move back and forth quickly behind our eyelids.

10. Although REM sleep is only about as deep as stage one, we do all our dreaming during the REM stage.

EXERCISE 5
Your answers may differ depending on how you chose to separate the clauses.

1. White buffalos are very rare, and they are extremely important in Native American folklore.

2. Many American Indian tribes feel a strong attachment to white buffalos because they are viewed as omens of peace and prosperity.

3. One farm in Wisconsin is famous as a source of white buffalos. Three of them have been born on this farm since 1994.

4. The owners of the farm are Valerie and Dave Heider, and they are as surprised as anyone about the unusual births.

5. The Heiders' first white buffalo was a female calf who was named Miracle.

6. After Miracle became a local attraction, visitors to the Heider farm raised tourism in the area by twenty-two percent in 1995.

7. A second white calf was born on the farm in 1996; however, it died after a few days.

8. Miracle survived until 2004; she lived for ten years.

9. In September of 2006, the Heider farm yielded a third white buffalo calf, but it was a boy.

10. The odds against one white buffalo being born are high; the odds against three being born in the same place are astronomical.

REVIEW OF FRAGMENTS AND RUN-ON SENTENCES (P. 90)

Your revisions may differ depending on how you chose to correct the errors.

With the focus on cleanliness lately in advertising for soaps and household cleaning products, people are surprised to hear that we may be too clean for our own good. This phenomenon is called the "hygiene hypothesis," and recent studies support its validity. For instance, one study shows the benefit of living with two or more pets. Babies may grow up with healthier immune systems and be less allergic if they live with a dog and a cat or two dogs or two cats. The old thinking was that young children would become more allergic living with many pets, but they don't. Somehow the exposure to pets and all their "dirty" habits gives youngsters much-needed defenses. There may be as much as a seventy-five percent lower allergy risk, according to this study.

IDENTIFYING VERB PHRASES (PP. 93–98)

Exercise 1

1. Scientists of all kinds have been learning a lot lately.

2. Those who study traffic safety have recently discovered a puzzling truth.

3. People drive more safely when they encounter fewer traffic signs and traffic lights.

4. The reason behind the "Shared Space" theory is easy to explain.

5. Drivers will regulate their speed and pay closer attention to other drivers when they are not told to do so by signs and lights.

6. Traffic signs and signals give drivers a false sense of security that often leads to recklessness.

7. When no signs or signals exist, drivers think about their own safety and drive more cautiously.

8. Many towns in Europe and America have already taken steps to test the truth of this theory.

9. In some cases, all lights, signs, and barriers have been removed so that all drivers and pedestrians must negotiate with each other to proceed through the town.

10. These changes have usually resulted in lower speeds, fewer accidents, and shorter travel times.

EXERCISE 2

1. Have you ever felt a craving for art?

2. Have you said to yourself, "I need a new painting, or I will lose my mind"?

3. If you do find yourself in this situation, you can get instant satisfaction.

4. I am referring to Art-o-Mat machines, of course.

5. These vending machines dispense small pieces of modern art.

6. You insert five dollars, pull a knob on a refurbished cigarette dispenser, and out comes an original art piece.

7. The artists themselves get fifty percent of the selling price.

8. Art-o-Mat machines can be found at locations across the country.

9. Art-o-Mats are currently dispensing tiny paintings, photographs, and sculptures in twenty-eight states and in Canada and Austria.

10. The machines have sold the works of hundreds of contemporary artists.

EXERCISE 3

1. During my last semester of high school, our English teacher assigned a special paper.

2. He said that he was becoming depressed by all the bad news out there, so each of us was asked to find a piece of good news and write a short research paper about it.

3. I must admit that I had no idea how hard that assignment would be.

4. Finally, I found an article while I was reading my favorite magazine.

5. The title of the article was a pun; it was called "Grin Reaper."

6. I knew instantly that it must be just the kind of news my teacher wanted.

7. The article explained that one woman, Pam Johnson, had started a club that she named The Secret Society of Happy People.

8. She had even chosen August 8 as "Admit You're Happy Day" and had already convinced more than fifteen state governors to recognize the holiday.

9. The club and the holiday were created to support people who are happy so that the unhappy, negative people around will not bring the happy people down.

10. As I was writing my essay, I visited the Society of Happy People Web site, *www.sohp.com*, and signed my teacher up for their newsletter.

EXERCISE 4

1. I have always wondered how an Etch A Sketch works.

2. This flat TV-shaped toy has been popular since it first arrived in the 1960s.

3. Now I have learned the secrets inside this popular toy.

4. An Etch A Sketch is filled with a combination of metal powder and tiny plastic particles.

5. This mixture clings to the inside of the Etch A Sketch screen.

6. When the pointer that is connected to the two knobs moves, the tip of it "draws" lines in the powder on the back of the screen.

7. The powder at the bottom of the Etch A Sketch does not fill in these lines because it is too far away.

8. But if the Etch A Sketch is turned upside down, the powder clings to the whole underside surface of the screen and "erases" the image again.

9. Although the basic Etch A Sketch has not changed since I was a kid, it now comes in several different sizes.

10. Best of all, these great drawing devices have never needed batteries, and I hope that they never will [need batteries].

EXERCISE 5

1. Scientists successfully cloned a dog for the first time in 2005.

2. Cloning experts had been attempting to clone a dog for many years.

3. They had had success with horses, cats, and even rats before they could clone a dog.

4. The scientists who eventually succeeded were from Seoul National University in South Korea.

5. They <u>named</u> the cloned dog Snuppy as a tribute to the university where the accomplishment <u>was made</u>, and they <u>pronounced</u> the name "Snoopy."

6. Of course, Snuppy <u>could thank</u> his "parent" dog, a three-year-old Afghan hound, for all of his great physical features.

7. Both dogs <u>had</u> long glossy black fur that <u>was accentuated</u> by identical brown markings on their paws, tails, chests, and eyebrows.

8. Unfortunately, the cloning procedure <u>does</u> not <u>guarantee</u> that the clone of a dog <u>will share</u> the unique features of the original dog's personality.

9. Nevertheless, now that dog cloning <u>has been achieved</u>, many people <u>have shown</u> an interest in cloning their own dogs.

10. Although some people <u>may</u> not <u>be</u> happy with just a physical copy of a beloved pet, for others, a copy <u>is</u> better than nothing.

[The word forms "cloning," "to clone," and "cloned" in "the *cloned* dog," are not acting as real verbs, but as *verbals*. To learn more, see page 125.]

REVIEW EXERCISE (P. 98)

My <u>brain</u> <u>feels</u> (like a computer's central processing unit). <u>Information</u> is continually <u>pumping</u> (into its circuits). <u>I</u> <u>organize</u> the data, <u>format</u> it (to my individual preferences), and <u>lay</u> it out (in my own style). As <u>I</u> endlessly <u>sculpt</u> existing formulas, <u>they</u> <u>become</u> something (of my own). When <u>I</u> <u>need</u> a solution (to a problem), <u>I</u> <u>access</u> the data that <u>I</u> <u>have gathered</u> (from my whole existence), even my preprogrammed DNA.

Since <u>I</u> <u>am</u> a student, <u>teachers</u> <u>require</u> that <u>I</u> <u>supply</u> them (with specific information) (in various formats). When <u>they</u> <u>assign</u> an essay, <u>I</u> <u>produce</u> several paragraphs. If <u>they</u> <u>need</u> a summary, <u>I</u> <u>scan</u> the text, <u>find</u> its main ideas, and <u>put</u> them briefly (into my own words). <u>I</u> <u>know</u> that <u>I</u> <u>can accomplish</u> whatever the teachers <u>ask</u> so that <u>I</u> <u>can obtain</u> a degree and <u>continue</u> processing ideas to make a living.

<u>I</u> <u>compare</u> my brain (to a processor) because right now <u>I</u> <u>feel</u> that <u>I</u> <u>must work</u> (like one). As <u>I</u> <u>go</u> further (into my education), my <u>processor</u> <u>will be</u> continually <u>updated</u>. And (with any luck), <u>I</u> <u>will end</u> up (with real, not artificial, intelligence).

USING STANDARD ENGLISH VERBS (PP. 99–104)

EXERCISE 1
1. end, ended

2. does, did

3. am, was

4. votes, voted

5. have, had

6. shop, shopped

7. are, were

8. pick, picked

9. do, did

10. have, had

EXERCISE 2
1. is, was

2. do, did

3. have, had

4. asks, asked

5. have, had

6. learn, learned

7. are, were

8. does, did

9. plays, played

10. am, was

EXERCISE 3
1. started, like

2. offers

3. are, have

4. finished, needed

5. run, do

6. advise, comfort

7. enjoy, are

8. completed, expected

9. have

10. thank

EXERCISE 4
1. have

2. play

3. plays

4. play

5. practices, do

6. is, wins

7. am, is, am

8. remind

9. follows

10. have, am, is

EXERCISE 5
1. gave

2. handed

3. had

4. showed

5. was

6. imagined

7. filled

8. did

9. looked

10. received

PROOFREADING EXERCISE
Yesterday, when I ~~walk~~ *walked* on campus to go to my classroom, I ~~notice~~ *noticed* a problem that needs to be fixed. Every morning, there is a long line of students in their cars waiting to enter the parking lots because the light at the corner ~~do~~ *does* not change fast enough. It ~~change~~ *changes* too slowly, so cars start to stack up on the side streets. Anybody who ~~walk~~ *walks* to school is affected, too. Drivers get desperate when they are stuck in traffic. Many of them don't watch where they're going and almost run over people who ~~is~~ *are* walking in the crosswalks and driveways.

USING REGULAR AND IRREGULAR VERBS (PP. 105–113)

EXERCISE 1

1. eat
2. eat
3. eating
4. eaten

5. ate
6. eats
7. eaten (past participle as adjective)

8. eating
9. ate
10. eat

EXERCISE 2

1. drive, driven
2. thinking, thought
3. take, takes
4. told, telling

5. wrote, written
6. knew, know
7. wave, waves

8. torn (past participle as adjective), tear
9. ridden, rode
10. made, make

EXERCISE 3

1. took, supposed
1. took, supposed
3. called, told, feel
4. thought, was

5. leaving, drove, saw
6. felt, knew, tell
7. tried, went

8. been, undo
9. wishes, take
10. used, called, does

EXERCISE 4

1. use, puts
2. does, do
3. transfers, spend
4. is, like, choose

5. does, wants
6. trusts, is
7. imagine, made

8. talking, asked, worries
9. looked, said, lived, understand
10. wonder, is

EXERCISE 5

1. lying, fell
2. was, done
3. wearing, shielded
4. lain, woke, realized, happened

5. felt, started
6. passed, turned, began
7. describe, experienced

8. was, felt, saw
9. looked, taped, was, protected, wearing
10. had, felt

PROGRESS TEST (P. 114)

1. B. (incorrect verb form) As soon as I *finished* the test, the bell rang.

2. A. (fragment) Textbooks *are* available online.

3. A. (run-on) Our class took a field trip to the museum, and I loved it.

4. B. (incorrect word form) I should *have* gone to the library sooner.

5. A. (incorrect word form) We were *supposed* to lock the door after class.

6. B. (incorrect word form) *They're* going away for spring break, and I'm staying at home.

7. B. (incorrect word form) We were *surprised* that it was delivered on time.

8. A. (incorrect verb form) In my math class, we've already *taken* three quizzes.

9. B. (run-on) Nothing worked, so we all got off the bus and waited for another one.

10. A. (fragment) *Although I don't like the taste of grapefruits or lemons,* I do like cleaning products citrus scents. [Connect the fragment to the sentence.]

MAINTAINING SUBJECT-VERB AGREEMENT (PP. 115–121)

EXERCISE 1

1. is, has, portray
2. is
3. include, spark, are
4. give

5. rank
6. have
7. gets, has, is, is

8. signifies, are
9. is, make
10. has

EXERCISE 2

1. gives
2. sounds, begins, is
3. connects
4. says, means

5. forecasts
6. are, mean
7. are, foretell

8. means
9. are
10. seem

EXERCISE 3

1. are, involve
2. suffer
3. are
4. come, lead

5. start, works, plays
6. starts
7. are

8. cause
9. is
10. warn

EXERCISE 4

1. are
2. has
3. are
4. is

5. involves, are
6. enter
7. includes

8. set, receive
9. has, have
10. is

EXERCISE 5

1. is, call
2. is, are, has
3. is, are, is
4. have, is

5. are, are
6. experiences, has
7. are, functions

8. determine
9. seems
10. affect, tend

PROOFREADING EXERCISE

Unfortunately, tension between members of the public ~~are~~ *is* common these days. When two people at a movie theater ~~irritates~~ *irritate* each other or have a disagreement, the whole audience ~~suffer~~ *suffers*. Everyone who is sitting around the troublemakers ~~want~~ *wants* to move immediately to another section. However, if anyone ~~get~~ *gets* up to sit somewhere else, then everyone else ~~start~~ *starts* to get nervous. So most people just ~~waits~~ *wait* until one of two fighting people ~~calm~~ *calms* down. After that, the members of the audience ~~forgets~~ *forget* about the disturbance and enjoy the rest of the movie. The same pattern ~~repeat~~ *repeats* itself in stadiums and ballparks, too.

AVOIDING SHIFTS IN TIME (PP. 122–124)

1. Back in the early 1900s, Sears Roebuck sold houses through the mail. In the famous Sears catalog, these mail-order houses ~~are~~ *were* listed along with the rest of the products. The house kits arrived in thousands of pieces, and people ~~can~~ *could* put them together themselves, or they ~~hire~~ *hired* a builder to help them. In 1919, one company, Standard Oil, placed an order for an entire town's worth of homes for its employees. The house kits even ~~include~~ *included* the paint that the homeowners ~~use~~ *used* to paint the houses when they ~~finish~~ *finished*. The ability to order a whole house from the Sears catalog ended in 1940, but thousands of these houses are still standing in communities across America.

2. The paragraph is correct.

3. Plastic surgery helps many people look better and feel better about themselves. Of course, there ~~were~~ *are* stories of unnecessary surgeries and even heartbreaking mistakes. People make their own decisions about whether plastic surgery ~~was~~ *is* right for them. Dogs, however, can't communicate what they ~~wanted~~ *want*. Nevertheless, some people ~~took~~ *take* their dogs in for cosmetic surgeries, such as tummy tucks and face-lifts. Just like humans, dogs sometimes ~~needed~~ *need* surgery to correct painful or unhealthy conditions. A dog with a low-hanging tummy ~~could~~ *can* get an infection from scratches that *are* caused by rocks on the ground. And another dog may need a face-lift to help it stay clean when it ~~ate~~ *eats*. Animal lovers ~~were~~ *are* worried that some canine plastic surgeries ~~were~~ *are* done without good reasons.

RECOGNIZING VERBAL PHRASES (PP. 125–131)

EXERCISE 1

1. Mark Twain lived [to become one of the most [admired] Americans of his time].

2. [Traveling across the U.S. and to countries around the world], Twain formed [unwavering] opinions, both favorable and unfavorable, of the people and places he visited.

3. Twain began [to write his autobiography] in the last years before he died in 1910.

4. [Hoping [to be honest and thorough]], he decided [to dictate his thoughts] as they struck him.

5. However, he knew that it might be impossible [to be as honest] as he wanted [to be].

6. [Being truthful] meant [including statements that could hurt or upset the people] that he knew, and he knew almost everyone.

7. Twain thought of a way [to avoid [causing that potential pain or embarrassment]].

8. He decided not [to publish his autobiography until 100 years after his death].

9. In that way, Twain did not need [to hold back any of his strong opinions].

10. In 2010, the first volume of *The Autobiography of Mark Twain* was finally released, [making it one of the most [anticipated] books of all time].

EXERCISE 2

1. The idea of [home-schooling children] has become more popular recently.

2. Many parents have decided [to teach kids themselves] instead of [sending them to public or private school].

3. There are many different reasons [to choose [home-schooling]].

4. In Hollywood, for instance, child actors often must use [home-schooling] due to their schedules.

5. The [home-schooling] option allows for one of their parents, or a special teacher, [to continue] [to instruct them on the set].

6. Other parents simply want [to be directly involved in their child's [learning]].

7. Many school districts have special independent study "schools," [offering parents the structure and materials] that they need [to provide an appropriate curriculum on their own].

8. Children do all of their [reading] and [writing] at home, with their parents [guiding them along the way].

9. The family meets with the independent study school's teacher regularly [to go over the child's work] and [to clarify any points of confusion].

10. Many parents would like [to have the time] [to home-school their children].

EXERCISE 3

1. Philippe Halsman was a well-[known] portrait photographer [working in the twentieth century].

2. Halsman's photographs were good enough [to appear on the cover of *Life* magazine 101 times].

3. [Capturing the essence of famous people on film] was Halsman's specialty.

4. The list of celebrities that Halsman was asked [to photograph] included Marilyn Monroe, Albert Einstein, and Winston Churchill.

5. Halsman found that [taking good pictures of such powerful people] was not easy.

6. He often tried [to find new ways] [to loosen them up].

7. In 1952, Halsman asked one of his elite clients [to jump in the air] while [being photographed].

8. Halsman loved the results, and he started a series of [jumping] pictures.

9. Who doesn't like [to see famous people like Richard Nixon] [jumping up like a little boy in a photograph]?

10. Halsman gathered the best of the [jumping] photographs in a book [called *Philippe Halsman's Jump Book*].

EXERCISE 4

1. Some travelers want [to know how [to behave in other countries]].

2. *Behave Yourself!* is a book [written [to help such people]].

3. It outlines what [to do] and what not [to do] in countries around the world.

4. In Austria, for example, [cutting your food with a fork] is more polite than [cutting it with a knife].

5. In Egypt, [nodding the head upward]—not [shaking the head from side to side]—means "no."

6. In the Netherlands, [complimenting people about their clothes] is not a good idea.

7. An Italian diner will fold lettuce into a bite-size piece with the fork and knife instead of [cutting it].

8. A common mistake that people <u>make</u> in many countries <u>is</u> [to stand with their hands on their hips].

9. This posture and [pointing at anything with the fingers] <u>are thought</u> [to be very rude] and even [threatening].

10. Travelers <u>should study</u> any country before [visiting it] in order [to avoid [confusing] or [offending] anyone].

EXERCISE 5

1. John Steinbeck, author of *The Grapes of Wrath,* <u>was</u> the first native of California [to receive the Nobel Prize for literature].

2. [Calling his hometown of Salinas "Lettuceberg,"] Steinbeck's [writing] <u>made</u> the area famous.

3. At the time, not everyone <u>liked</u> the attention [brought by his portrayals of life in *Cannery Row* and other works].

4. Steinbeck's father <u>was</u> the treasurer of Monterey County for ten years, [working also for the Spreckels company].

5. John Steinbeck <u>tried</u> [to find satisfaction in his birthplace], [enrolling in and quitting his studies at Stanford University many times].

6. Finally, Steinbeck <u>moved</u> to New York, [distancing himself from his California roots].

7. Steinbeck <u>won</u> the Nobel Prize in 1962, [revealing the literary world's esteem for his work].

8. Not [writing anything of the caliber of the Salinas stories] while [living in New York], Steinbeck <u>did return</u> to California before he <u>died</u> in 1968.

9. In 1972, the Salinas library <u>changed</u> its name, [to be known thereafter as the John Steinbeck Library].

10. The house Steinbeck <u>was born</u> in <u>became</u> a restaurant and then a full-[fledged] museum [chronicling the life of Salinas' most [celebrated] citizen].

PARAGRAPH EXERCISE

CHRISTO AND JEANNE-CLAUDE (1935-, 1935-)

It <u>started</u> as an obsession with [wrapping]. The Bulgarian-[born] artist Christo <u>spent</u> years [swaddling bicycles, trees, storefronts, and women friends] before [moving on] [to wrap a section of the Roman Wall, part of the Australian coastline, and eventually all twelve arches, plus the parapets, sidewalks, street-lamps, vertical embankment, and esplanade, of Paris' Pont Neuf]. And yes, together they <u>did wrap</u> the Reichstag. But Christo and his wife/manager/collaborator Jeanne-Claude

<u>are</u> quick [to insist] that [wrappings] <u>form</u> only a small percentage of their total oeuvre. There <u>were</u>, for instance, those twenty-four and a half miles of white nylon, eighteen feet high, they <u>hung</u> from a steel cable north of San Francisco; the eleven islands in Biscayne Bay, Florida, they "<u>surrounded</u>"—not <u>wrapped</u>, <u>mind</u> you—with pink polypropylene fabric; and the 3,100 enormous blue and yellow "umbrellas" they <u>erected</u> in two [corresponding] valleys in California and Japan. Not [to mention] their 2005 blockbuster, "The Gates," 7,503 sixteen-foot-tall saffron panels they <u>suspended</u>, to the delight of almost everybody, over twenty-three miles of footpaths in New York's Central Park.

So, what<u>'s</u> their point? <u>Rest</u> assured, you<u>'re</u> not the first [to ask]. And no one <u>is</u> more eager [to tell you] than the artist formerly [known] as Christo (now, officially, "Christo and Jeanne-Claude") whose art <u>is</u> nothing if not Open to the Public. In fact, [taking art public]—that <u>is</u>, [taking it away from the Uptown Museum Gallery Complex] by [making it too big] [to fit in studios, museums, or galleries]—<u>was</u> part of the original idea. Christo and Jeanne-Claude <u>will tell</u> you that their point <u>is</u>, literally, [to rock your world.] By temporarily [disrupting one part of an environment], they <u>hope</u> [to get you] [to "perceive the whole environment with new eyes and a new consciousness."]

SENTENCE WRITING

Your sentences may vary, but make sure that your verbals are not actually the main verbs of your clauses. You should be able to double underline your real verbs, as we have done here.

1. [Thinking of a good title] <u>takes</u> time.

2. We <u>spent</u> the morning [folding laundry].

3. I <u>enjoy</u> [skiing], but golf relaxes me.

4. I <u>was taught</u> that [marking up a book] <u>is</u> wrong.

5. I <u>would love</u> [to take you to school].

6. I <u>need</u> [to get a good grade on the next quiz].

7. Yesterday, I <u>started</u> [to paste my old photos in a scrapbook].

8. He <u>doesn't have</u> any desire [to exercise].

9. The school <u>canceled</u> the [planned] [parking] lot next to the library.

10. [Given the opportunity], my dog <u>will escape</u> from our yard.

CORRECTING MISPLACED OR DANGLING MODIFIERS (PP. 132–136)

Answers may vary. Corrections are in *italics*.

EXERCISE 1

1. *While I was walking to my car,* I noticed an iPad on the ground.

2. The sentence is correct.

3. People will wait for hours to ride the new roller coaster *that's full of 360-degree loops.*

4. The flight attendant helped a six-year-old boy *find his seat.*

5. The sentence is correct.

6. We have found several travel bargains *by shopping on the Internet.*

7. Angelica finally spotted her lost keys *that were hidden by the long curtains.*

8. *After she got help from a specialist,* her knee began to improve.

9. The sentence is correct. *or* With a low-cost data plan, I can't use my phone *to go online very often.*

10. Students couldn't read the bulletin board *because it had faded from direct sunlight.*

EXERCISE 2

1. The sentence is correct.

2. *Before we could ask for an extension,* the teacher gave us a few extra days to turn in our papers.

3. *Looking through their binoculars,* they spotted a hawk and its babies.

4. The sentence is correct.

5. I called the doctor *while I was on the roof.*

6. The sentence is correct.

7. *After it screeched to a stop,* I got on the bus and grabbed a seat.

8. I can't eat a hamburger *without pickles.*

9. The sentence is correct.

10. We had to write a paragraph *in our notebooks, and the topic was the weather.*

Exercise 3

1. They finally found their lost credit card *that had been lying under the table for a week.*

2. *Walking down the hall, she located the door to the auditorium.*

3. The sentence is correct.

4. *My doctor told me to drink extra water after taking an aspirin.*

5. The sentence is correct.

6. Our mail carrier *tripped on a crack in the sidewalk and fell.*

7. *Since we argued nonstop,* the road trip was not as much fun as we hoped it would be.

8. The sentence is correct.

9. The sentence is correct.

10. The students immediately liked their substitute teacher, *who smiled nicely at everyone.*

Exercise 4

1. The sentence is correct.

2. Filled with the perfect amount of air, *the new tires made my car handle really well on the road.*

3. After three weeks of waiting, *I finally received the textbooks that I bought online.*

4. He cooked all of his meals *while he was wearing* his slippers.

5. The sentence is correct.

6. *As we drove past the park,* a ball bounced into the street between two parked cars.

7. *I didn't even want the tiny pieces of that torn quiz paper near me.*

8. The sentence is correct.

9. The sentence is correct.

10. I saw an army of ants walking in the cracks of the sidewalk.

Exercise 5

1. *Because I felt the thrill of a day at the amusement park,* my blisters didn't bother me.

2. My friends and I saw the new tearjerker, *which is full of touching scenes.*

3. The sentence is correct.

4. Practicing for an hour a day, *she improved her piano playing.*

5. The sentence is correct.

6. *While she was sitting on a bench all day,* an idea came to her.

7. They discovered a new outlet mall *on the road to their cousins' house.*

8. *From his parents,* he felt the pressure of trying to get a good job.

9. The sentence is correct.

10. The sentence is correct.

PROOFREADING EXERCISE

Corrections are *italicized.* Yours may differ slightly.

I love parades, so last year my family and I traveled to Pasadena, California, to see one of the biggest parades of all—the Tournament of Roses Parade on New Year's Day. It turned out to be even more wonderful than I expected.

Although we arrived one day early, the city was already crowded with people. *By nightfall,* lots of families were setting up campsites on Colorado Boulevard. We didn't want to miss one float in the parade, so we found our own spot and made ourselves at home. When the parade began, I had as much fun watching the spectators as the parade itself. I saw children *sitting on their fathers' shoulders* and pointing at the breathtaking horses and floats. *The floats were decorated completely with flowers or plant material.* I couldn't believe how beautiful they were and how good they smelled.

The crowd was overwhelmed by the sights and sounds of the parade. Everyone especially enjoyed hearing the school bands, *marching and playing their instruments with perfect precision.* They must have practiced for the whole year to be that good.

My experience didn't end with the parade, however. After the last float had passed by, I found a twenty dollar bill *as I walked down Colorado Boulevard. I framed it as a souvenir of my trip to the Rose Parade, and now it hangs on my wall at home.*

FOLLOWING SENTENCE PATTERNS (PP. 137–143)

EXERCISE 1

    S LV   Desc
1. Sleep is an important part (of life).

      S   S   AV Obj
2. Animals and humans use sleep (as a vacation) (for their brains and bodies).

        S   AV   Obj
3. Some facts (about sleep) might surprise people.

     S   AV   Obj   S AV
4. Large <u>animals</u> <u>require</u> less sleep than small <u>animals</u> <u>do</u>.

       S   AV
5. A typical <u>cat</u> <u>will sleep</u> (for twelve hours) (in a day).

         S   AV
6. An ordinary <u>elephant</u> <u>will sleep</u> (for only three hours).

       S AV   Obj   Obj
7. Smaller <u>animals</u> <u>use</u> their brains and bodies (at higher rates).

        S AV   Obj
8. Therefore, <u>they</u> <u>need</u> many hours (of sleep).

        S LV Desc
9. The <u>reverse</u> <u>is</u> true (for large animals).

      S AV
10. <u>Humans</u> <u>fall</u> (between cats and elephants) (for their sleep requirements).

EXERCISE 2

      S   LV   Desc
1. <u>Erasto Mpemba</u> <u>is</u> a big name (in science).

            S AV   Obj
2. (In the early 1960s), <u>he</u> <u>observed</u> an odd phenomenon.

         S LV   Desc
3. (At the time), <u>he</u> <u>was</u> a high school student (in Tanzania).

      S   AV   Obj
4. <u>Mpemba</u> <u>made</u> ice cream (for a school project).

     S AV   Obj   AV Obj
5. <u>He</u> <u>boiled</u> the milk and <u>mixed</u> it (with the other ice cream ingredients).

       S AV   Obj
6. Then <u>he</u> <u>put</u> this boiling hot mixture directly (into the freezer). [*Boiling* is a verbal.]

     S   AV Obj...   S AV
7. <u>He</u> *discovered that the hot <u>liquid</u> <u>froze</u> very fast*. [Note: This *dependent clause*

is the object in the sentence. It is *what* Mpemba discovered.]

         S   AV   Obj   Obj

8. Mpemba told his teachers and fellow students (about his discovery).

         S   AV

9. They laughed (at the idea) (of hot liquid) freezing quickly. [Note: *Freezing*

quickly is a verbal phrase in this sentence. See page 125 for more about verbals.]

            S   AV   Obj

10. Now all scientists call this phenomenon the "Mpemba effect."

EXERCISE 3

                    S   AV   Obj

1. (In late September), the Stade de France (in Paris) hosted an unusual spectacle.

       S   AV

2. Hundreds (of actors, stunt people, and extras) reenacted the famous chariot

   Obj

race (from the classic film *Ben-Hur*).

           S   AV   Obj   Obj

3. The same show included live gladiator fights and a galley ship assault.

       S   AV   Obj

4. Promoters also encouraged participation (from the audience).

     S   AV

5. Many (of the 60,000 audience members) attended (in traditional Roman costumes).

       S   AV   Obj

6. The stadium sold toga-like robes (in advance) (along with the tickets).

               S   LV   Desc

7. Obviously, the live chariot race was the highlight (of the show).

        S   AV

8. Participants (in the dangerous race) rehearsed (for nine months).

          S   AV

9. The chariot race lasted (for fifteen minutes).

   S LV   Desc

10. It was the final event (of the night).

EXERCISE 4

               S   LV   Desc

1. Horatio Greenough was a sculptor (in the 1800s).

          S   AV   Obj

2. Greenough created a controversial statue (of George Washington).

            S   LV   Desc   S   LV   Desc

3. The statue weighed twelve tons, but its weight was not the reason (for the

controversy).

                          S   AV   Obj

4. The controversial aspect (of the statue) involved Washington's clothes.

          S   AV   Obj

5. The statue portrayed Washington (in a toga-like garment).

          S   S   S   LV Desc   Desc

6. His stomach, chest, and arms were bare and very muscular.

          S   AV

7. One part (of the toga) draped (over the statue's raised right arm).

                  S   AV

8. The bare-chested statue (of Washington) stood (in the rotunda) (of the

Capitol) (for only three years).

          S   AV   Obj

9. Officials moved the statue many times.

             S   AV

10. (In 1962), it arrived (in its final home) (at the American History Museum).

EXERCISE 5

          S   LV   Desc   Desc   Desc

1. Charles Osgood is a writer, TV host, and radio personality.

     S LV   Desc

2. He is also the editor (of a book) (about letters).

              S LV   Desc

3. The book's title is *Funny Letters (from Famous People)*.

　　　　　　　　 S　　　AV　　　　　　Obj
4. (In his book), <u>Osgood</u> <u>shares</u> hilarious letters (from history).

　　　　　　　　　　 S　　　　　　　AV
5. <u>Thomas Jefferson</u> <u>wrote</u> (to an acquaintance) (about rodents) [eating his wallet].

　　　　　　　　　　 S　　　　　　　AV　　　　　　　　　　　　　 Obj
6. <u>Benjamin Franklin</u> <u>penned</u> the perfect recommendation letter.

　　　　　　　　 S　　　　　　 AV　　　　　　　　 Obj
7. <u>Franklin</u> <u>did</u> not <u>know</u> the recommended fellow (at all).

　　　　　　　 S　　　　　AV　　　 Obj
8. <u>Beethoven</u> <u>cursed</u> his friend bitterly (in a letter) one day.

　　　　　　　　　　　　　　　　　　　 S　　　　 AV　　　　　 Obj
9. (In a letter) the following day, <u>Beethoven</u> <u>praised</u> the same friend excessively

　　　　　　 AV　 Obj
and <u>asked</u> him (for a visit).

　　　　　 S　　 AV　　　 Obj　　　　　　　　　　　　　　　　　　　 AV　　　 Obj
10. <u>Osgood</u> <u>ends</u> the book (with a letter) (by Julia Child) and <u>includes</u> her secrets

(for a long life).

PARAGRAPH EXERCISE

　　　　　 S　　　　　AV　　　 Obj　　　　　　　　　　　　　　　　　　　　　　　AV
　　<u>Armstrong</u> <u>released</u> his grip (on the handrail) (of the ladder) and <u>stepped</u>

　　　　　　　　　　　 S　　　　　　　　　　 AV　　　　　　 Obj DC...
fully (off the foot pad). <u>Walter Cronkite</u> proudly <u>told</u> his CBS audience that a

　　　　　　　　　 S　　　　　　　　　 AV
38-year-old <u>American</u> <u>was</u> now <u>standing</u> (on the surface) (of the Moon). When

　　　 S　　　　　 AV　　　 Obj　　　　　　　 S　 AV　　 Obj DC...
<u>Armstrong</u> <u>scraped</u> his foot (across the surface), he <u>noticed</u> that the dark powdery

　　　 S　　　　AV　　　　 Obj　　　 S　 LV Desc　　 Desc　 S　　 AV Obj
material <u>coated</u> his overshoe. "The <u>surface</u> <u>is</u> fine and powdery. <u>I</u> can <u>kick</u> it up

　　　　　　　　　　　　 S　　 AV
loosely (with my toe). <u>It</u> <u>adheres</u> (in fine layers) (like powdery charcoal) (to the

S   AV

sole and sides) (of my boots)." Although his <u>boots</u> only slightly <u>impressed</u> the

Obj   S   AV   Obj   S   AV

surface, the <u>material</u> <u>preserved</u> the imprint (of his boots) very well. "I only <u>go</u> in

S   AV

a small fraction (of an inch)—maybe one-eighth (of an inch)—but <u>I</u> <u>can see</u> the

Obj   Obj

prints (of my boots) and the treads (in the fine, sandy particles)."

AVOIDING CLICHÉS, AWKWARD PHRASING, AND WORDINESS (PP. 144–148)

Your answers may differ from these possible revisions.

1. I've been trying to help my son finish his first-grade homework every night, but it isn't easy. Of course, I know that he is smart, but he doesn't always show it. I can get him to sit for a few minutes with his workbooks, but he runs off as soon as I turn around. I tell him stories of how strict teachers were about homework when I was his age. Unfortunately, my son's teacher uses stickers as motivators, and they just don't work. I really hope that my son will learn the value of keeping up in school.

2. Today, many shoppers buy only organic meats, fruits, and vegetables. They get excited whenever they see an organic label on a can, box, or package. I work at a busy supermarket, and I see customers with and without a lot of money buying these foods to avoid eating pesticides and hormones. Ordinary folks have started to care more about what they and their children eat. Admittedly, organic eggs do taste better, and it feels good to know that the eggs come from happy, free-ranging chickens. Of course, budget-conscious shoppers will always care more about price and will rarely buy organic foods if they cost more.

3. I have a friend who used to be a struggling actor, but now she has become a professional house sitter. First, she joined an organization that advertises house-sitting opportunities. My friend's first house-sitting job was in Malibu. Unbelievably, she was paid to live in a house on the beach, eat free food, and watch free movies. All she had to do was stay at the house and feed the owners' indoor cat. Now my friend is house sitting in Sedona for friends of the owners of the Malibu house. I am thinking seriously of becoming a house sitter myself.

CORRECTING FOR PARALLEL STRUCTURE (PP. 149–154)

Your revisions may vary.

EXERCISE 1

1. Preparing for emergencies involves two steps: planning for anything and gathering certain supplies.

2. The sentence is correct.

3. The sentence is correct.

4. Where would you go, and how would you get there?

5. Have you made a list of phone contacts inside and outside the area?

6. Do the adults, teenagers, and children in the family carry those phone numbers with them?

7. Are the most important supplies ready at hand, including water, food, flashlight, radio, and batteries?

8. Have you assembled your own first-aid kit or bought a ready-made one?

9. Do you stay prepared by reading, understanding, and updating your important insurance policies?

10. By planning for anything and stocking up on the right supplies, you can prepare yourself and your family for emergencies.

EXERCISE 2

1. Taking driving lessons was exciting but nerve-wracking.

2. At first, I learned how to start, steer, and stop the car smoothly.

3. Between driving lessons, I studied the manual, watched driving videos, and practiced emergency hand signals.

4. My instructors taught me, tested me, and encouraged me.

5. The sentence is correct.

6. Finally, my teachers decided that I had learned enough and that I was ready to take the test for my driver's license.

7. I arrived at the testing location, waited in the lobby for a few minutes, and heard someone call my name.

8. During the test, I changed lanes, made right and left turns, and parallel parked like a professional driver.

9. The man who tested me said that I knew the rules and that I must have had good teachers.

10. The sentence is correct.

EXERCISE 3

1. The Internet is full of information about new gadgets and technology.

2. People want to have the coolest phones, the clearest photos, and the best travel accessories.

3. The sentence is correct.

4. The ring doesn't use technology to help people do something more easily or live more comfortably.

5. Instead, it helps people avoid doing something—forgetting their anniversary.

6. The "Remember Ring" is designed for people who love gadgets but tend to forget special occasions.

7. It includes several hi-tech features: a perpetually charging battery, a clock run by a microchip, and a tiny heating element.

8. The built-in heating element activates at a preprogrammed time and reminds the wearer about an upcoming anniversary.

9. The sentence is correct.

10. The Remember Ring comes in seven styles in both white and yellow gold.

EXERCISE 4

1. To begin, decide which person or family you want to focus on.

2. Make a blank chart that includes spaces for all of a person's important information.

3. Then visit a relative who knows a lot of family history and hopefully saves papers and mementos.

4. Plan to spend a lot of time with any such valuable resource.

5. Gather information from and about one individual at a time.

6. Ask about every part of the person's life—marital status, children, religion, occupation, and travel.

7. Thank your resources for providing you with valuable information.

8. Visit the attics or the dusty old cupboards of anyone who has documents relating to your family.

9. Don't forget the local records office in the town where a relative grew up.

10. Purchase books that provide preprinted worksheets and family tree templates to make your family tree come together faster.

EXERCISE 5

Your revisions may differ.

1. The sentence is correct.

2. First, avoid getting frustrated if you have to wait a long time in the reception area or the exam room.

3. Always answer the doctor's questions first; then ask your own questions.

4. Inquire about a referral to a specialist if you think you need one.

5. Find out about other treatments besides the one the doctor first recommends.

6. Ask about any tests that the doctor orders and determine how to get in touch with the doctor about the results.

7. Take the time to ask about prescription drugs' side effects and optional medicines.

8. Try to be calm in your discussions with the doctor.

9. Finally, be prepared to wait in a long line at the pharmacy.

10. If you follow these suggestions when visiting a doctor, you will be more informed and feel more involved in your own treatment.

PROOFREADING EXERCISE

   The world knows relatively little about the life of William Shakespeare. Stanley Wells' book *Is It True What They Say about Shakespeare?* addresses the questions that people continue to have about the famous poet and playwright. Because of Shakespeare's talent and reputation, everyone wants to know when he was born, which schools he went to, where he traveled, who his friends or lovers were, what he looked like, as well as how and when he wrote each of his poems and plays. Wells starts with the basic question "Is it true that . . .?" Throughout the book, he identifies commonly held beliefs about Shakespeare, discusses the historical evidence, and judges each belief to be "true," "untrue," or something in between. Wells even examines the numerous theories that someone else wrote the works of Shakespeare but finds no evidence strong enough to convince him of their validity.

USING PRONOUNS (PP. 155–161)

EXERCISE 1

1. I

2. she (*does,* a missing verb)

3. she and I (or replace the pair with *we*)

4. I

5. she and I (or replace the pair with *we*), me

6. she

7. I

8. I

9. her and me (or replace the pair with *us*)

10. me, her

EXERCISE 2

1. its

2. its

3. its

4. their

5. his or her (One day last week, *the passengers* had to gather *their* belongings. . . .)

6. their

7. their

8. his or her, his or her (*The passengers* did their best to hide *their* annoyance. . . .)

9. him or her, his or her (As *the passengers* stepped off the bus at the end of the line, the driver thanked *them* for *their* patience and understanding.)

10. it

EXERCISE 3

1. me

2. he (. . . taller than *he was.*)

3. She and he (or *They* are working. . . .)

4. The dentists received gift bags full of toothbrushes and dental floss. (To avoid wordiness, we deleted the *his or her* pronouns, as well as *Each of* in the beginning.)

5. their

6. I (*I* was the person responsible. . . .)

7. The audience expressed its opinion of the performances with its applause. (To avoid wordiness, we changed the subject to *audience* and used the pronoun *its.*)

8. its

9. I (. . . better than *I do.*)

10. she

EXERCISE 4

1. I (. . . as *I am.*)

2. she (. . . than *she does.*)

3. she

4. their

5. its

6. Everyone must use *a* password to enter the network.

7. me (. . . or *by me.*)

8. she (*She* and Justin were the winners. . . .)

9. their

10. us (. . . judge sent *us* a message.)

EXERCISE 5

1. me

2. Students will buy *their* own materials for the jewelry class.

3. their

4. I

5. Due to the holiday, everyone was allowed to turn *the* essay in late.

6. she

7. he (. . . than *he is.*)

8. I

9. me

10. her

PROOFREADING EXERCISE

Corrections are *italicized.*

Rude drivers have one thing in common. Whether they are male or female, they all they think that they know how to drive better than anybody else. The other day, as my friends and ~~me~~ *I* were driving to school, we stopped at an intersection. A very old man who used a cane started to walk across ~~it~~ *the intersection* in front of my friends and ~~I~~ *me* just before the light was ready to change. So we waited. But while we waited for him, an impatient driver behind us started to honk his horn since he couldn't see ~~him~~ *the old man.* I wondered, "Does ~~he~~ *this driver* want us to hit ~~him~~ *the old man,* or what?" Finally, ~~it~~ *the intersection* was clear. ~~He~~ *The angry man* pulled his car up beside ours, opened his window, and yelled at us before he sped away. The old man reached the other side safely, but ~~he~~ *the rude driver* hardly noticed.

AVOIDING SHIFTS IN PERSON (PP. 162–164)

PROOFREADING EXERCISE

1. ~~We have all~~ *You have probably* seen images of astronauts floating in their space capsules, eating food from little silver freeze-dried cube-shaped pouches, and sipping Tang out of special straws made to function in the weightlessness of space. Now you can buy that same food and eat it yourself on earth. NASA has gone online with a site called thespacestore.com, and all ~~one has~~ *you have* to do is point and click and get these space munchies delivered to your door. If ~~people~~ *you* want NASA souvenirs or clothing, ~~they~~ *you* can purchase them at the same site. [Note that we chose to revise this paragraph in second person.]

2. I was reading about superstitions for my psychology class, and I learned that a lot of these beliefs concern brooms and sweeping. One superstition says that, whenever ~~you~~ *people* change ~~your~~ *their* residence, ~~you~~ *they* should get a new broom. People should not take their old brooms with them because the brooms might carry any bad luck that was swept up at the old place and bring it to the new one. Also, if ~~you~~ *people* sweep dirt out an open door, *they should* make it the back door so that the bad luck will depart forever. If ~~you~~ *they* sweep dirt out the front way, the same bad luck will come right back in again. Finally, ~~I learned never to~~ *people should never* walk across a fallen broomstick unless ~~I~~ *they* never want to get married, for that is the fate for anyone who steps over a broomstick. I bet most people would be surprised by how many things can go wrong when ~~you~~ *they* pick up a broom. [Note that we chose to revise this paragraph to report the details about brooms using third person pronouns.]

3. The paragraph is correct.

REVIEW OF SENTENCE STRUCTURE ERRORS (PP. 164–167)

1. B. incorrect verb form (They're *supposed* to be relaxing. . . .)

2. A. incorrect pronoun (. . . *luckier than I*, meaning *luckier than I am.*)

3. B. awkward phrasing (. . . *but have never given up my weekends.* or *but will never give up my weekends.*)

4. B.   run-on sentence (He put them on the podium *and immediately started lecturing.*)

5. B.   fragment (*Too many people wander in if we don't.*)

6. A.   wordy and cliché (People usually avoid getting involved in strangers' lives.)

7. A.   incorrect pronoun (The library renewed the books that my friend and *I* had checked out.)

8. A.   wordy (The store was offering a free coffee maker.)

9. A.   shift in time (My essay is full of interesting details and *has* a strong thesis.)

10. B.   pronoun agreement (Everyone at the party *looked shocked.*)

11. A.   subject-verb agreement error (Some of the new furniture *has* scratches on it already.)

12. B.   fragment and wordy (They can be as small as a baby bottle or as large as a magnum of champagne.)

13. B.   misplaced modifier (We saw a beautiful metallic *kite hanging from the top of a tree.*)

14. B.   run-on sentence (However, there is one big difference between them; Shawn is not as ambitious as Sharon is.)

15. A.   wordy (Whenever I plan a *meal* around a single ingredient, the *different dishes* don't taste good.)

PROOFREADING EXERCISE
Revisions are *italicized.* Yours may differ.

Let's Get Technical

In my child development classes, I'm learning about ways to keep girls interested in technology. Studies *show* that girls and boys begin their school years equally interested in technology. After elementary school, *girls lose interest.* Because boys keep up with computers and other technology throughout their educations, *boys* get ahead in these fields. Experts have come up with some suggestions for teachers and parents to help *girls stay involved in technology.*

Girls need opportunities to experiment with computers. Girls spend time on computers, but they usually just do their *assignments; then* they log off. Since computer games and programs are often aimed at *boys, parents* and teachers need to buy computer products that will challenge girls not only in literature and art, but also in math, science, and *business.*

Another suggestion is to put computers in places where girls can socialize. One reason many boys stay interested in technology is that *they can do it on their own.* Girls tend to be more interested in working with others and *sharing* activities. When computer terminals are placed close to one another, girls work at them longer.

Finally, parents and teachers need to *provide positive role models*. *They need to teach girls* about successful women in the fields of business, *science*, and technology. And the earlier *girls get interested* in these fields, the better.

PUNCTUATION

PERIODS, QUESTION MARKS, EXCLAMATION POINTS, SEMICOLONS, COLONS, DASHES (PP. 168–175)

EXERCISE 1

1. Do you know how many resources go into making the jeans that we all love to wear?

2. Here are a couple of the details: the dyeing process uses about a pound of harsh chemicals and 15 dye baths to create a single pair of jeans.

3. Would you believe that it also takes 2,500 gallons of water to finish that one pair?

4. Of course, each movement of the jeans through the process requires electricity.

5. Luckily, textile scientists in Switzerland have come up with a "greener" method of jeans production.

6. The result is called Advanced Denim, and its environmental benefits are staggering!

7. The scientific and environmental communities are excited, and who wouldn't be?

8. This new denim requires only one trip through a dye vat and finishes the fabric with eco-friendly substances.

9. The Advanced Denim process uses 30 percent less energy and over 90 percent less water than traditional denim.

10. Can you imagine the positive effects it could have when multiplied by the 2 billion pairs of jeans produced each year?

EXERCISE 2

1. Have you noticed that light bulbs don't last as long as they used to?

2. Some seem to burn out after only a month or two.

3. Would you believe that one light bulb has lasted for 110 years?

4. Well, it's true—believe it or not! (or)

5. At a fire station in Livermore, California, the same bulb has been burning since 1901.

6. The now famous light bulb is treated like a celebrity by the firefighters.

7. They are proud of its history, and who wouldn't be?

8. The famous bulb doesn't get cleaned or covered by any type of shade; no one wants to risk damaging it or making it burn out after so many years.

9. The Livermore Light Bulb, as it's called, has even made it into the *Guinness Book of World Records* as the longest running light bulb.

10. Anyone who wants to see this famous bulb in action can visit its 24-hour webcam online.

EXERCISE 3

1. The sentence is correct.

2. This young woman—a very controversial figure in Washington, D.C.—began her career as a sculptor in 1863 at the age of sixteen.

3. Miss Ream was a student of the famous sculptor Clark Mills; he is perhaps best known for his statue of Andrew Jackson located across from the White House.

4. Vinnie Ream started to work with Mills in his studio in the basement of the Capitol building; soon members of Congress were volunteering to sit for Miss Ream, and she sculpted busts of them.

5. Her fame and reputation grew in the late 1860s; that's when she was awarded a ten-thousand-dollar commission to create a life-size statue of Abraham Lincoln.

6. Vinnie Ream had known Lincoln; in fact, before his assassination, President Lincoln would allow Miss Ream to sit in his office within the White House and work on a bust of him as he carried out the business of running the country.

7. The sentence is correct.

8. Vinnie Ream's relationships and the works she produced were not accepted by everyone; Ream's youth and physical beauty led to much of this harsh criticism.

9. Some people questioned her motives; others even questioned her abilities.

10. The sentence is correct.

EXERCISE 4

1. The sentence is correct.

2. The sentence is correct.

3. One relatively safe place is inside a building that has plumbing pipes or electrical wires; those channels can absorb the electrical energy unleashed by lightning.

4. Of course, once inside such a building, people should stay away from the end sources of plumbing and wiring: faucets, hoses, phone receivers, and computer terminals.

5. Buildings without pipes or wires are not safe shelters during lightning strikes; these might include pergolas, dugouts, and tents.

6. Outside, lightning can move over the ground; therefore, you should be aware of a position that emergency officials call the "lightning squat."

7. The sentence is correct.

8. The sentence is correct.

9. Lightning is electrical energy; consequently, it can travel far from the actual storm clouds.

10. The sentence is correct.

EXERCISE 5

1. What do math and origami—Japanese paper folding—have to do with each other?

2. Erik Demaine and other origami mathematicians would answer, "Everything." (or "Everything!")

3. If you have never heard of the field of origami mathematics, you're not alone.

4. Origami math is a relatively new field; back in 2003, Demaine won a "genius" award partly due to his work with origami and its applications in many fields.

5. The MacArthur Foundation awarded Demaine more than just the title "genius"; it awarded him half a million dollars. (or !)

6. At twenty, Demaine was hired as a professor by the Massachusetts Institute of Technology; he became the youngest professor MIT has ever had.

7. Erik Demaine has his father to thank for much of his education: (or ;) Martin Demaine home-schooled Erik as the two of them traveled around North America.

8. Erik was always intensely interested in academic subjects; during his travels, he and his father would consult university professors whenever Erik had questions that no one else could answer.

9. Erik Demaine continues to investigate one area in particular: the single-cut problem.

10. This problem involves folding a piece of paper—then making one cut; the result can be anything from a swan to a star, a unicorn, or any letter of the alphabet.

PROOFREADING EXERCISE

Who hasn't seen one of those inflatable jumping rooms at a park or in the front yard of a house hosting a child's birthday party? These jumpers are popular for several reasons: children can have fun playing with their friends; adults can keep an eye on many children at once, and everyone gets a lot of exercise. In 2007, a freak accident occurred on a beach in Hawaii; it involved an inflated castle-shaped bouncer, a few brave adults, and several lucky children. As the kids bounced around as usual, a strong gust of wind—a whirlwind, according to one witness—lifted the castle straight up into the air and knocked all but two of the children out instantly. Then the castle bounced on the sand once before flying fifty yards out into the ocean. As the castle flew, another child dropped out of it; luckily, he was unhurt. Many adults—both lifeguards and others—jumped in to save the two-year-old girl who remained inside the castle. One man was able to reach her; incredibly, she was not seriously injured!

COMMAS USED TO SEPARATE ELEMENTS (PP. 176–182)

EXERCISE 1

1. The young actor named Sabu began his career in 1937, and he became famous for his unique background and abilities.

2. The sentence is correct.

3. The sentence is correct.

4. In real life, Sabu understood elephants very well, for his father was an owner and trainer of elephants.

5. Sabu's first film was called *The Elephant Boy,* and it made him an instant celebrity.

6. The sentence is correct.

7. The sentence is correct.

8. The sentence is correct.

9. Sabu's version of *The Jungle Book* was made twenty-five years before Disney's animated version, but it captured the essence of the mysterious jungle even more vividly with real actors and animals.

10. The sentence is correct.

EXERCISE 2

1. I finished high school on June 23, 2012, in Houston, Texas.

2. My favorite English teacher was young, enthusiastic, and highly motivated.

3. We read essays, stories, poems, novels, and research articles in her class.

4. My group even opted to to read a play, memorize all of its parts, and perform it for everyone.

5. The sentence is correct.

6. The sentence is correct.

7. We each wrote letter of complaint about a product, a service, or an experience that was unsatisfactory to us.

8. Then we sent copies of our letter to the company's business address, to our home address, and to Ms. Kern's school address.

9. Ms. Kern assured us that we would receive a response from the company if we explained our dissatisfaction clearly, asked for a reasonable solution, and used a respectful tone.

10. My company replied to my letter with a note of apology, a bumper sticker, and an impressive gift card to use at any of the company's stores.

EXERCISE 3

1. As if people don't have enough to worry about, Melinda Muse wrote a book called *I'm Afraid, You're Afraid: 448 Things to Fear and Why*.

2. In her book, Muse points out the dangers of common places, objects, foods, months, days, and activities.

3. If people go to Vegas regularly, they should worry because paramedics can't reach people as quickly in large crowds or huge buildings.

4. The sentence is correct.

5. In the comfort of our homes, unwashed new clothes may transfer dangerous chemicals to people's eyes, skin, and lungs.

6. Among the foods to avoid, grapefruit juice can interfere with certain medications' effectiveness.

7. Thanks to Independence Day celebrations and outdoor picnics, July ranks highest of all the months in accidental injuries and food poisonings.

8. Being linked with more suicides and heart attacks than any other weekday, Mondays are the most dangerous days of the week.

9. Believe it or not, singing in a choir can even permanently damage people's ears.

10. After reading *I'm Afraid, You're Afraid,* it's possible to be afraid of almost everything.

EXERCISE 4

1. The United States introduced the Susan B. Anthony dollar in 1979, making her the first woman on a circulating coin.

2. No one deserved this honor more than Susan B. Anthony, having led the fight for women's voting rights in America.

3. The Anthony dollar quickly became unpopular, however.

4. People disliked certain features of the coin, not the person on the coin.

5. This dollar coin was too much like a quarter, nearly the same size and color with the same rough edge around it.

6. The sentence is correct.

7. In 1999, the government stopped issuing Susan B. Anthony dollars, preferring to introduce a new golden dollar coin instead.

8. The new coin portrayed the image of a famous American woman, just as the Anthony dollar did.

9. The Sacagawea "golden dollar" has suffered from its own lack of popularity, unfortunately.

10. Women haven't had much luck as images on coins, have they?

EXERCISE 5

1. Fish may be considered "brain food," but I've never liked it.

2. While everyone is saying how delicious a big salmon steak is or how yummy the shrimp tastes, you'll find me grimacing and munching on the bread.

3. Part of the problem with fish is the smell, but my friends who love to eat fish also love the smell of fish cooking.

4. I always thought that was strange, but it makes sense, doesn't it?

5. If someone hates the taste of onions, that person probably also hates the smell of onions cooking.

6. Come to think of it, my husband hates to eat sweets and doesn't like the smell of them either. (You could also use a comma before *either* to make it a tag.)

7. When we walk into a bakery together, he practically has to hold his nose the way I would in a fish market.

8. To me, that's odd, but my aversion to fish must seem weird to someone who loves it.

9. Our daughter adores the taste of bacon, but she hates the smell of bacon frying.

10. The sentence is correct. [Note that a *fanboys*—in this case *So*—can begin a sentence, and it does not need a comma after it.]

PARAGRAPH EXERCISE

After the commas, we have identified the elements that they separate.

There I was in the pilot's seat of a small airplane. I had signed up for a course in flying at the aviation school, [*2 independent clauses (ICs) with fanboys*] but I didn't really expect to get my pilot's license. Learning the instruments took the most time. Once we began training in the cockpit, [*introductory dependent clause (DC)*] the instructor told us what to do, [*2ICs with fanboys*] and we did it. When I turned the yoke to the right, [*intro. DC*] the plane banked right. When I turned it to the left, [*intro. DC*] the plane went left. Actually, [*intro. word*] it was very similar to driving a car, [*tag contrast*] only much more fun. I'm exaggerating about it being easy, [*tag comment*] of course. My favorite type of practice involved landings, [*tag description*] bringing the plane in softly and safely. After many hours of supervised flying, [*intro. phrase*] my time to solo came, [*2ICs with fanboys*] and I was nervous but excited. [or "I was nervous, but excited" as a *tag contrast*] I covered my checklist on the ground, [*list*] took off without any problems [*list*], and landed smoothly in the middle of the runway. On a cold day in October 2012, [*intro. phrase*] I became a licensed pilot. Now I can work toward my next dream of becoming a private pilot for a rock star.

SENTENCE WRITING

Here are some possible combinations. Yours may differ.

I like to watch golf and tennis, but I love to play baseball and soccer. [*2ICs with fanboys*]

Tutors do not correct students' essays, but they can explain how to clarify ideas, add stronger details, and improve organization. [*2ICs with fanboys* and a *list*]

When my parents were growing up in the 1960s, most cars had seatbelts, but not airbags or car seats for children. [*intro. DC* and *tag contrast*]

COMMAS USED TO ENCLOSE ELEMENTS (PP. 183–189)

For Exercises 1 and 2, correct sentences remain in the answers without commas for the sake of comparison.

EXERCISE 1

1. The first person who guessed correctly won a trip to the Grand Canyon.

2. Professor Jones, who guessed correctly, won a trip to the Grand Canyon.

3. Cookies that contain nuts may be harmful to people with allergies.

4. My cookie recipe, which does not contain nuts, is safe for people with allergies.

5. Students who take the train to school catch a shuttle from the station to campus.

6. Melissa, who takes the train to school, catches a shuttle from the station to campus.

7. The teacher explained the answer to the question that everyone missed.

8. The teacher explained the answer to question 14, which everyone missed.

9. The gorilla, an animal on many endangered species lists, has an average lifespan of 30 to 50 years.

10. Koko, the gorilla who became famous for learning to communicate through sign language, turned 42 years old in July 2013.

EXERCISE 2

1. We hope, of course, that people will honor their summons for jury duty.

2. Of course we hope that people will honor their summons for jury duty.

3. People who serve as jurors every time they're called deserve our appreciation.

4. Thelma and Trevor Martin, who serve as jurors every time they're called, deserve our appreciation.

5. We should therefore be as understanding as we can be about the slow legal process.

6. Therefore, we should be as understanding as we can be about the slow legal process.

7. A legal system that believes people are innocent until proven guilty must offer a trial-by-jury option.

8. The U.S. legal system, which believes people are innocent until proven guilty, offers a trial-by-jury option.

9. With that option, we hope that no one will receive an unfair trial.

10. With that option, no one, we hope, will receive an unfair trial.

EXERCISE 3

1. The story of Dracula, the frightening Prince Vlad Tepes, has been fascinating people across the world for hundreds of years.

2. He was held as a prisoner in Bran Castle, a medieval fortress in Transylvania in the 15th century. [This sentence needs only one comma; the end of the sentence is the end of the "scoopable."]

3. Bran Castle, also called Dracula's Castle, has become a popular tourist attraction.

4. The sentence is correct.

5. The sentence is correct.

6. The sentence is correct.

7. It was given to Marie, Queen of Romania, in 1920.

8. The sentence is correct.

9. The sentence is correct.

10. Queen Marie's grandson, Dominic von Habsburg, now owns the castle, along with his two sisters, Maria Magdalena and Elizabeth.

EXERCISE 4

1. Arthur S. Heineman, a California architect, designed and built the world's first motel in the 1920s.

2. He chose the perfect location, the city of San Luis Obispo, which was midway between Los Angeles and San Francisco.

3. Heineman, an insightful man of business, understood the need for inexpensive drive-in accommodations on long motor vehicle trips.

4. Hotels, which required reservations and offered only high-priced rooms within one large structure, just didn't fulfill the needs of motorists.

5. Heineman envisioned his "Motor Hotel," or Mo-Tel, as a place where the parking spaces for the cars were right next to separate bungalow-style apartments for the passengers.

6. Heineman's idea was so new that, when he put up his "Motel" sign, several residents of the area told him to fire the sign's painter, who couldn't even spell the word *hotel*.

7. The sentence is correct.

8. Heineman's Milestone Mo-Tel, the world's first motel, opened in San Luis Obispo in 1925.

9. Before Heineman's company, the Milestone Interstate Corporation, could successfully trademark the name "Mo-Tel," other builders adopted the style and made *motel* a generic term.

10. Some of the original Milestone Mo-Tel building, now called the Motel Inn, still stands on the road between L.A. and San Francisco.

EXERCISE 5

1. I bought a book, *The Story of the "Titanic,"* because I am interested in famous events in history.

2. This book, written by Frank O. Braynard, is a collection of postcards about the ill-fated ocean liner.

3. The book's postcards, four on each page, can be pulled apart and mailed like regular ones.

4. The sentence is correct.

5. The blank sides, where messages and addresses go, include brief captions of the images on the front of the cards. (Note: This sentence could be left without commas.)

6. The book's actual content, the part written by Braynard, offers a brief history of each image relating to the *Titanic*.

7. One of my favorite cards shows the ship's captain, Edward Smith, and its builder, Lord Pirrie, standing on the deck of the *Titanic* before it set sail.

8. Another card is a photograph of *Titanic* passengers on board the *Carpathia,* the ship that rescued many survivors.

9. There is also a picture of two small children, survivors themselves, who lost their father in the disaster but were later reunited with their mother.

10. The most interesting card, a photo of the ship's gymnasium, shows that one of the pieces of exercise equipment for the passengers was a rowing machine.

PARAGRAPH EXERCISE

Do you know, Ryan, that there is a one-unit library class that begins next week? It's called Library 1, Introduction to the Library, and my friends recommended it. The librarians who teach it will give us an orientation and a series of assignment sheets. Then, whenever we finish the assignments, we turn them in to the librarians for credit. Ms. Kim, the librarian that I spoke with, said that the course materials cover really valuable library skills. These skills, such as finding books or articles in our library and using the Internet to access other databases, are the ones universities will expect us to know. I therefore plan to take this class, and you, I hope, will take it with me.

SENTENCE WRITING

Here are some possible combinations. Yours may differ.

Samantha Jones, a great boss, recognizes hard work and rewards dedicated employees. [or] Samantha Jones is a great boss who recognizes hard work and rewards dedicated employees.

She plans to buy herself an expensive watch by Tag Heuer, her favorite brand. [or] She plans to buy herself an expensive Tag Heuer watch.

Only two people, the manager and an actor, were in the store when the commercial was filmed. [or] The manager and an actor were the only people in the store when the commercial was filmed.

COMMA REVIEW EXERCISE (P. 190)

I'm writing you this note, Melanie, to ask you to do me a favor. [5, name] Before you leave for work today, would you take the chicken out of the freezer? [3, intro.] I plan to get started on the appetizers, drinks, and desserts as soon as soon as I wake up. [2, list] I will be so busy, however, that I might forget to thaw out the chicken. [6, interrupter] It's the first time I've cooked all the food for a party by myself, and I want everything to be perfect. [1, 2ICs with fanboys] The big round baking pan, the one in the cupboard above the refrigerator, should be the best place to keep the chicken as it thaws. [7, scoopable] Wish me luck, seriously! [4, tag]

Thanks for your help.

QUOTATION MARKS AND ITALICS/UNDERLINES (PP. 191–196)

EXERCISE 1

1. A film crew was setting up in the park by my house, and I saw a sign that said, "Extras holding."

2. I found someone who didn't look too busy and asked, "Are you looking for extras?"

3. "Yes," she answered, "if you want to be in a crowd scene, just fill out the paperwork and sit over there."

4. I didn't even think twice and told her, "Sure, I'd love to be in it."

5. I found out from another extra that we were filming the pilot for a new TV comedy series along the lines of <u>Desperate Housewives</u>.

6. When I asked what I was supposed to do, he said, "They'll give you a picket sign, and you'll wave it. That's it."

7. I held my sign that said, "No more cuts to education!" and waved it when I was told to.

8. While it was happening, I kept telling myself, "You're going to be on TV—just try not to look stupid."

9. I heard someone ask, "Did anyone else hear that the title of the series is going to be <u>Tangle Square</u>?"

10. We all shook our heads; then I added, "But that's an interesting title, if it's true."

EXERCISE 2

1. I am reading a book called <u>Don't: A Manual of Mistakes & Improprieties More or Less Prevalent in Conduct and Speech</u>.

2. The book's contents are divided into chapters with titles such as "At Table," "In Public," and "In General."

3. In the section about table don'ts, the book offers the following warning: "Don't bend over your plate, or drop your head to get each mouthful."

4. The table advice continues by adding, "Don't bite your bread. Break it off."

5. This book offers particularly comforting advice about conducting oneself in public.

6. For instance, it states, "Don't brush against people, or elbow people, or in any way show disregard for others."

7. When meeting others on the street, the book advises, "Don't be in a haste to introduce. Be sure that it is mutually desired before presenting one person to another."

8. In the section titled "In General," there are more tips about how to get along in society, such as "Don't underrate everything that others do, and overstate your own doings."

9. The <u>Don't</u> book has this to say about books, whether borrowed or owned: "Read them, but treat them as friends that must not be abused."

10. And one can never take the following warning too much to heart: "Don't make yourself in any particular way a nuisance to your neighbors or your family."

EXERCISE 3

1. Emilie Buchwald once noted, "Children are made readers on the laps of their parents."

2. Have you read Mark Twain's book <u>The Adventures of Tom Sawyer</u>?

3. I took a deep breath when my counselor asked, "How many math classes have you had?"

4. "Let's start that again!" shouted the dance teacher.

5. Last night we watched the Beatles' movie <u>Help</u>! on DVD.

6. "Books," wrote Jonathan Swift, "are the children of the brain."

7. Voltaire stated in <u>A Philosophical Dictionary</u> that "Tears are the silent language of grief."

8. Why do dentists ask questions like "How are you?" as soon as they start working on your teeth?

9. "Time is the only incorruptible judge" is just one translation of Creon's line from the Greek play <u>Oedipus Rex</u>.

10. My favorite essay that we have read this semester has to be "The Pie" by Gary Soto.

EXERCISE 4

1. <u>Women's Wit and Wisdom</u> is the title of a book I found in the library.

2. The book includes many great insights that were written or spoken by women throughout history.

3. England's Queen Elizabeth I noted in the sixteenth century that "A clear and innocent conscience fears nothing."

4. "Nothing is so good as it seems beforehand," observed George Eliot, a female author whose real name was Mary Ann Evans.

5. Some of the women's quotations are funny; Alice Roosevelt Longworth, for instance, said, "If you don't have anything good to say about anyone, come and sit by me."

6. "If life is a bowl of cherries," asked Erma Bombeck, "what am I doing in the pits?"

7. Some of the quotations are serious, such as Gloria Steinem's statement, "The future depends on what each of us does every day."

8. Maya Lin, the woman who designed Washington D.C.'s Vietnam Veterans Memorial, reminded us that, as she put it, "War is not just a victory or a loss. . . . People die."

9. Emily Dickinson had this to say about truth: "Truth is such a rare thing, it is delightful to tell it."

10. Finally, columnist Ann Landers advised one of her readers that "The naked truth is always better than the best-dressed lie."

EXERCISE 5

1. In Booker T. Washington's autobiography <u>Up from Slavery</u>, he describes his early dream of going to school.

2. "I had no schooling whatever while I was a slave," he explains.

3. He continues, "I remember on several occasions I went as far as the schoolhouse door with one of my young mistresses to carry her books."

4. Washington then describes what he saw from the doorway: "several dozen boys and girls engaged in study."

5. "The picture," he adds, "made a deep impression upon me."

6. Washington cherished this glimpse of "boys and girls engaged in study."

7. It contrasted directly with his own situation: "My life had its beginning in the midst of the most miserable, desolate, and discouraging surroundings."

8. "I was born," he says, "in a typical log cabin, about fourteen by sixteen feet square."

9. He explains, "In this cabin I lived with my mother and a brother and sister till after the Civil War, when we were all declared free."

10. As a slave at the door of his young mistress's schoolhouse, Booker T. Washington remembers, "I had the feeling that to get into a schoolhouse and study in this way would be about the same as getting into paradise."

PROOFREADING EXERCISE

We were allowed to choose a book to review in our journals last week. The teacher specified that it should be a short nonfiction book about something of interest to us. I found a great book to review. It's called <u>Tattoo: Secrets of a Strange Art</u>. Albert Parry breaks the contents down into chapters about tattoo legends, techniques, and purposes. A few of the chapter titles are "The Art and Its Masters," "The Circus," "Identification," and "Removal." The book also includes illustrations and photographs of tattoo designs and tattooed people and animals throughout history, including Miss Stella: The Tattooed Lady, The Famous Tattooed Cow, and Georgius Constantine. Parry describes Constantine's tattoos in the following way: "the most complete, elaborate, and artistic tattooing ever witnessed in America or Europe." Parry continues, "There was almost no part of his body, not a quarter-inch of the skin, free from designs." Needless to say, since I love tattoos, I loved Parry's book about them.

CAPITAL LETTERS (PP. 197–201)

In this section, titles of larger works are *italicized* rather than <u>underlined</u>.

EXERCISE 1

1. I have always wanted to learn another language besides English.

2. Recently, I have been watching a lot of films from India.

3. Some people call them "Bollywood movies."

4. Whatever they are called, I love to watch them.

5. One part of these movies that I love is their language: Hindi.

6. I have to use English subtitles to understand the dialogue most of the time.

7. But sometimes I can catch what's happening without the subtitles.

8. Because of my intense interest in Hindi-language films, I plan to take a Hindi class.

9. I have already bought a book that explains the Devanagari writing system.

10. Now I will enroll in a class and learn Hindi as a second language.

EXERCISE 2

1. When people think of jazz, they think of *Down Beat* magazine.

2. *Down Beat*'s motto may be "Jazz, Blues & Beyond," but some people think that the magazine has gone too far "beyond" by including two guitarists in the *Down Beat* Hall of Fame.

3. The two musicians in question are Jimi Hendrix and Frank Zappa.

4. Jimi Hendrix was inducted into the Hall of Fame in 1970.

5. *Down Beat* added Frank Zappa to the list in 1994.

6. Since then, readers and editors have been debating whether Hendrix and Zappa belong in the same group as Duke Ellington, John Coltrane, and Miles Davis.

7. Those who play jazz guitar have some of the strongest opinions on the subject.

8. Russell Malone, Mark Elf, and John Abercrombie all agree that Hendrix and Zappa were great guitarists but not jazz guitarists.

9. Others like Steve Tibbetts and Bill Frisell don't have any problem putting Hendrix on the list, but Tibbetts isn't so sure about including Zappa.

10. It will be interesting to see who *Down Beat*'s future inductees will be.

EXERCISE 3

1. Many consider *The Diary of Anne Frank* to be one of the most important books of the twentieth century.

2. Anne Frank wrote her famous diary during the Nazi occupation of Holland in World War II.

3. The building in Amsterdam where the Frank family and several others hid during the two years before their capture is now a museum and has been recently renovated.

4. Visitors to the Anne Frank House can stand before her desk and see pictures of movie stars like Greta Garbo on her wall.

5. They can climb the stairs hidden behind a bookcase that led to the annex where Anne lived with her mother, Edith; her father, Otto; and her sister, Margot.

6. One of the others hiding with the Franks was Peter van Pels, who was roughly the same age as Anne.

7. Anne writes of her relationship with Peter in her diary.

8. Visitors to the museum can enter the room where Peter gave Anne her first kiss just a few months before the Nazis discovered their hiding place in 1944.

9. Anne's family and Peter's were both sent to concentration camps in Germany.

10. Only Anne's father lived to see the Anne Frank House open as a museum for the first time on May 3, 1960.

EXERCISE 4

1. I recently saw the movie *V for Vendetta*, and I wanted to learn more about it.

2. I found out that it's based on an extensive series of comic books.

3. They were written by Alan Moore and illustrated by David Lloyd.

4. The original episodes of *V for Vendetta* were published in black and white within a British comic series called *Warrior*.

5. Once the series caught on in the United States, DC Comics began to publish it.

6. At that time, the creators added color to the drawings.

7. The letter V in the title *V for Vendetta* stands for the main character, a mysterious costumed figure who calls himself V.

8. However, many other connections between the letter V and the Roman numeral 5, which is written as a V, come up throughout the story.

9. V wears a mask that people in the United Kingdom refer to as a Guy Fawkes mask.

10. Guy Fawkes was an English historical figure famous for his involvement in the Gunpowder Plot, which failed on the fifth of November in 1605.

EXERCISE 5

1. When my art teacher asked the class to do research on Frida Kahlo, I knew that the name sounded familiar.

2. Then I remembered that the actress Salma Hayek starred in the movie *Frida*, which was about this Mexican-born artist's life.

3. Frida Kahlo's paintings are all very colorful and seem extremely personal.

4. She painted mostly self-portraits, and each one makes a unique statement.

5. One of these portraits is called *My Grandparents, My Parents, and I*.

6. Kahlo gave another one the title *The Two Fridas*.

7. But my favorite of Kahlo's works is *Self-Portrait on the Borderline between Mexico and the United States*.

8. In an article I read in *Smithsonian* magazine, Kahlo's mother explains that after Frida was severely injured in a bus accident, she started painting.

9. Kahlo's mother set up a mirror near her daughter's bed so that Frida could use herself as a model.

10. In the *Smithsonian* article from the November 2002 issue, Kahlo is quoted as saying, "I never painted dreams. I painted my own reality."

REVIEW OF PUNCTUATION AND CAPITAL LETTERS (P. 202)

1. We couldn't leave San Antonio, Texas, without visiting its most famous site: the Alamo.

2. My teacher asked, "Have you ever seen the first episodes of *The Simpsons?*"

3. The Bridges have remodeled their garage; now their son uses it as an apartment.

4. When Eric, my older brother, gets a traffic ticket, he always goes to traffic school.

5. We have refunded your money, Ms. Jones, and have sent you a confirmation.

6. One of the teachers who visited the library left his wallet on the checkout counter.

7. The United Parcel Service, better known as UPS, was hiring on campus yesterday. [or] The United Parcel Service—better known as UPS—was hiring. . . .

8. Even though I am enjoying my Latin class, I wish I had taken Chinese instead.

9. You always misremember the date of my birthday: you think it's in May.

10. Pink, normally a calming color, can have the opposite effect when it's neon.

11. "Stopping by Woods on a Snowy Evening" is a famous poem by Robert Frost.

12. Finding a good deal for a new car online takes time, patience, and luck. [or !]

13. My friend is reading the play *Taming of the Shrew* in her women's studies class.

14. I wonder how much my *History of Textiles* book will cost.

15. The foreign film club needs people to pass out flyers—let's volunteer!

COMPREHENSIVE TEST (PP. 203–204)

1. (p) I wonder if I can get an earlier registration date.

2. (ww/apos) The bookstore has updated *its* checkout system again.

3. (//) *Kids' movies and TV shows* usually have better stories than the ones made for adults.

4. (sp/ww) The fencing coach gives great *advice* to help students improve quickly.

5. (p) "Welcome," the teacher said to all of us, "are we ready to begin?"

6. (wordy) Depending of the price of gas, I either ride my bike or drive to school.

7. (cap) Both math and *English* require intense concentration.

8. (ro) Reunions seem like a good idea, but they seldom live up to expectations.

9. (unclear pro) *The microwave* blew a fuse when I was making my lunch.

10. (cs) We volunteered to read books to children at the library*;* it was really fun.

11. (shift) Students often throw their notes away when *they* should always keep them.

12. (s-v agr) Either the employees or the company *has* to take a cut in earnings.

13. (ww) We ordered business cards with *our* new logos printed on them.

14. (s-v agr) Each of the candidates *receives* the questions in advance.

15. (c) As we stepped outside, the sunlight hurt our eyes.

16. (adj) She felt *bad* when her sister didn't get a scholarship.

17. (mm) Our group studied for *only* an hour; that's why we failed.

18. (sp/ww) The critique of our sculpture projects took much longer *than* I expected.

19. (frag and awk) An error *occurred* while *I was uploading* the video on YouTube.

20. (ww and wordy) *They're* going to pack on Wednesday and move on Friday.

WRITING

EXERCISE 1: IDENTIFY A TOPIC, FACT, OR THESIS (P. 223)

1. FACT
2. TOPIC
3. FACT
4. THESIS
5. THESIS
6. THESIS
7. TOPIC
8. TOPIC
9. THESIS
10. THESIS

WRITING EXERCISE 9: WRITE A PARAGRAPH THAT INCLUDES TRANSITIONS (P. 226)

Previously (or *In the past*), I used to plan my long road trips by going through the following routine. *First*, I made sure that I had a map of the highways so that if I got lost along the way, I wouldn't panic. *Then*, even if I did have a map to the city of my destination, I would call the hotel for specific driving directions from the highway. *Another* way that I planned ahead was to check my car's tires and have its engine serviced, if necessary. *Also*, I never forgot to bring my cell phone because I had learned how important they are on long drives. *Finally* (or *As the final step*), before I left my house on the day of the trip, I checked the Highway Patrol updates to see if there were any road closures on my route. This routine always worked for me; *however*, I can give it up now that I have a car with its own navigation system. I just need to figure out how it works!

WRITING EXERCISE 14: WRITE A SUMMARY OF A READING (P. 245)

In "Christo and Jeanne-Claude (1935-, 1935-)," Judy Jones and William Wilson explain how these two married artists work as a team to make their mark on the world. Christo and Jeanne-Claude literally use the whole world as an art studio and gallery. Their art works are usually large-scale events that highlight buildings or public places with fabric and color. They want their work to touch everyone, especially people who don't usually go to museums or galleries. To Christo and Jeanne-Claude, the possibility to make and see art is, and should be, everywhere.

Index